THE *last* LONE WOLF

THE *last* LONE WOLF

RECOVERING THE LOST SACRAMENT OF FRIENDSHIP

DERRICK STEELE

Published by Kingsmen Publishing in association with The Warriors Path, Ltd.

All Scripture quotations, unless otherwise indicated, are taken from the Holy Bible, New International Version®, NIV®. Copyright ©1973, 1978, 1984 by Biblica, Inc.™ Used by permission of Zondervan. All rights reserved worldwide. www.zondervan.comThe "NIV" and "New International Version" are trademarks registered in the United States Patent and Trademark Office by Biblica, Inc.™

Scripture quotations noted ESV are from the ESV® Bible (The Holy Bible, English Standard Version®), Copyright © 2001 by Crossway, a publishing ministry of Good News Publishers. Used by permission. All rights reserved.

Scripture quotations taken from the (NASB®) New American Standard Bible®, Copyright © 1960, 1971, 1977, 1995, 2020 by The Lockman Foundation. Used by permission. All rights reserved. www.lockman.org

ISBN 979-8-9850025-2-2 (hardcover)
ISBN 979-8-9850025-1-5 (ebook)
ISBN 979-8-9850025-0-8 (pbk.)

For David,
without whom there would have been nothing to say.

CONTENTS

INTRODUCTION

But in the interest of truth-telling, there seems to be no risk
that Shakespeare is not willing to run as if from the conviction
that if the truth is worth telling, it is worth making a fool of
yourself to tell.
(Frederick Buechner, *Telling the Truth*)

From the outset I must admit my fear that a book of this size is
almost certain to come across as startlingly—perhaps even offen-
sively—far too narrow in its scope to satisfy the modern Christian
critic. This is because quite naturally for brevity's sake I have been
forced into making a series of unspoken assumptions so momentous as
to be quite nearly unforgivable. That being said, with at least one eye
towards avoiding undue misunderstanding through my liberal use of
brevity, allow me to preface what follows with an equally brief
disclaimer:

*God is our ultimate Good. He is our Final Need, the only Ultimate
Source of Life that ever was or ever could be available to us, the
creatures of His making.*

That is the core assumption that must be understood, and to
which we will return as need occasions in the pages ahead. But I
want to be clear from the very outset that what follows is not a

creative attempt at circumventing that ultimate preeminence of our need for our Creator. God forbid that anyone misconstrues the message of this book as some new form of thinly veiled Humanism. To follow the path set out within these pages is not to find oneself on an aimless detour, nor to wander down a lesser tributary of the Greater Stream known as the River of Life. I will repeat again and again—there is no life apart from God, and the more intimately our life becomes intertwined with His, the closer we come to experiencing true life, Eternal Life, life as it was meant to be: Life to the full.

This ultimate goal, then, being—let us hope—universally accepted, the question may yet fairly remain open to discussion, *"Through what methods is the goal to be best and most fully attained?"*

How? How is it done? How is the long slow ascent Godward to be made? By what methods can such a thing be accomplished? For surely by now you have noticed that, in spite of the simplified spiritual equations often offered in the Sunday morning sermon, the pursuit of deep intimacy with God is neither an obvious nor an easy thing. Certainly not something that can be solved through cold logic, five-step programs founded upon a childish pleasure for alliteration, or mathematical thinking. Spiritual things transposed into solvable equations may make sense to a society born and bred upon a scientific mindset, but what we seek is far too relational for that sort of thinking to carry us very far. Certainly not as far as is needed. As G.K. Chesterton once so memorably wrote concerning St. Francis of Assisi, "His religion was not a thing like a theory but a thing like a love-affair." So must our religion be, if we are to unlock any of its most profound secrets, if we maintain any hope that we might one day progress, as they say in Narnia, "further up and further in". (C.S. Lewis, *The Last Battle*)

What I have written has been dedicated to a fuller understanding of just one of the methods for this ascent that God has placed at our disposal, one of the methods that He eagerly intended us to use.

There are, perhaps, higher methods than the one I have chosen to discuss; there are, to be sure, many lower ones. But few methods have been so pushed to the margins of modern life as the one I have proposed, and therefore few are in need of such special 'rehabilitation'. My readers will, I hope, understand if it seems that I have ignored a vast cornucopia of equally significant means and ways towards experiencing *Life to the full* in order to attempt to bring home my particular thesis with extreme emphasis. So, you will notice, are almost all books of non-fiction written. It would seem that it is the rightful prerogative of authors to make their arguments seem more singular, more alone at the top of the pyramid of priorities, than they truly are, objectively speaking. Nor do I think authors can be faulted for doing so. After all, don't we seem to learn best by intensive immersion? By soaking and marinating in one idea at a time; one idea that, for that moment, must command all our attention, must demand that we take it seriously enough to be worth the rare and fleeting moments that we have for such things? Anything less than this, and our minds have wandered off to the 'next' thing before the last page has even been turned. Sherlock Holmes may have famously possessed a 'mind palace' in which he was able to store vast amounts of information, but I think most of us have little more than a mere subway terminal in comparison, a place in which "one thought drives out another", as Tolkien's bumbling innkeeper Barliman Butterber so aptly noted of his own mental failings.

And yet, I don't think that I'm guilty of any gross exaggeration in emphasizing my particular topic. (I know, I know: every author would say the same thing, just as every criminal on trial would exclaim that he's innocent.) If anything, I'm haunted by the fear that I haven't done enough: that I've missed something pivotal, have failed to handle this high and holy task deftly and poignantly with the urgency it so greatly deserves. What I have written, I've written under the solemn burden of knowing that such a topic, in such a style as this, may only have one chance in a generation of receiving a fair hearing—and that is a weight of responsibility that I have never taken lightly.

In times past far greater authors have noted that, as a book about everything would be a metaphysical and logical impossibility, the restriction must be made—and accepted—that each particular book has to be about a very particular something. The something that I have written this book about is *Friendship*. Its value and necessity. Its goodness and delight. Its original high place in the vast hierarchy of possible human experiences—so clearly contrasted by its present impoverished position in today's world, where it now has been pushed to the furthest, far-flung margins of adult life.

I believe this particular something is begging for a great book to be written that has the power to reawaken the childish heart slumbering deep within all of us—the heart that once upon a time desired no greater pleasure than being in the company of dear friends as often as our parents would allow—as often as it could possibly be managed, notwithstanding the very minor demands that life placed upon our youthful freedom. (My oldest son turned twelve last month, and if I needed a fresh reminder of how strong that desire to be with friends really was for all of us at that age, I've got it in spades. Listening to him you'd think there could be no joy left in life without the company of at least one friend.)

I'm sure that it's too great a glory to hope that this might be that much needed book, that book that I myself would like to turn to when I need to be reminded of those sweet, innocent times. Nevertheless, my heart compels me to do the best that I can, and pray that at the very least it may turn out to be, to take another quote from Tolkien's enduring fantasy, "like the falling of small stones that starts an avalanche in the mountains."

—

Whenever I am confronted in a social setting with the common conversation opener, "Tell me a little about yourself?", within two minutes I'll be regaling my new acquaintance with stories and adventures in which David Anderson, my lifelong, oldest and dearest friend, prominently figures. I could hardly tell my story without including him. In recent years such necessity of inclusion has become also true of my young family, my wife and three boys. You see, I can't really give a fair and useful description of who I am without talking about *the relationships that form the context of my life.* If I were suddenly to cease to be Tristan, Nathaniel, Cody and Gwendolyn's father, who then would I be? The simple experiment of a weekend at home while the rest of the family is away—the ensuing awkward aimlessness, the existential angst that accompanies suddenly being ripped from one's relational context—this is proof enough to me that we are set adrift when we lose touch with the unique role we have been set to play on Life's enormous Stage. Unique, and irreplaceable. Seven billion people on the planet, but my wife will never have another husband, my children will never have another Daddy, and I will never have friends that can replace the ones I have already walked through the better part of my life with.

Naturally, I realize that where I differ—where I have always differed from the majority of the people I have known—is in defining my own unique role on Life's Stage not primarily by things like my personality, ambition, or accomplishments, but rather *by my relationships.* To most people in our current society, it would seem almost self-deprecating to answer the question, "What makes you unique?" with the response, "Let me tell you about my best friend; let me tell you about my sons." And yet I make this response without excuse and without shame, and thank the college professors in Intercultural Studies I had a great number of years ago for the freedom to do so. It was under their tutelage that I learned that the way we do things in America is not the only—or necessarily the best—way that things can be done. Through them I learned about the many people from diverse cultures and times who in fact did believe that their relationships most significantly defined them. It wasn't, after all, sheer madness on my part to want to do the same.

Of course I realize that in our culture we have all been led to believe that our own personal journey is so much bigger than the relational context we happen to find ourselves in at any one stage of that journey. *We* are the Center. *We* are the constant. When it comes to the other Players who happen to share the Stage with us in any given scene, we must never forget that we are, after all, merely 'passing through'. Our pride and our belief in our own autonomy combine to tell us that we need no one in order to be our fullest selves. Our fear of being labeled 'codependent' by a society of would-be psychologists has contributed to our unhealthy phobia of 'need-ing' anyone. A layman's mistaken understanding of Cloud and Townsend's popular teaching that says it is wise to live with boun-daries has led many to mistakenly live instead with walls. Despite God's contradicting social commentary, we apparently remain quite desperate to prove that it is, in fact, good to be alone.

Thankfully I have found in myself an instinctive rebelliousness to the status quo wherever I have run up against it—be it in the culture, the church, or the family. Subsequently I have felt more freedom than most to actually own up to my personal insufficiency, my inter-dependence: in short, the humbling truth of my need for others. Rather than succumbing to the societal pull towards feeling embar-rassed at the first sign that I am not 'fully autonomous', I have instead freely embraced the actual truths that actually living life has shown me (and I think would show others if they were open to receive the truth of it). Even when those truths contrast the popular 'empowerment' catch phrases and hashtags circulating on social media. Of course my experience may not ring true for anyone else. Still, I offer it as a potentially helpful window into a fuller expression of human experience than that which any single, individual one of my readers has known.

Whether we have given it much thought or not, we are all children of a particular time and place, a unique moment in history, a specific culture that has provided us with a lens through which to view, interpret, and make sense of the world around us. While it is not my intent to wage a full scale assault on the particular time and place that we happen to find ourselves in as twenty-first century citizens of Western culture, I can hardly proceed without admitting that a reha-bilitation of both the necessity and goodness of deep, lifelong friend-ships is going to set us at odds with many of our underlying cultural values.

But that should not deter us from our chosen path. Why should it? The utterly mad thing is to be at all surprised that such com-plications have arisen. *Of course they have.* Ours is a crazy, mixed-up, fallen and hurting world. Truth be told, a great many of the cultural assumptions into which we were born are going to require some correcting if we are to discover that narrow path that leads to the desire of our hearts—to the arms of our loving Father, to the well-spring of the Life we were born to know yet have been searching our whole lives to find.

Life in these Shadowlands, it could fairly be said, is a slow and arduous—but essentially central—ascent back to the heart of God. And although each individual soul must, as an individual, choose to take up or refuse this journey, my prayer is that through this little book many fellow "travellers between life and death" will experience the turn of sudden joy unlooked for that comes when we realize, be-yond all hope, *that it was never a journey we were meant to take alone.*

PROLOGUE

There is a friend that sticks closer than a brother.

Proverbs 18:24

(An excerpt from Kenneth Grahame's *The Wind in the Willows*)

The call was clear, the summons was plain. He must obey it instantly and go. 'Ratty!' he called, full of joyful excitement, 'hold on! Come back! I want you quick!'

'O, come along, Mole, do!' replied the Rat cheerfully, still plodding along.

'Please stop, Ratty!' pleaded the poor Mole, in anguish of heart. 'You don't understand! It's my home! My old home! I've just come across the smell of it, and it's close by here, really quite close. And I must go to it, I must, I must! O, come back Ratty! Please, please come back!'

The Rat was by this time very far ahead, too far to hear clearly what the Mole was calling, too far to catch the sharp note of painful appeal in his voice. And he was much taken up with the weather, for he too could smell something—something suspiciously like approaching snow.

'Mole, we mustn't stop now, really!' he called back. 'We'll come for it tomorrow, whatever it is you've found. But I daren't stop now—it's late, and the snow's coming on again, and I'm not sure of the way! And I want your nose, Mole, so come on quick, there's a good fellow!' And the Rat pressed forward on his way without waiting for an answer.

Poor Mole stood alone in the road, his heart torn asunder, and a big sob gathering, gathering, somewhere low down inside him, to leap up to the surface presently, he knew, in passionate escape. But even under such a test as this his loyalty to his friend stood firm. Never for a moment did he dream of abandoning him. Meanwhile, the wafts from his old home pleaded, whispered, conjured, and finally claimed him imperiously. He dared not tarry longer within their magic circle. With a wrench that tore his very heartstrings he set his face down the road and followed submissively in the track of the Rat, while faint, thin little smells, still dogging his retreating nose, reproached him for his new friendship and his callous forgetfulness.

With an effort he caught up the unsuspecting Rat, who began chattering cheerfully about what they would do when they got back, and how jolly a fire of logs in the parlour would be, and what a supper he meant to eat; never noticing his companion's silence and distressful state of mind. At last, however, when they had gone some considerable way further, and were passing some tree-stumps at the edge of a copse that bordered the road, he stopped and said kindly, 'Look here, Mole, old chap, you seem dead tired. No talk left in you, and your feet dragging like lead. We'll sit down here for a minute and rest. The snow has held off so far, and the best part of our journey is over.'

The Mole subsided forlornly on a tree-stump and tried to control himself, for he felt it surely coming. The sob he had fought with so long refused to be beaten. Up and up, it forced its way to the air, and then another, and another, and others thick and fast; till poor Mole at last gave up the struggle, and cried freely and helplessly and openly, now that he knew it was all over and he had lost what he could hardly be said to have found.

The Rat, astonished and dismayed at the violence of Mole's paroxysm of grief, did not dare to speak for a while. At last he said, very quietly and sympathetically, 'What is it, old fellow? Whatever can be the matter? Tell us your trouble, and let me see what I can do.'

Poor Mole found it difficult to get any words out between the upheavals of his chest that followed one upon another so quickly and held back speech and choked it as it came. 'I know it's a—shabby, dingy little place,' he sobbed forth at last, brokenly: 'not like—your cosy quarters—or Toad's beautiful hall—or Badger's great house—but it was my own little home—and I was fond of it—and I went away and forgot all about it—and then I smelt it suddenly—on the road, when I called and you wouldn't listen, Rat—and everything came back to me with a rush—and I wanted it!—O dear, O dear! —and when you wouldn't turn back, Ratty—and I had to leave it, though I was smelling it all the time—I thought my heart would break—We might have just gone and had one look at it Ratty—only one look—it was close by—but you wouldn't turn back, Ratty, you wouldn't turn back! O dear! O dear!'

Recollection brought fresh waves of sorrow, and sobs again took full charge of him, preventing further speech.

The Rat stared straight in front of him, saying nothing, only patting Mole gently on the shoulder. After a time he muttered gloomily, 'I see it all now! What a pig I have been! A pig—that's me! Just a pig—a plain pig!'

He waited til Mole's sobs became gradually less stormy and more rhythmical; he waited till at last sniffs were frequent and sobs only intermittent. Then he rose from his seat, and, remarking carelessly, 'Well, now we'd really better be getting on, old chap!' set off up the road again, over the toilsome way they had come.

'Wherever are you (hic) going to (hic) Ratty?' cried the tearful

Mole, looking up in alarm.

'We're going to find that home of yours, old fellow,' replied the Rat pleasantly; 'so you had better come along, for it will take some finding, and we shall want your nose.'

'O, come back, Ratty, do!' cried the Mole, getting up and hurrying after him. 'It's no good, I tell you! It's too late, and too dark, and the place is too far off, and the snow's coming! And—and I never meant to let you know I was feeling that way about it—it was all an accident and a mistake! And think of River Bank, and your supper!'

'Hang River Bank, and supper too!' said the Rat heartily. 'I tell you, I'm going to find this place now, if I stay out all night. So cheer up, old chap, and take my arm, and we'll very soon be back there again.'

– Kenneth Grahame, *The Wind in the Willows*

Desperado, why don't you come to your senses?
Come down from your fences, open the gate
It may be rainin', but there's a rainbow above you
You better let somebody love you (let somebody love you)
You better let somebody love you before it's too late.
-The Eagles, "Desperado"

It is not good for the man to be alone.
Genesis 2:18

ONE

BEGINNINGS

"Then I was young and unafraid,
And dreams were made and used and wasted.
There was no ransom to be paid,
No song unsung, no wine untasted."
"I Dreamed a Dream", *Les Mis*

The child is father of the man:
And I could wish my days to be
Bound each to each by natural piety.
W. Wordsworth

The only thing more tragic than the tragedy that
happens to us is the way we handle it.
John Eldredge, *Wild at Heart*

"*Well, I guess the best years of my life are over now. It's time to grow up...*"

It was the Spring of 1990. Our family's twelve-passenger Ford Econoline van was cresting out on the railroad tracks that ran like an iron spine along the southern ridge separating the quiet Midwestern suburb from the serenely idyllic college campus that my older brother and I had been attending for the past two years. The view from this last vantage point on the way out of campus was iconic. Sublime. Postcard perfect. And better: it was like standing on the lip of a gigantic postcard photograph, but it was a three-dimensional one you could leap into, like one of Bert the Chimney Sweep's sidewalk chalk drawings in the classic film *Mary Poppins*.

Although the view from the ridge always possessed a degree of sublime attraction, it was on certain azure-skied days of perfect May weather that it was at its incomparable best. And such a day it was, as we looked back over our shoulders to catch one more glimpse of our happy home away from home.

Below and to the left the white spire of the imposing four-story, red brick Billy Graham Center loomed nearest and largest to our vantage point. Directly ahead, great ancient trees verdant with young leaves towered over the lush green of the Front Lawn that ran up from the street below to yet another ridge, up to the feet of the great limestone castle that was Blanchard Hall: the iconic soul of the one-hundred-and-thirty year old college. To the right, the newly resurfaced red rubber track encircling McCully Football Field, and just beyond that, on the edge of our vision, our own dear 'field of dreams', East McCully soccer stadium.

Some of what I remember of that place is gone now. The soccer field has been renamed Bean Stadium in recent years, and the sweet pungent smell of fresh cut grass will not come there again as it did once upon a time to us, for in the intervening years artificial turf has taken its place. And that sublime, postcard view from the southern ridge, while still accessible on foot or bike, can no longer be the last thing seen by a graduating senior as his family van turns one last time for home, for the road up that last ascent has been lost to time and what is sometimes erroneously called 'progress'.

Ah, happy hills ah, pleasing shade!

Ah, fields beloved in vain!

Where once my careless childhood stray'd,

A stranger yet to pain!

I feel the gales that from ye blow

A momentary bliss bestow,

As waving fresh their gladsome wing

My weary soul they seem to soothe,

And, redolent of joy and youth,

To breathe a second spring.

-Thomas Gray, *Ode On A Distant Prospect of Eton College*

It might not have been Eton, but the love and longing we felt for our own alma mater could not have been described with any less poignant words than those of Thomas Gray, the eighteenth century poet.

"Well, I guess the best years of my life are over now. It's time to grow up..." Although in that moment it was not me, but my older brother, who spoke those unforgettable words, they drove into my own heart with deadly precision. For his own part, my older brother spoke those words with his familiar crooked half-smile and a blunt matter-of-factness that belied any sincere emotion. But I was not fooled. This was my only brother and I knew him well enough to realize that he was masking a deeply felt pain, masking it behind the same old nonchalant persona he had been relying on since the day the safe haven of our home had come crashing down around us thirteen years prior...

DISNEY AND DEPARTURE

Now *that* full story need not here be told in all its sordid detail. But the simple fact is that our lives *do* resemble the characters in a story to a larger degree than we generally take the time to consider. Okay, maybe not always in the stirring sense that our lives appear —in a way perceptible to ourselves, anyway—to possess a cohesive, discernible plot. Or even some clear continuous movement towards any sort of a climax or resolution for that matter. But then, if there's one thing that we all lack any real clarity on, it's ourselves, our own story. As author John Eldredge points out, "We have no idea who we really are, why we're here, what's happened to us, or why." And we all say a hearty amen to that feeling. *Story? What story? There's no story here.* Just some apparently disconnected bits and bobs and a great deal of aimlessness. If anything we are tempted to agree with the less hopeful philosophy expressed by the fictitious film character Forrest Gump, who famously suggested that in fact "maybe we're all just floatin' around, accident-like on a breeze".

But if we can just open our minds to this idea and believe that beyond the fogginess we experience in the moment we are in, that there *is* a clarity which one day may enable us to read back over the episodes and adventures of our life like the pages of a cohesive story, then I think we can at least admit this much: the things that happen to us in Chapters 1-5 (our early years) clearly have had a powerful impact on the kind of people we are—and the kind of choices we make—in Chapters 6-10 (the portion of our life's story we happen to be in at the present.)

Certainly that was true for us, my brother and I: for the ghost of that cold December day in 1977 was there on that graduation day, peeking out from beneath my brother's crooked smile even as we took that one last look back on our beloved campus as it disappeared from view behind the crown of the hill as we turned for home.

That winter day long ago had been a day that started like many others in our childhood home: with all the signs that a storm of substantial size was brewing behind the double doors at the end of the upstairs hall leading to my parent's bedroom. In a thinly veiled attempt to get us out of harm's way we were shipped off to the movies, chaperoned by our oldest sister—too rare a treat on both scores to not arouse the suspicion of even the most trusting second grader yet unwise to most of the harsher ways of the world. Whatever the reasons behind the unexpected boon, I for one was eager to take the path of escape offered, for my lifelong fear of conflict was already deeply entrenched, and I wasn't about to look a gift horse—or dragon, as in this instance it was—in the mouth.

Perhaps the latest Disney film, *Pete's Dragon*, turned out to be shorter than expected; perhaps the storm behind those double doors at the end of the hallway took longer to reach its full fury than had been anticipated. Perhaps it was both. Perhaps it was neither, but merely chance or fate or the powers of Evil that conspire to destroy the children of God before they are old enough to defend their weakest and most precious border—the one surrounding their heart. Whatever the case, two blameless boys of seven and nine came through the front door that evening, alive and soaring high with the magic of Disney, just in time to pass their father on the threshold—a threshold he was crossing for the very last time.

It wasn't precisely an abandonment—it was more accurate to call it an eviction. But those are meaningless technicalities to a child. What mattered was knowing that something central and essential to our world had been decided without us, and the stark sense of utter helplessness was both tangible and terrifying in its intensity. We, whom this decision would most affect in the years to come, were powerless to stop it. Dad was moving out. That horrible, shadowy spectre haunting the halls of our elementary school in low whispers and grave tones, that frightening and mysterious family-destroyer whose name was invoked with such sorrow, 'divorce', was moving in.

That night we stood by helplessly and watched the sanctuary of Home broken forever. In a hundred lifetimes a boy's heart does not forget a moment like that, though his conscious mind may bury it deep within the soul's graveyard of broken dreams. But if one thing was clearly true, it was that the breaking of our world in that early chapter now echoed in both my brother's words and in the crooked, nonchalant smile masking the emotion that lay behind them.

THE VOWS OF THE HEART

You see, by his own admission in later years, my brother's subconscious response—the inner vow of his nine year old heart—to the ending of all that was supposed to be the bedrock foundation of a growing child just learning the ways of the world, had been that he must now live his life in such a way as to never truly need anyone again. *Move fast, play it loose, and don't let people get close enough to you to get in a position to hurt you. Need is weakness, so don't need anyone.* Or whatever version of those ideas a nine year old's heart is able to internally verbalize. It wasn't the best response to our situation, mind you, but I suspect it has a familiar ring: haven't most of us found similar ways over the years to attempt to manage our own hurts, disappointments and betrayals by telling ourselves not to be quite so trusting, so vulnerable, so naively defenseless to suffer from the "slings and arrows of outrageous fortune"?

Of course we have. We *all* make promises to ourselves, promises that we will be wiser, more cautious, more guarded the next time we face a similar potential for disappointment, hurt, or heartbreak. Fool me once, shame on you; fool me twice—well, you know how the saying goes. The fact is that we are perpetually promising our tender selves that we 'will do' or 'won't do' whatever we have imagined will protect us from being hurt in the same way a second time. These promises are generally called 'inner vows', but I expect you already know much about them. It's basic stuff really for anyone with some experience with either Christian counseling or inner healing ministry, and I know I'm only grazing the surface of a subject that is too deep, too rich, and too vital to be given such cursory mention.

In passing though let me just point out that it is commonly believed that the deepest, most life-altering of these inner vows take place in our childhood. They are, for the most part, unintentional. We are far too young and lacking in self-awareness to know what we are doing, and by no means is it common for us to know that we are making them at the moment we are, in fact, making them. As John Eldredge points out about these vows, and our other core convictions about the world and about ourselves,

> Our deepest convictions—the ones that really shape our lives—they are down there somewhere in the depths of our hearts. Certainly we'd reject the more disabling beliefs if we could; but they form when we are vulnerable, without our really knowing it, like a handprint in wet cement, and over time the cement hardens and there you have it.
>
> *(Waking the Dead)*

Nor even, in later years, is there any guarantee that most people will necessarily recognize the impact these inner vows continue to have in their lives. The hurts that cause us such pain are deep hurts, often too deep for thoughts or words. Like the shifting of tectonic plates, an unstable fault line now runs across the foundation of our soul, so deep that it is hidden from the average person's powers of self-awareness. As G.K. Chesterton wrote,

> One may understand the cosmos, but never the ego; the self is more distant than any star. Thou shalt love the Lord thy God, but thou shalt not know thyself.   *(Orthodoxy)*

Or, as the Scriptures put it: "The purpose in a man's heart is like deep water" (Proverbs 20:5 ESV), and much like the iceberg that sank the White Star Line's indestructible Titanic, the real devastating magnitude of our soul's worst collisions are almost always deceiving from our perspective here upon the surface of the waters, for we have truly only seen the 'tip of the iceberg'.

My life, no less than my brother's, was permanently impacted by the broken relationships in our would-be safe haven of home—only it took me nearly thirty years to realize that this was the case. I'm embarrassed to admit it now, but I remember how I responded throughout high school and college years to questions about my parent's divorce—always with a dismissive shrug: *"It was a long time ago. It wasn't a big deal. I'm fine."*

I expect that some of that was posing, which we of the fallen race of Adam seem to know how to do from an early age. But mostly I think I really believed that I was supposed to be too strong a person to suffer any lasting influences from some past heartache. What did my parent's divorce have to do with me? It was their sad tale, not mine. An unfortunate and often unpleasant complication for my life, certainly: but couldn't I limit its impact to that and nothing more, if I only tried hard enough to rise above it?

My coping style was echoed in the words that Frederick Buechner wrote concerning the death of his father, a tragic event that happened in 1936 when he was just ten years old:

> When somebody you love dies, Mark Twain said, it is like when your house burns down; it isn't for years that you realize the full extent of your loss. For me it was longer than for most, if indeed I have realized it fully even yet, and in the meanwhile the loss came to get buried so deep in me that after a time I scarcely ever took it out to look at it at all, let alone to speak of it.
>
> (Frederick Buechner, *The Sacred Journey*)

Looking back, I'm a little surprised more people weren't compelled to call me out on my attitude of bald-faced denial. Why didn't someone inform me that my nonchalance displayed either an overabundance of childish naivety, or an equally unsupportable amount of youthful pride? I suppose it's possible that they were mostly just as naive as I was. Perhaps at that point in time the prevailing wisdom of the culture was best summed up in John Candy's words in the film *Home Alone*? Trying to console Mrs. McCallister for accidentally leaving her eight-year-old son Kevin home all by himself for the Christmas holidays while the rest of the family jetted off to Paris, Candy's character Gus Molinski recounts the time he had accidentally left one of his children all day in a funeral home, alone with a corpse. "Poor little guy didn't speak for months. But he's okay now. They bounce back. Kids are resilient like that."

On the surface it's funny—"good humor", as we used to say—but below the surface we have carelessly ingested a dangerous lie. Kids are the *opposite* of resilient, as John Eldredge pointed out in the aforementioned wet cement analogy. They aren't bouncing back; rather they are receiving input that is making a permanent impression on their open, undefended hearts. Convictions are forming. Promises (vows) in response to those convictions are being made. And, as is usually the case in life, our ignorance to these soul-truths doesn't protect us from experiencing their harmful, even at times devastating, effects.

THE VOW OF THE LONE WOLF

If we do ever become aware of our own inner vows, it is often much later, when we have reached an age where mature self-examination is even possible. Along with the requisite age and maturity, learning to see the deep impact that these early vows have

made on our present lives often necessitates our becoming the kind
of imaginative people who can learn to read the days of their life in
terms of a running, connected thread, like one would expect to find
in a book, film, or story of any kind.

Even then, uncovering the causes and beginnings of our deeply
rooted attitudes and approaches to life may not happen without the
external aid of gifted, Spirit-led counselors, very wise friends, and the
healing presence of Jesus. Yes, ultimately it is He who will be the key
architect of our journey of self-awareness as He works to "bind up the
brokenhearted"—a ministry He promised to perform in that memorable moment when he announced to the Jewish people of His day
that the words found in the prophet Isaiah (61:1) were being
fulfilled through Him before their very eyes. Some of that "binding
up" work is going to be dealing with broken places buried deep in
our past. The hurt, the wound, the brokenness happened somewhere
back there in the earlier chapters of our story, and to there He must
take us to usher in His healing. And that means one of the things we
can expect that Jesus will be up to in our lives is opening our eyes to
those past events, and revealing to us the protective vows we once
made that have since had so many detrimental effects on our hearts.

Understand, these unspoken vows, or inner resolves, are a very
natural human response to the brokenness of this imperfect, fallen,
and all-too-often dangerous world. Pain and sorrow strike, and we
quite naturally recoil, as if we have touched a hot stove, or disturbed
an unseen snake in our path. *Whatever I just did, I want to make sure
I don't do it again*, a voice whispers within. *I must guard myself more
carefully next time.* Honestly, I think everyone has done this to some
degree. After all, getting hurt is the occupational hazard of living on
the "rebel planet" we call Home. In fact, it feels like this protective
reaction is almost too common to be singled out as an object for our
concern or pity, doesn't it? Seriously, who hasn't made some similar
silent agreement in an attempt to guard their heart from another

painful wound? And to be perfectly fair, on the surface our reaction feels wholly appropriate to the situation: *like who would really expect us to respond any differently?* That's what makes the whole plot against the human heart so diabolical—we are so fully justified in closing ourselves off, making protective vows, guarding our hearts against further wounding. But there is no healing, no true freedom or deep joy to be found once we start travelling down that path.

Yes, these inner vows are common to us all. And my brother's sub-conscious resolve to protect his heart from loss, pain, and loneliness by learning to make it on his own was one of the most common of them all.

I call it *the vow of the Lone Wolf.*

Does it sound familiar? Have you, like so many, found that the determination to go through life as a Lone Wolf both works, and somehow *doesn't* work? That it protects, and yet does so with deva-stating effect? That needing no one turns out to be a safe but hor-rible thing?

ONE FOR ALL?

"Well, I guess the best years of my life are over now. It's time to grow up..." So said one who had held a very deep commitment to the Vow of the Lone Wolf. And yet, on this day when, luggage in hand, he too had crossed a threshold for the last time—leaving behind the old Victorian home where he and seven of his closest friends had lived for the past nine months—here he was, keenly aware that life had to offer a far happier option than that of the Lone Wolf. And yet, barely having surrendered his native defenses to the beauty of this new life, now the dream was fading away from him like the windswept clouds racing toward the eastern horizon even as our family van began the long pursuit of a sun hurrying its way into the west.

For my brother the 'fantasy' of college was ended, and the 'real world' now beckoned—the 'real world' of work and career and adult responsibility. Graduation Day, with all its pomp and circumstance—what had it turned out to be for him but the last note of youth's spring song? One final memory to place in the vault beside the others, the vault that was now to be slammed forever shut with the words "The Time of Our Lives" inscribed over the threshold?

Looking back on the photos of that day, I see the crowds of smiling faces, the exultant expressions as arm-in-arm my brother and his closest friends laugh carelessly into the camera and, by extension, into the face of the unknown challenges of the future that await them. It was like looking at a youthful version of Alexandre Dumas' immortal heroes of myth and legend, the Musketeers Athos, Porthos, and Aramis. Romantic as I am, it was no large imaginative leap for my mind's eye to replace those flowing, blue graduation gowns blousing in the hot blast of an early summer wind with the embroidered cassocks and plumed hats that would have been on display at a seventeenth century graduation of Musketeers in training—if such a thing there ever was. The jubilant faces shining in the sunlight of a future day when untold glory would be theirs and the world would lie conquered at their feet; the raw youthful courage to face head-on whatever challenges the world, the flesh, and the Devil might throw their way; the unmistakable depth of the bond of brotherhood forged through years of shared study, work, laughter and tears: was it any wonder that I imagined I could see the ghosts of another time weaving amongst the happy throng filling the plaza and spilling up and down the stone steps of the old campus chapel?

> Had the world by the tail
> good would prevail
> Starships would sail
> and none of us would fail in this life

Not when you're young
We were drawn to whoever
could keep us together
And bound by the Heavens above
And we tried to survive
travelling at the speed of love.

Woah, when we were young
When we adored the fabulous
Woah, when we were young
We were the foolish fearless
Woah, when we were young
We didn't know it wouldn't last
Woah, when we were young
(Take That, *"When We Were Young"*)

So went the words of a song from the most recent film retelling of the Musketeer legend. *We were drawn to whoever could keep us together and bound by the Heavens above.* Beautiful sentiment. I listen to the song often, and am moved every time, transported to a time and place of deep fellowship and great adventure. *I want this*, my heart whispers. But we don't live in the seventeenth century, and I reckon we don't much bother to believe in the things that Musketeers once believed in—or the things they lived and fought and died for, for that matter. Old Things. Grand Things. Things that could to a great extent be embodied in their now famous cry, *"One for All, and All for One!"* Even now, in this age of cynicism and cold pragmatism, just speaking those words aloud can still make the youthful heart in me leap to its feet and rush to the window of my soul in eager expectation, like the provincial peasant boy in the old story who rushes to the garden gate at the rumour of the passing of some great King.

"One for All, and All for One!" Was there truly such a time when lives could be lived according to such a beautiful, adventurous, and deeply relational ideal?

Whether there was such a time or not, one thing was clear on that warm spring day in the last decade of the twentieth century: *this* was not that time. And now when I look a little closer at those fading graduation photos, I'm sure that I can discern a shadow behind the smiles, and a suggestion in those eyes that they may well have recently been shedding tears—tears that were not all tears of joy.

Perhaps it is only my imagination, but I can't help but see the traces of sorrow lining those smiling faces, for ultimately my brother and his friends knew that, unlike a class of musketeers in training entering together into the long awaited adventure of a lifetime, this graduation was in almost every way that truly matters more about the *ending* of an adventure than the beginning of one. After endless hours, days, weeks, months, sharing every detail of life in one another's company, their little Fellowship was now parting ways, parting never to be together in the same way again.

> Here they talked of revolution,
> Here it was they lit the flame,
> Here they sang about tomorrow,
> And tomorrow never came.
> Phantom faces at the window,
> Phantom shadows on the floor,
> Empty chairs at empty tables
> Where my friends will meet no more.
> Oh my friends, my friends don't ask me
> What your sacrifice was for
> Empty chairs at empty tables
> Where my friend will sing no more.
>
> ("Empty Chairs at Empty Tables", *Les Misérables*)

Sure, my brother and his friends were leaving with diploma in hand. And who could underestimate the importance of that little piece of paper in today's world? It is the *Golden Ticket* that provides entrance into adulthood. *You may now get a job that pays higher than minimum wage; perhaps, if you are lucky, the job will even be in the field of your choice.* Whether you find success and satisfaction in your career, or even find a career at all, is now up to you. The point is that you have the means and the societal permission to take the next step in the journey towards pursuing the blessed and all powerful American Dream: the dream of becoming an independent, autonomous, self-sufficient member of society.

After all, that was the point of those raucous, deeply relational college years, wasn't it? Those unforgettable times of fellowship and brotherhood and shared adventure, that sense that we might live "bound by the heavens above": that was merely just a happy accident, a meaningless byproduct of our true heart's desire. Wasn't it all really about achieving our dream of autonomy? Wasn't this what my brother had been laboring towards since the age of nine—a day when his determination to need no one would become a fully attainable adult reality? The day when he could finally and fully embrace his identity as 'The Lone Wolf'?

THE AMERICAN SPIRIT

It's true that most of us have grown up in an American culture that is crazy over the idea of 'autonomy'. We're just nuts for this idea of self-sufficiency, this approach to life that protects us from needing anyone but ourselves. All our years of education took this as a basic assumption—this mysterious word 'autonomy', which was fed to us as a psychologically indisputable and definitive solution to the age old question of the ancient catechism, *"What is the chief end of man?"* long before we were old enough to understand what the word meant, or why it was universally accepted as our Ultimate Good.

Looking back, I can't ever recall hearing a single lesson taught on why autonomy was the highest pursuit of the healthiest people, only that it unquestionably was. It was one of those things in life that was always assumed, but never explained. Even at church, where man's desperate dependence on God for even his next breath was well known, there was still no full frontal assault mounted against the cultural assumptions regarding personal autonomy.

It wasn't until college, in some psychology or sociology class—I cannot remember now which—that I found myself thinking one day, *"The definition of human health sure relies heavily on this 'autonomy' business. Where did we get this idea from anyway? A whole lot of what we are being taught would fall like a house of cards if we were to take another basic assumption for our ground zero starting point—like family, or community, or interdependence..."*

Now, I'll be honest: until recently I wasn't entirely sure I understood what the definition of the word 'autonomy' really even was. But at the risk of sounding postmodern, I don't suppose it really matters what the word means to those who fully understand it nearly so much as what impression it left upon us common folk through our formative schooling years. We are, after all, imaginative souls. I believe it was Chesterton who said, "Man is more myth than fact," and as such it stands to reason that we learn more readily and deeply through the impressions of myth more than the mere presentation of facts.

Perhaps it was the undefined nature of 'autonomy' that gave it such strength and weight—that allowed it to burrow so deep into our psyche, achieving that magical position of unassailable truth. Whatever the case, I know that the impression left by the word was that it was, in layman's terms, a scientific, psychological, and sociological stamp of approval on our American thirst for 'independence'.

And independence: what a magical word, that! Reaching nearly mythic proportions itself, the word acts like an incantation which ushers in starry, patriotic visions of heroism and bravery of the highest order. Simply speak its name, and good Americans everywhere snap to attention, ready to salute the "good old rugged American independent spirit that made this fair nation the greatest place on Earth". We have our Declaration of Independence, our Independence Day, our independent spirit. We are strong; we can do anything, we believe in ourselves, and we know how to pull ourselves up by our own bootstraps.

It's heady stuff, isn't it? And in case you've never stopped to look closely, you might not have noticed that it's everywhere. There's no escaping it. Perhaps even more closely guarded than the concept of 'autonomy', there's even less room for discussion on this one. If Americans have a Sacred Cow, 'independence' is it.

THE COWBOY

When my father left home I was only seven, and the way that it affected me was not the same as the way it had affected my brother. He gravitated towards protection—finding an independence that would require no one. But something deep inside me shifted towards needing people even more than ever. Now, that isn't to say the temptation to idolize the way of the Lone Wolf wasn't there at all. (Given our national culture, how could it not be?) I remember sometime during my seventh grade year being introduced to the works of the famous western writer of the day, Louis L'Amour. Like most boys my age, I immediately fell in love with his version of the rugged, independent hero: those rough-and-tumble adventurers of the Old West who could survive alone for weeks in hostile Indian country, holed up in a cave in the dead of winter with no food, no water, a broken leg, and three bullet wounds: all of which, even as singular episodes, would have been fatal to all but the most self-sufficient of truly Manly Men.

I especially loved L'Amour's saga of the Clinch Mountain Sack-etts. During that early teen period I read and reread the adventures of William Tell, Orrin, Tyrell—brothers, but still mostly solitary, lonely men travelling the rugged, lonely terrain of the uncharted West in search of fortune, freedom, and a place to call their own. And there were stories of their equally adventurous, equally in-dependent Sackett cousins: Nolan, Flagan, Galloway, and of course Milo Talon, protagonist of a book, the title of which became a sort of private password among our small group of friends in those early years: *Ride The Dark Trail*. Yep, to me these hombres were the ultimate examples of the iconic American hero. They had no home and no lasting commitments. They lived with no barriers and no boundaries, nothing to stop them from doing whatever they wanted whenever they liked. What freedom! It was so beautiful in its simplicity, and it went a far way with me in glorifying the prevailing cultural value of autonomy. *A real man doesn't need anyone,* I thought. *No, sir, no how. No one, except maybe his horse...*

> "It was a rough, hard, wonderful life, and it took men with the
> bark on to live it. We didn't ask anything of anybody..."
>   -(Louis L'Amour, *Galloway*)

And so, despite my own half-awareness of some deep longing within me to experience lasting, intimate relationships, by the end of middle school some equally strong cultural influences had driven me far along the path to believing that the Lone Wolf was in fact the greatest of masculine heroes that one could aspire to become.

And it wasn't just the westerns, though they were strong tonic to a young man in search of a masculine hero. There were plenty of other role models on offer that glorified the life of the Lone Wolf. I think we all know of one off the top of our heads: the world's most famous fictional secret agent. Let's face it: James Bond? He didn't need *anyone*. You didn't even *want* to be one of his friends or associates. My goodness, anyone remotely connected to James was expendable and was, as a rule, usually dead fifteen minutes after we had been introduced to their character. We quickly learned not to grow attached to any friend, associate, or paramour of this iconic masculine hero, this man among men who barely had a moment to mourn his losses before proving once again that he could take down the bad guys, save the world from destruction, and look great doing it—all by himself.

THE LONE WOLF: LOSS AND LEAVING

Fast forward back again with me six years on from my middle school infatuation with those rugged, solitary heroes of the Wild West, and my first introduction to the heroics of British agent 007, back to that heartbreaking spring day when we cleared the last remaining salvageable possessions out of the old Victorian house my brother and his seven housemates had called home for the previous nine months. It was clearly a day I haven't easily forgotten. Up until that point in my life I had felt a unity and bond with my brother so intense that at times it amounted almost to a vicarious sharing of his experiences. It is even possible that I felt certain passages in my brother's life more keenly than he did himself, as we often do with those we know and care about most. That is partly true because we are rarely able to distance ourselves from our own story long enough to be aware of our most significant moments—not until long after, when the golden hue cast by nostalgia replays those moments in the theatre of our memories for what they had always been, but what we were blind to in the moment. It is for most of us, as C.S. Lewis noted it was for himself, that no experience was enjoyed fully in the moment, not "until it had been down in the cellar for a while".

This day, however, there were signs that the significance of the moment was not wholly lost upon my brother. Nor upon me. For on this day I saw autonomy and independence and *'a real man doesn't need anyone'* go to war with Something Else—some human desire that runs deeper than culture and stronger than society's norms. And for all the talk of New Beginnings, I could only see an End, and the End seemed to me to be full of more sorrow and loss than the promise of the New Beginning.

> This is the time to remember
> Cause it will not last forever
> These are the days to hold on to
> Cause we won't
> Although we'll want to
> These are the times
> But time is gonna change
> I know we have to move somehow
> But I don't want to lose you now
>
> -Billy Joel, *"This is the Time"*

And although that Something Else I saw go to war that day had no weapons with which to win this particular fight against the cultural status quo and the ways of the world, in my own heart that day I learned that it was in fact the stronger of the two desires.

And why should it not be? For the vow to "never need anyone" is always born out of the pain of a wounded heart, not the deepest longings of a healthy one. And if we know anything about the animal kingdom, it's that a Lone Wolf is merely that kind of wolf who has forgotten all the best parts of what a wolf was designed by God to do and to be.

Perhaps we are, many of us, more like the Lone Wolf than we ever intended to be, in ways we haven't even acknowledged. In our wounding, in our hurt, in the brokenness of this world, do we even remember all the best parts of what we as humans—as intrinsically relational beings—were designed to be? And if we could remember this precious, deeply relational portion of our humanity, is it even recoverable in a world such as ours?

I don't suppose that on that sad spring day I was mature enough to be asking these deeper questions, but I've been asking them ever since, and I'm asking them now. For some of us who have travelled a fair distance down life's Road it may feel like too many bridges have been crossed, too many ships burned, to ever hope or dream of recovering this precious, child-like piece of ourselves in any significant way—this buried piece of our humanity that cowers in submission beneath the cold, stoic stare of the Lone Wolf gazing back at us from the bathroom mirror each day.

I won't pretend that the eventual success of such a difficult rehabilitation is a foregone conclusion. Our thirst for autonomy and independence runs so deep; our relational instincts have been buried deeper still. But it remains my ardent hope that some of you might be bold enough to ask some of these questions along with me: that we might discover together that the pursuit of 'autonomy' need not, *ought not,* always have the last word on the kind of choices we make, and ultimately, on the kind of people we become...

TWO

ALONE

"Yes! in the sea of life enisled, With echoing straits
between us thrown, Dotting the shoreless watery wild,
We mortal millions live alone.
                                        - Matthew Arnold

I n the beginning—back in the Garden of goodness and delight
and perfection that was Mankind's first and intended home—the
opening chapter of the Holy Scriptures tells us that God paused to
survey all that He had just finished creating, and announced that He
was pleased as punch with all that he saw. (Of course the Hebrew is a
bit technical, and my grandmother and all her generation weren't
around just yet, so you'll just have to accept "pleased as punch" as
more or less a loose translation. Okay, more loose, less translation. But
I'd say it captures the essence of the thing.)

Much as you might expect, everything God made turned out
good. Anywhere you dip into this brief description of the Creation

account that has been passed down through the ages from the mouth of God to the tablets Moses first made on Mount Sinai, you will find example after example of how good it truly is. Verse sixteen tells us that He separated the waters, and made the land appear. Just imagine: from out of the watery depths rise all the lands we know, with all the wild and fantastic geography that covers our planet—the majestic Rocky Mountains, the other-worldly heights of the Himalayas, the heartbreaking beauty of the Swiss Alps, England's Lake District, the White Cliffs of Dover, the Scottish Highlands, to name just a handful of my personal favorites. And by raising the mountains out of the Deep and gathering the dry lands together, by logical necessity God was also forming the boundaries for where the waters were to remain: the fathomless vast oceans, the balmy azure seas, the turbulent rivers—to surround and border and weave in and out of these new landscapes in all their rushing, babbling, sparkling delight.

Can you imagine? What an understatement to call all of that extravagant, creative, breathtaking beauty simply "good"! And that's only the beginning. It gets better. Much better.

Next comes all vegetative life. You'd need a lifetime of botanical studies to even begin to describe in adequately—how shall I put it—*flowery* language, the extravagance going on in this brief bit of creativity described in the eleventh verse of the first chapter of Genesis. Trees—deciduous and evergreen, whole forests of them miles upon miles wide, filling the countryside, covering hill and dale, climbing up the sides of those but newly-made mountain ranges still reveling in their infancy. The towering Great Sequoias of California, the rolling forests of the Appalachian and the Allegheny mountains, the stately, white barked sentinels of a Rocky Mountain aspen grove thousands upon thousands strong, with their quaking autumn leaves turned breathtaking hues of yellow, gold and orange. Maple, oak, poplar, ash, hawthorn, birch and willow. The variety is stunning, the lavish abundance defying description. Trees by the millions—billions—and each and every one of them its own majestic marvel worthy of unending happy contemplation.

BACK UP THE SUNBEAM TO THE SUN

I remember there being a couple of trees I used to pass on that paradisiacal Midwestern college campus I mentioned earlier, during the habitual prayerful, emotion-filled walks so common to that period of my life. I used to stop and allow myself to drink those trees in, really focusing on them as individual creative acts, and say, "God, I wonder if anyone has ever praised, thanked, and adored you for the wonder and beauty of THIS particular tree?!!" Passers-by might well have labeled me a tree-hugger if they had noticed the way I stood and gaped in delight at one gnarled old solitary oak that grew along the northern border of the park we used to hold our college soccer training sessions; but I felt that the gift so easily ignored and so swiftly dismissed deserved something more than it commonly received from the hurried, preoccupied, and self-absorbed recipients of that singular gift. Here was a miracle, and we were missing it. Perhaps a deep ache inside myself, knowing what it was to be 'missed' by those around me, drew an ever deeper connection for me towards the old oak, and the other forgotten trees I stopped to delight in. It felt like I was discovering a precious signpost of God's character and His goodness hidden right there in plain sight. As C.S. Lewis wrote:

> Gratitude exclaims, very properly "How good of God to give me this."
> Adoration says, "What must be the quality of that Being whose far-off and
> tiny coruscations are like this!" One's mind runs back up the sunbeam to
> the sun.

If I could always be what I aim at being, no pleasure would be too ordinary or too usual for such reception: from the first taste of the air when I look out of the window—one's whole cheek becomes a sort of palate—down to one's soft slippers at bedtime.

(C.S. Lewis, *Letters to Malcolm*)

As I write this, it is autumn here in the Midwest—one of the few seasons we tend to boast of in these parts. This morning, half-awake and virtually blind without the aid of either glasses or contacts, I opened my eyes to neither the startling brilliance of sunlight, or—which is so common for six months out of our year—to the dull, semi-darkness of a heavy gray overcast sky. Actually it *was* overcast. Going to rain before the day was out, dollars to doughnuts. But it wasn't the clouds that I noticed. (Remember I'm working with eyes about as helpful as a bat's at this point, so I'm not really *seeing* anything.) Instead, I had the overwhelming sense of being immersed in an enchanting, deeply-hued bath of color that pulsated and coursed through our small home.

Curiosity piqued, I reached for my glasses. Streaming in from the large picture window across from where I lay was an absolute riot of colors so intense that for a moment I wondered if I wasn't still dreaming—if I hadn't wandered into a fairy land, or perhaps some-how awoken in the great forest of Lothlorion of the High Elves of Tolkien's imagination. Half the view out the wide window was filled with the burning bush in the foreground that had turned the color of a ripe Gala apple—deep red, mottled with the hint of lingering green. Further out the Japanese maple and the barberry bush had both turned a deeper red than the burning bush: tinged with just a dusting of purple. And across the street a grand old maple rising more than fifty feet into the sky was the centerpiece of the land-scape—every one of its thousands upon thousand leaves the most perfectly pumpkin orange you could hope to imagine.

Just another dark, rainy autumn morning? Not on your life; though I might have missed it, if I hadn't been praying so consistently the past few weeks for God to open the eyes of my heart. The richest king in the world could not have had any better, were he to order all the kingdom's wealth to be melted down and used to wash his castle with paints of pure gold. Extravagant goodness to be sure, and my mind was "running back up the sunbeam to the sun", both delighting and adoring in one fluid, indivisible act.

THE TASTE OF GOODNESS

Returning to the Genesis account, friends: we haven't even begun to talk about all the equally marvelous, endless variety of trees that produced edible objects—imagine that! (We are so used to the idea, we don't even consider how strange and unexpected it all was. Would you have thought of doing that—designing part of the landscape in such a way that living creatures could pluck bits of it out of the whole, put them in their mouths, and experience both pleasure and renewed strength? Would you have thought to write a play in which parts of the very stage could be uprooted and consumed by the actors—to the general delight of all?)

> And the best part is, almost everything is eatable—edible.
> You can EAT it!   - (Gene Wilder, *Willie Wonka*)

> And the Lord God made all kinds of trees grow out of the ground -
> trees that were pleasing to the eye and good for food.
>
>   Genesis 2:9

Apples and oranges. Peaches, plums and pears. Bananas and pineapples. Olives and figs. The mind boggles, and the mouth waters at the very naming of them. We certainly don't need to walk by faith to know about God's goodness, or the goodness of His creativity for us here in this—we have literally *tasted* and *seen* how truly *good* these things are!

It's all been said before by much better writers down through the ages; but it bears repeating. I daresay we are compelled to repeat it. Often, constantly, with an eye towards reawakening the faculty of delight that rusts within us all. Endless praise isn't just a religious concept: it's the natural description of the riot in our hearts at the contemplation of what kind of Being must have left His signature here in all of this vibrant, exuberant, extravagant creativity.

And really, even still, we've hardly started to get going here. We've only just scratched the surface of Creation in all its bounty, and every bit of it is good, good, good. *Grass?* Soft, and oh so good, especially between your toes. *Hawaii?* Not too shabby either, as far as tropical paradises go. *Stars?* Breathtakingly good, in just about the most epic, romantic, haunting way imaginable. *The Sun?* Sort've like life-sustaining good, and a thousand other goods that would take too long to enumerate. *Fish? Birds? Animals of every kind?*

Wow.

It's incredible beyond words.

And it's all really just setting the stage.

What? This is all just a prelude?

Oh yeah. The best is yet to come.

COMETH THE HOUR, COMETH THE MAN

Now, as we move forward into the next part of the creation account, I don't want any of you to be sidetracked by the *'It's not about me'* religious trend making its way around the Church these days. I understand the sentiment behind the movement, and of course as a posture of pride and arrogance, people living their lives thinking *'me, me, me'* all the time is not only narcissistic, it's also way out of touch with reality. It doesn't take a very robust sense of humor to agree that even the very best of us would make a pretty miserable Center of the Universe. So yeah, I get it. A self-centered individual who hasn't submitted his life to Jesus and to the service of the Kingdom of God is going to need a healthy dose of reorientation in which he learns that 'it's not about me.'

But there's also something else going on in the 'it's not about me' movement—a worldview that we've adopted unwittingly from the prevailing mood of materialism and godless evolution in the society around us. If 'worldview' is so strong a word that we would adamantly deny our own adherence, then call it a *mood* if you will. I myself would be tempted to call it more of a *malaise* than a mood. What is it I'm referring to? It's this insidious idea that we—as the product of one random series of mutations out of a trillion other such mindless movements—are nothing more than a piece of the universe, and not in any way distinct from the Whole. The atheist scientist tells us that we are of such insignificance in the Universe that it is pure human arrogance to imagine that we are special in any way. While the Christian would humble himself before a loving Father, the Accidental Materialist would have us all humble ourselves before an empty void stretching endless light years in every direction, until we are deeply rooted in the idea that we are little Nothings lost in the middle of a never ending Nowhere.

But contrary to the currently popular macro-evolutionary driven attitude that 'it's not about us', when we take a close look at the 'why' of Creation—the deep purposes in the heart of God—we come to understand that the real point of all of this indescribable creativity we've been taking a brief look at is still yet to be revealed. Wait for it:

> Then God said, "Let us make man in our own image,
> in our likeness..."   (Genesis 1:26)

And there it is. In today's parlance, it's the cosmic mic drop. From inanimate objects we've moved on to vegetative life, then on to sentient life, and finally, at the crescendo of God's Magnum Opus, cometh the Man himself, the being created in the very image of God, animated by the breath of God Himself, intended for a high and holy destiny that has been hidden even from the Heavenly Host.

I'll bet you can guess what God had to say about this climax of Creation, can't you?

And it was Good.

Notice (how could you fail to?) that according to the way God chose to record the Creation story, there is an obvious theme that's pretty hard to miss: when He makes something, it's Good. And I'm convinced that it is both appropriate and wise for us to be *looking* for a 'theme' in what we have been given in Genesis Chapter One. There's something more creative going on in this writing than just cold, hard. academic facts. Remember, this is hardly an exhaustive account here folks—we just witnessed the creation of everything in the material universe crammed onto one page of text. *One page!* It would seem that of all the millions of things God could have told us about the Beginning, he decided to boil it down to one vital essential that we were desperately going to need to understand in order to live out of a firm grasp of Who We Were, Where We had Come From, and How We had Gotten Here. And even though we live mostly unaware of the deep significance that 'beginnings' bear on all these issues, God Himself has surely not forgotten their importance. As Ben Affleck's character in the film *Shakespeare in Love* so eloquently exclaimed, on returning to The Globe Theatre after time away traveling the play houses of England and hearing that his friend Will Shakespeare had a new production waiting in the wings: "What is the play, and what is my part?"

In order to play one's role well, the first order of business is to know the Story. And the most sensible place to start understanding any story is, quite logically, to go back and see its beginning. Odds are you're going to find some vital information back there at the beginning, without which you don't have much hope of understanding even half of what's going on at this point in the story.

NOT SO GOOD?

Now, I don't mean to be condescending here. I think it's safe to assume that none of you are probably strangers to the Genesis account of Creation, or to the belief that, crassly put, *"God don't make no junk."* To be honest, we are pretty desensitized to a lot of what I'm saying at this point. We assume that since God made it, of course it's good. There's no surprise in that, really. Nothing to see here. Move along.

But then notice what an incredibly strange thing the story tells us next (I think we often miss the incongruity of what's being replayed before our imaginations here).

> The Lord God said, "It is not good for the man to be alone."
>
> (Genesis 2:18)

Whoa. What do we have here? Did I understand that correctly? God, in His infinite wisdom, His unparalleled creativity, His perfection, is actually looking down at the world—at the unfallen Paradise of Eden, mind you—and saying, *"Uh-oh. Hold on. Big problemo! There's something wrong with this picture..."*

While I'm not willing to go so far as to suggest that God, in the midst of doing 'quality control', discovers an oversight on His part, we have to admit that *something extremely significant* is going on here. "And it was good." "And this was good." "And that was good." "And everything was good."

Good, good, good.

It's all good.

Until suddenly...

...*it's not.*

Now, assuming, as I suppose most of us would, that God knew He was going to make both a Man and a Woman all along, then what's up with the dramatic tension? I mean, come on now: why not just do it at the first whack, bring both of them out onto the stage at the same time, and save us all from the ridiculous feeling that somehow the All-Knowing Creator of the Universe just did a 'whoopsie-daisy'? Why does He put a pause in the creative process, right in the midst of declaring how good everything is, to point out to us (I suppose in that moment He was pointing it out to Himself, to the Son, and to the Heavenly Hosts?) that something amidst all this Garden Paradise is yet amiss?

Stick with me here. I realize we are battling against a bored, non-plussed familiarity with this bit of the Creation account that is whispering to us even now, *"Yeah, yeah. Everything was good. And then it wasn't so good. And so God created women and invented marriage, blah, blah, blah. I've heard this one at every wedding I've ever been to..."* But let's push past that and go a little deeper this time. I mean, this seems so...well, *odd.* What was God up to here? Maybe understanding His actions as they are described in the Genesis account is beyond our human comprehension—but what about making some sense of why He chose to have Moses record things just as he did? If we got beyond the mechanical knee-jerk response of saying "The Bible says it, and that's all you need to know", and began to ask, "Why are these facts reported in so curious a manner?" then might we agree that at the very least this inex-plicably odd juxtaposition of the one not good thing—the form-breaker, the pattern-defier, the iconoclastic exception to the rule—is meant to startle us out of our lethargy and warn us that something vital to the entire explanation of *essential* human nature is about to

be expressed? Is it possible even that all those short, swift and unsatisfying descriptions of Creation were glossed over in such an apparently unscientific manner because, in the context of the account God
is offering to us, they were intended merely as part of the backdrop?
Part of a build up to the thing He *really* wanted to tell us?

(Wouldn't that explanation be a great relief to all those who
struggle with the simplistic summation that they find in Genesis 1 of
how Everything in the material universe came into existence? Instead of fearing some errancy in the account because no intelligent,
modern, enlightened person could find the recorded events remotely
satisfying to their hunger to know and understand, wouldn't it be
great to discover that it never did satisfy this intellectual curiosity,
even to a middle-eastern tribe of humble, uneducated people some
3,500 years ago—because it was never meant to?)

A STUDY IN ANCIENT POETRY

In college one of my Bible professors was Dr. Leland Ryken, a thin,
dour-faced academic type, who was constantly involved in a playful
war of words with the other professor who shared the teaching load in
that class, Dr. James Wilhoit. They were an odd couple, those two, and
the class was always entertaining—watching the good-natured clash of
personalities at play. Dr. Ryken had written a book entitled *"How to
Read the Bible as Literature"*, and early in the semester he began to
teach from the basic premise of his book—that to understand the
Bible correctly, one must read each section with a view for the actual
literary form in which it was written. As a naive nineteen-year-old
Christian who was quite zealous about my faith (as I understood it),
I remember responding with a furious and indignant defensiveness
to everything the good professor was trying to teach. *What?* I
spluttered. *Heretic! Backslider! Libertine! I can't believe they're letting
him teach here! In a Bible class of all places!*

Obviously my reaction to the good professor's thesis was a tad extreme, to say the least. I think at that point I still held the Bible in a sort of simplistic reverence that bordered on idolatry. I thought that it would devalue some of the 'magical' quality I always attributed to the Bible to give too much consideration to the individual authors, or the genres in which they wrote. I feared that this approach would give more respect to the intentions of the human authors than was appropriate. God was speaking through them: did it really matter what *they* thought they were writing? Thankfully, as the years went by I did come off that particular high horse that was a form of Bibleolatry, and discovered how much it actually aided in biblical interpretation to recognize the various *genres* present within its pages.

And looking at the Creation Story of Genesis through this lens—through this idea that there is more than simply naked, textbook-like *truth* on display here, but a deliberate and painstakingly developed *literary form* as well—it should be clear that God was highlighting an essential Idea through the form that He used.

Most of us know enough about western forms of poetry to know that *rhyme* and *rhythm* are some of its key building blocks. But back in the times of Moses when the first five books of the bible—the Law, or Torah—were written, their primary poetic devices were *repetition* and *parallelism*. Although in our translations, and by our classical western standards, the Creation account hardly comes across as a poem, we can't help but notice the use of these other, more foreign to our understanding, artistic devices: most especially the glaring, impossible-to-miss repetition in the frequently used phrases, *"And there was evening, and there was morning"*, and the satisfied proclamation: *"And He saw that it was good."*

If we had needed any more evidence that the startling revelation of there being, in fact, one thing that was not good, was somehow significant—perhaps pivotal—to what God meant to communicate through the Creation Story, I think we have it. This is Truth, to be sure: I am making no judgement here at all against those who hold a Literalist view of each detail given in the Genesis account. On such matters I have no desire to quibble. But whether you lean towards the literal viewpoint or the figurative viewpoint of the Truths expressed, one thing cannot be denied: what we have here is not only Truth, but also creative storytelling, carefully shaped and crafted— an artistry of words and ideas that is poetry to its very core. Keeping that fact in mind, we also cannot deny that it is no mistake that the pattern ends as it does: *"It is not good for the Man to be alone."*

Now, in our incessant need to boil the magic and mystery of the human adventure down to easy-to-understand axioms and culturally relevant ideas, we have in the Church today accepted this as meaning that marriage is the prescribed panacea for the solving of this existential crisis, this reality about our humanity that runs deeper than mere brokenness: for it was part of our nature before the breaking of the world, even in the golden summer glory of Paradise when no Shadow yet lay upon even the outermost hedges of the Garden of God. And while in the narrative the "realization" on God's part of this trouble in Paradise leads to the creation of the Woman and immediately upon the heels of that, her union with the Man, it would be naive and willfully stubborn not to admit that from this union would spring all Mankind. In short, God did not solve Adam's aloneness merely by giving him a wife, but in so doing setting into motion the system through which He would also give to them both sons and daughters, grandchildren, great-grandchildren: generation upon generation unto the ending of the World.

Might we dare to say then, that while Christian teaching has been quick to say that God solved the great dilemma raised in the Creation narrative ("It is not good for the Man to be alone") by giving to the Man a Wife, it would perhaps be equally true to point out that He has solved Man's loneliness by giving him Mankind?

THE DAY GOD WASN'T ENOUGH

There have always been in the Church those who preach a philosophy that emphasizes detachment from the world and singular devotion to God. And our initial reaction is to think that it sounds, well....so *religious*. So *good*. So *correct*. Like if we were really committed to living the lives God wants us to live, this is *exactly* the sort of place we would end up sooner or later. After all, the natural tendency of our Fallen Race is to live apart from God, to not even *begin* to give Him the attention or the time He deserves, much less the worship, obedience, or mastery over our lives. In contrast, when we come to Him through Jesus and the Good News that our sins are forgiven and our Creator waits to welcome us back into relationship with Him with arms flung wide, we immediately begin to see the necessity for a major overhaul of those old, mistaken priorities. The God who we thought to be merely an inconsequential component of the Whole we refer to as 'our life' turns out to be the very Ground of our being, the Foundation on which all the rest of 'our life' stands. "He must become greater" is a natural and necessary mindset during this time of transition out of our vain and foolish humanism.

And as His star rises, the pseudo-importance of a great many things we once valued above Him are eclipsed in comparison. As a tendency—a trend, a direction—thus followed to its logical conclusion, we may begin to project forward in our imagination that the ultimate End of All Things would be the renunciation of everything that is not God—even the world He created for our good pleasure.

I remember feeling this way myself during my junior year of college, when through a series of painful circumstances I lost every external conduit of 'life' that had become more important to me than God Himself. It began when I was unceremoniously dumped by the young woman I loved and hoped to marry. Then, while still reeling from the break-up, my bid to achieve another dream—a call-up from the reserve college soccer team to the Varsity squad—was derailed by a season-ending ankle injury. Almost on the very heels of that disappointment, the many late-night walks in rain and inclement weather—the sole pleasure remaining to a hopeless romantic wallowing in his own brokenheartedness—led to a debilitating bout of pneumonia.

Oh, what a pathetic picture I painted! Part Old Testament Job, part Shakespeare's Romeo Montague, part Dumas' Edmond Dantes—I played the role of the love-sick poet with 'nothing left to live for' to melodramatic perfection.

But through this dark time I discovered an intimacy with God that I had never known or, at that point in my journey, even imagined possible. It began during those late-night, rain-soaked wanderings across the deserted, silent campus—a campus whose lonely lamp-lit paths I haunted in deliberate search of solitude. In the beginning my conversation with God was nothing more than an endless soliloquy, beseeching Him with sighs and tears to intervene in the affairs of Men (and more to the point, Women) on behalf of my broken heart. But the words, the cries, the tears were more fervent than any tears I had shed before in the context of 'prayer', and the angst of those moments inevitably drove me closer to the One who appeared to be my last hope of consolation. I knew as I had never known before that He was listening, that He cared. And after a while—many months (I was far too much a devotee to the cause of romantic love to miss this chance to revel in all the emotions of unrequited love as long as my heart could sustain the necessary maelstrom of emotions)—it began to dawn on me that the pain of losing *her* had been a small price to pay for the new found joy of gaining *Him* in this deeper and more intimate sense.

It was at the height of this spiritual awakening that I believed I was beginning to understand certain famous words spoken by the Apostle Paul:

But whatever was to my profit I now consider loss for the sake of Christ.
What is more I consider everything to be a loss compared to the sur-
passing greatness of knowing Christ Jesus my Lord, for whose sake I
have lost all things.

(Philippians 3:7-8)

Enraptured in the first flush of this new awakening, I began to
imagine that the ultimate consummation of my spiritual journey
would be to one day sit in the presence of God Himself, contem-
plating His completeness in rapturous devotion—wanting, needing,
desiring nothing else, nothing more. I would exist in some uncrea-
ted, formless spiritual dimension, infused with this cloudy, silver
haze of glory, possessing this complete satisfaction that now and for
the rest of eternity I would have no thought for anything but God
Himself. All else I had ever known or loved or delighted in was
merely a mirage, a fleeting phantom that would one day flutter and
fade and dissolve into shreds of smoke and nothingness—to reveal
that only One Thing in fact remained. I was convinced that this is
the destiny He was moving me towards. Of course these were very
natural feelings, born as they were out of an experience very similar
to that which we have all felt in the context of romantic love—when
all the commonplace world fades from view and we have eyes for nothing but the object of our rapturous, glorious obsession.

And even in the years long after the first flush of this 'spiritual
high', had passed (all such moments of life-halting obsession must
fade, or all star-crossed lovers would die of starvation), I still carried
the same image in the back of mind of what the highest Good must
look like—eternal separation from the material universe; a lonely,
disembodied, exclusive contemplation of God and God alone. But
then I held that old imaginative picture of the Consummation of All
Things more or less at arm's length, and with a secret discomfort, for
the new things I seemed to be discovering about the Goodness of

God were larger and fuller and vibrantly teeming with unexpected Life and Beauty: a living, breathing kaleidoscope of People, a delightful deluge of Places, an extravagant cornucopia of Things. Life, in all its variety of experiences, was Good, just as God had said it was from the very beginning. Still, the old vision was slow to be cast out, and I was often visited by a sense of horror at the fear that the 'good' God had prepared for me was not the tangible Good for which my soul now desired.

And yet...how odd, and beautiful, and so like our God that *His own Words*—so exquisitely and purposefully chosen—would be the source of our protection from our own narrow, one-dimensional 'religious' instincts.

> The Lord God said, "It is not good for the man to be alone." (Gen. 2:18)

Do you see it? It's there, staring back at us from out of the depths of Time. Once upon that far away Time, God created a Thing in His own image, in the Imago Dei, to be with Him, to see His face and to walk with Him amongst the flowers of Paradise. That is to say, everything we tend to imagine would be necessary to achieve the ultimate fulfillment of our existence was pretty much already happening there for Adam, the firstborn of the Race of Man. And yet it was there, in that exact, seemingly perfect, moment and time and place that one of the unexpected, fathomless mysteries in the heart of God was announced to the breathlessly watching heavenly host: having God was not everything that God wanted for the Man. Remember now: the Man *had* God, had Him at a level of intimacy you and I can only dream of. And yet in some significant way God was still able to describe the Man as being *alone*. By His own choice, in His uncontested sovereignty and ability to do all things, God chose to make a Man that needed more than God.

He chose to make a Man that also needed Men.

THREE

A GOODNESS
BIG ENOUGH

"A great good is coming, is coming, is coming to thee,
Anodos."
- George Macdonald, *Phantastes*

I t was a hot humid day in the summer of '83. With an odd mixture of euphoric excitement and anxious trepidation, I carefully unstuck the heat-warmed edges of the Buck Rogers plastic decal on my favorite t-shirt, hitched my three-stripe tube socks (color coordinated to match my terry-cloth wristbands) up as close to my knees as they would stretch, and double-checked one last time that my fashionably tight shorts were not showing too much of my bean pole legs. Then, heaving a piece of the family's green, hard-sided Samsonite luggage into my arms, I took a deep breath and headed across the parking lot toward the bus that was to convey me to one of the most memorable weeks of my still-so-brief life: Junior High Church Summer Camp.

With every step I knew that I was leaving safety, comfort—and any possibility of boredom—behind. Frenetic, overly stimulated pre-pubescent teens ran amok through the church parking lot, ranging in packs and herds in and out of the double doors that led to the old Fellowship Hall where pre-trip registration matters were being fina-lized. Luggage was flying. Footballs were flying. Bodies were flying. Those were freer days, when physical contact, wrestling, dogpiles—even affectionate touch: hair tousling, headlocks, hugs—were looked on with an innocence appropriate to the place in the world that our young and simple hearts yet belonged.

Now, one of the benefits of growing up in a thriving mega-church was the weekly training it afforded in acquiring all the skills nec-essary to slip with serpentine agility and sublime deftness through the smallest gap in a tightly bunched moving mob of people. To antici-pate the next gap before it even materialized, and to commit to the necessary move as an act of faith, courage, and supreme self-confi-dence. Anything less and the rest of 'the gang' (if in fellowship), or the 'hunted quarry' (if in pursuit) would be lost around two turns, up a staircase, and into the parking lot headed for home before you could even exclaim: "The game is afoot!" It was great fun; a highlight of church to be sure, like playing a real life version of Tetris every Sunday morning, where the prize for winning was having the widest selection of donuts to choose from in the melee following Mr. Greenman's class in Knox Hall.

It was with a brilliant display of these hard-earned skills that I successfully fought my way through the pandemonium in Fellow-ship Hall to reach the registration table, Samsonite in tow. We had arrived late, as was the norm in those days for our family, and regi-stration was wrapping up.

"Here's your folder for the week with everything you need to know," chirped Anna Marie, the serious-minded, authoritative junior high director as she handed me my packet of information. "Maps, schedules, rules, journal space for quiet times. Oh," she added with a curiously suspicious smile, "and the pink page in the back has the cabin assignments."

Now, if there's one thing that junior highers understand better than just about any other people in the world it's that one's ultimate happiness is almost entirely dependent upon the people around you, and a week at summer camp with your closest friends can be the pinnacle of joyous delight, while a week spent run afoul of a gang of teenage miscreants can be a veritable living Hell. Having both the good and bad fortune to experience both, I can tell you that this is no exaggeration.

But this year that was mere formality! There wasn't really any reason to fear any more—no need to leave potential compatibility to the caprices of chance, the winds of fate, or whatever alphabetic equation the leadership came up with next. You see, over the past year David and I had been growing increasingly inseparable. By the summer of '83 we were really settling into one of those classic boyhood friendships that most children dream of. It would have been unthinkable for Anna Marie to have miscalculated our desire to make this week one of the golden highlights of an already golden youth.

"Did you see? Can you believe it?"

The voice calling to me through the cacophony of boisterous noise was unmistakably that of my best friend. He had materialized out of the crowd, hauling in a stray throw of a wildly mis-aimed Nerf football, then turning breathlessly to address me, all the while exuding the nonchalance that came so naturally to him.

"Did I see what?" I called back. It was my first glimpse of David since my frantic arrival, and my heart leaped with excitement in anticipation of the riotous times that were now about to commence.

A head shorter than many of us, David's baby face, Scandinavian blond hair, mischievous joie de vivre, and inherent self-confidence combined to make him the most sought-after companion in our junior high society. He was, in brief, the epitome of "cool"—mostly because he was too busy enjoying life to waste a moment's thought on whether or not he *was* cool. Fun and exuberance came so naturally to him, and it was contagious to all around him. To paraphrase a line from one of our favorite tv shows of that year, *Remington Steele*, I never minded being the second one through the door, so long as the first one through the door was David Anderson.

Back to the story. Having had no response to my first query, I tried again to be heard above the din.

"Did I see what?"

Already the mob of kids and counselors committed body and soul to the makeshift game of 'dogpile the person holding the football' had swarmed around and over us, and David was being carried away on a turbulent sea of testosterone when he somehow succeeded in shouting over his shoulder, *"Anna Marie put us in different cabins!"*

In the space of a heartbeat I felt all the blaze of a glorious summer camp experience worthy to be preserved in songs, ballads and epic poems for generations to come suddenly vanish into thin air. Was it really possible? If Anna Marie cared about us at all, wouldn't she have put us in the same cabin? I found myself wondering: was she merely clueless, or was she culpably heartless?

As soon as I had recovered from the initial shock, I strode back to the registration desk, emboldened by the obvious justice of my case.

"Anna Marie," I said, "You made a mistake. You put me and David in different cabins."

"Oh no, dear," she smiled back with a motherly I-know-what's-good-for-you expression on her face. "That wasn't a mistake. I separated you on purpose. I think it will be good for both of you to have to make some new friends."

Needless to say, I was speechless. Floored. Thunderstruck. I was no longer the victim of human error or a random injustice born of mere inattentiveness. This wasn't a mistake: *it was a plot*. A diabolical plot hatched to drive a wedge between me and my best friend. A misdirected plot, one that I now believe stemmed from a very specific attitude towards our friendship, and most likely towards friendship in general.

For the sake of brevity, I'll fast forward through the events of the following week and say that ultimately David and I very much did get the last laugh. Anna Marie's plot to 'take us out of ourselves' failed utterly. Backfired brilliantly. Oh, yes: we took her attempts to hinder our inseparable friendship as a direct challenge—one we overcame with every spare moment we were allowed. We were up before dawn—before even our counselors—plotting our own course for the day: joined at the hip in every activity together, every meal, every game, every teaching session. We got in trouble together, made lifelong memories together, even began falling in love with the same girl together. (That's a story for later.) And you know what? For thirty years that week has remained one of the iconic experiences upon which our lifelong friendship has been built.

A GRAVE MISUNDERSTANDING

Now, I realize that it's possible you may not see much more in this story other than the obvious and natural struggle between young boys who want to have fun and the adults responsible for teaching them the more mature ways of the world, or, as in this case, the ways of the church. *A wise and decisive bit of youth-pastoring,* you might be inclined to think. *The fact that it backfired with lifelong positive effect—that the deepest spiritual resource of your entire life has been this friendship—could hardly have been taken into account at the time.*

Right. Because no one could've seen that coming.

Or could they?

Let's say for argument sake that Anna Marie had been successful, that the bonds of my friendship with David had been weakened during that iconic week in the summer of '83 as we sacrificed our personal desires in order to dutifully pursue a more 'collective' attitude towards this larger, more ambiguous entity called 'the youth group'. That would have been the mature thing to do, right? The unselfish thing? And, now we come to it: the thing that would have pleased God the most?

So we bucked the system and we got lucky. I mean, let's be honest: we weren't even remotely considering the potential spiritual, moral, educational benefits of our friendship as a couple of zany, fun-loving junior high kids. So we bucked the system—the commonly accepted belief that friendship is an *incidental* by-product of a healthy youth ministry model—and we got lucky. Surely that's the exception and not the rule? A bad example to be eschewed, not a badge of honor to be paraded about in public? After all, what does obediently following God's laws have to do with something as *human*, as *natural*, as a really good friendship anyway?

WHAT A GOD WANTS

Now, I don't want to get sidetracked here, but I think we've hit on something that needs to be addressed. It feels like we've struck a vein of ore that leads straight through and down to the very foundation of our beliefs, something at the level of *elemental* truth. It's something that we touched on in the preceding chapter, but into which we didn't delve too deeply. It's an idea that can be summed up in the question: *Just what exactly are God's desires for us?*

As I've already alluded to, in college when something that might be called a 'religious fervor' fell upon me, my inclination—whether by instinct or by teaching—was to treat the process of 'surrendering to the Lordship of Jesus Christ' as a *negative* activity. By negative I mean the opposite of 'positive', if we can ascribe to 'positive' the idea of moving *up* a number chart, as when in the act of addition the number grows further away from zero, and thus become fuller, larger, more robust. If my 'life' in all its variation of interests, desires, and activities was made up of a sum total of, let's say, fifty parts, then it appeared to me that in order to please God my task was to self-sacrificially jettison from my life as many of those parts as possible—until ultimately nothing remained but one thing: God Himself.

As a case in point, you'll recall that I mentioned how badly I desired to one day make it onto the college soccer team. At that age I loved playing soccer more than doing just about any other thing in the whole world, and I dreamt often of the moment when all the blood, sweat, and tears would finally pay off and I would cross over into this 'promised land' I longed to enter: the moment when I would become a fully accepted member of the team—worthy at last, after many heartaches and humiliations, to join the ranks of this elite circle of talented athletes. After being cut from the squad two years in a row, I had finally scraped my way onto the reserve team in my junior season. Factoring in the seniors that would be graduating, I felt that the next year I had a real chance of making the varsity squad, if only as a willing benchwarmer. At long last I thought I was within touching distance of achieving my dream—even if only as the 'Rudy' of my college soccer team.

But then my life well and truly went to pieces in a manner that would have made even Humpty Dumpty cringe at the sight of it (painful breakup, season-ending ankle injury, pneumonia, etc.). Then, out of the ensuing dark night of the soul, I was thrown into the first true period of religious fervor, and for the better part of the next six months I think I was living on a spiritual mountain top. It wasn't long before I began acting like I was also living on a *physical* mountain top, far away from all the interests and activities of my past life—and human civilization in general. I grew enamored with the monastic attitude; you could even say I ran amok with monkish ideals. I was captivated by the words of one of our college campus alumni legends, the missionary/martyr Jim Eliot, who famously wrote, "He is no fool who gives up what he cannot keep to gain what he cannot lose."

(In passing it's curious to note how easy it is to praise the Way of Renunciation when life has already taken from you everything that you feared to lose. Was I surrendering anything, or just making something 'religious' out of my loss?)

And so, thus enamored, part way through the following spring term I came to the conclusion that in order to 'surrender' everything to God I had better give up my most prized possession of all—my dream to play college soccer. In what I imagined to be a romantic and noble act of self-sacrifice, I sat down with the coach and told him of my new decision: I wanted to stay in the program as a practice squad player and as the team chaplain, but I didn't want to officially be in contention to make the varsity squad. Being as expendable as I was, he 'graciously' accepted my proposal.

That following summer I was scheduled to spend living with missionaries in Jamaica—something required as an internship towards my degree. I know, I know: Jamaica, right? Palm trees, white sand beaches, azure seas. Hardly suffering for Jesus. But as it turned out the overseas experience got off to a horrible start, and in the first few days I was desperately homesick for people and places that I knew. Most of it is a story for another time, but suffice it to say I had a serious case of culture shock. For Pete's sake, a glimpse of the golden arches or a little slice of pizza would have doubled as a little slice of heaven. I felt an oppressive sorrow and loneliness in my spirit, and would have done anything to be allowed to go home.

But then one of the local Jamaican workers at our retreat center invited me out into the community for a pick-up game of soccer. I felt a migraine coming on, but I reluctantly accepted the offer anyway. I went. I played. And somewhere in the midst of that hot, humid, exhausting but good-spirited makeshift game of soccer played on a rocky, uneven cow pasture among a group of Jamaicans I had never met...I found my joy. In a moment my homesickness ended, and my summer adventure turned a corner.

That local Jamaican worker soon became my roommate at the retreat center, (we slept in a small room the size of a closet just behind the kitchen) and we spent the entire summer playing soccer together whenever our duties allowed us the free time. My roommate's name was Richard Coke (just 'Coke' to all who knew him), and although over the intervening years we've lost contact, we truly shared one of the happiest and most unforgettable summers of my life together. With his help I began to grow and improve as a soccer player. I made many more friends through the sport as the summer went on, and realized that my passion for the game was an open door to relationships in places where my missionary hosts simply could not find a breakthrough. And to be completely honest—all potential Kingdom usefulness aside—the game itself was simply a source of deep pleasure. It wasn't long at all before I began to regret my decision to 'surrender to God' my dream to play college soccer.

Nevertheless, after a halfhearted attempt to ask Coach if I could undo my previous offer, when I returned to campus that fall I reluctantly went forward with my original plan of voluntary martyrdom —hanging on the outer fringes of the team, participating in every training session and every practice, but only as the team chaplain. And although I enjoyed the role of chaplain, and applauded myself for the 'depth of my devotion to God', my heart ached for what I had denied myself in God's name, and a hard-to-shake doubt about His good intentions for me was allowed to set down deep roots in the unspoken places of my soul.

THE EXPANSIVE GOODNESS OF GOD

By the theory that I was acting on at the time, I was convinced that the kind of person who pleased God most was the man or woman who denied their heart's desires the most—who would deny even their body the necessary amount of food and sleep: rising before the dawn and fasting on even less than locusts and honey. Who would spend as much of the day as possible in private prayer and devotion, allowing themselves no other thought besides 'the happy contemplation of God'. This, I imagined, was God's desire for our lives: that we became people of but One Part, not fifty. Negation. Emptying. Detachment. Denial. These were the things, or so I had come to believe, that God loved best.

And then, over the course of many years—and by the boundless mercy of God—I found to my great relief that these 'religious' ideas hadn't taken into account the whole story at all: the whole story of what I now refer to as the *Expansive* Goodness of God.

Now, I know that I am stepping every nearer to what in certain religious circles is something of a sacred cow, and I want to move cautiously. I am not *in any way* suggesting we reject the clear teachings of Jesus that talk much of 'dying to self', 'taking up one's cross', 'losing one's life for his sake', etc. Whatever else we believe, these words most certainly remain, and must be taken into account by anyone who claims Jesus as Lord and Master.

It makes complete sense that to an unredeemed, fallen son of Adam or daughter of Eve who has known nothing in their life but the sinful arrogance of (imagined) self-rule, there is certainly a hard road ahead, for the path from self-rule to God's Kingdom does lead through self-denial. But notice I said *through* self-denial, not *to* self-denial. Because denial and sacrifice are not ends, but only means, and were never meant to be ultimate answers to the question: *"Just what exactly are God's desires for us?"*

The New Testament has lots to say about self-denial, but not about self-denial as an end in itself. We are told to deny ourselves and to take up our crosses in order that we may follow Christ; and to nearly every description of what we shall ultimately find if we do so contains an appeal to desire. If there lurks in most modern minds the notion that to desire our own good and earnestly to hope for the enjoyment of it is a bad thing, I submit that this notion has crept in from Kant and the Stoics and is no part of the Christian faith. Indeed, if we consider the unblushing promises of reward and the staggering nature of the rewards promised in the Gospels, it would seem that Our Lord finds our desires not too strong, but too weak."

(- C.S. Lewis, *The Weight of Glory*)

For many, this may seem like hairsplitting. Making a meal out of what is merely a nuance. And in some respects they are right. But the Christian life *is* a life of nuance. *All* of life is a nuance. In a world such as this, there are certain nuances that could be said to be the paving stones along the paths to Heaven or to Hell. Yes, Jesus' path led through a cross, and he told us to pick up our own crosses in order to follow him down that dangerous path which led to the Great Rescue of the human race. But does Jesus, we must dare to ask, at His deepest center of being, *like* carrying crosses? Does He *enjoy* placing them on the backs of those He loves? Is self-denial at the very *center* of what God wants for His children, or merely one of many tools He must pick up and sorrowfully wield when required, but is even more eager to set down again when its usefulness is past?

Now, in regards to that period in my own life I mentioned above, I want to be clear about something: I do believe that God moved me to release to Him some things in my life, including the soccer 'dream'. It had become something of an idol to me: I was placing it higher on the priority list than was healthy or wise. Some pruning in my life was required then, as it has been on numerous occasions since and will no doubt be in the future. Where I got it wrong was in thinking that the renunciation itself was the point, and that all true religion eventually flowed in that direction. I was picturing God as someone who wanted to take things away, and not as Someone who actually had an extravagant, lavish, boundless desire to give, and give, and give—beyond my wildest hopes or dreams.

I'm aware that most of us struggle with the role of self-denial in God's plan for our lives. We've heard so much about it, and very rarely is the message delivered with a cautious and deliberate concern for how our hearts receive that message, and how we reconcile the call to 'carry our cross' with a belief in the good heart of God. But when we actually turn to the Bible, I think we find that God Himself has been more kind and careful with us than our religious teachers have been. Look at what He says through the author of the book of Hebrews:

> Let us fix our eyes on Jesus, the author and perfecter of our faith, who for the joy set before him endured the cross, scorning its shame.
>
> (Hebrews 12:2)

Well now.

Really?

Yes, really. In no uncertain terms we are told here that Jesus *endured* the cross, endured it because it was the means that led towards something else, something very uncrosslike: towards freedom, life, redemption, and restoration for His people. And it led for all concerned, including Himself, to ultimate joy. The path led through pain, pain more terrible than you and I can probably imagine, for there was physical suffering as well as who-knows-what amount of spiritual suffering on that lonely executioner's hill the day that Jesus rescued the race of Man from eternal death. It led *through* pain, but for Jesus it was all about the End Game. And that End Game was *Joy*.

Friends, I really can't emphasize this enough. The Christian world is divided in many ways over many issues, not the least of which is the difference between those who live fixated on the often difficult *means* through which God must train His children, and those who have gone on, further up and further in, to a higher country where the prevailing breeze blowing through their soul is full of the sweet scent of ultimate *ends*. Yes, for the latter group surrender and sacrifice are still at times a part of their journey. But they understand what they are *for* and what they are *about*, and I daresay that mostly they hardly take them into account at all, so caught up are they in the vision of the place to which God is leading them. They have become like Bunyan's Pilgrim, who runs from all that he must leave behind without counting it as loss at all, for his heart is captivated by that which he seeks: *"Life! Life! Eternal Life!"*

> ...though Christianity seems at first to be all about morality, all about duties and rules and guilt and virtue, yet it leads you on, out of all that, into something beyond. One has a glimpse of a country where they do not talk of those things, except perhaps as a joke. (*Mere Christianity*)

"Joy," Lewis points out elsewhere, "is the serious business of Heaven." *That* is God's End Game; *that* is where He is leading us: into a Joy that has no bounds, a joy that does not end.

Joy. Did you catch that? Do you believe it? That God's ultimate desire for you personally is that all your sadness, sorrow and fear one day be swallowed in a vast ocean of limitless, boundless joy? That the whole Story—that *your* story—is intended by God to end in a joy that will never fade, falter, or fail? Joy like you've barely tasted, even ever so briefly, in this world ravaged by sin and death?

I'll be the first to admit that it's not easy to believe. Lewis even goes on to admit that it can feel like a 'truancy' to let oneself contemplate the shocking promise that happiness and joy are God's chief ends for us, the 'serious business' that we will be going about in God's King-dom. But, whether it feels irresponsible or not in a world such as the one we now have, it can't be denied that what Jesus offers is Life. Full, abundant, overflowing Life.

To doubt those good intentions—to refuse to look towards the promise of endless joy in the Kingdom to come—does not make you a better Christian, you know. As if only carnal Christians want to find happiness in the end, and truly holy people don't! It's not a sign of holiness to reject or reframe God's promises to fit our human under-standing of what religion 'ought' to look like. No; it is simply doubt and unbelief, and a distrust of the character of God. It is living from the spirit of the man in the parable who had only been given one bag of gold: "Master," he said, "I knew that you are a hard man, harvest-ing where you have not sown and gathering where you have not scattered seed. So I was afraid..." (Matthew 25:24-25).

And yet don't we still know far too many churches, religious organizations, and even individuals among our own friends and family, who give the consistent, (but mostly shadowy and un-spoken), underlying impression that long faces and somber tones, unselfishness and the killing of one's own desires are somehow the Highest Good—that these negative things are the things that please God the most and are nearest to His heart?

> If you asked twenty good men today what they thought the highest of the virtues, nineteen of them would reply, Unselfishness. But if you had asked almost any of the great Christians of old, he would have replied, Love. You see what has happened? A negative term has been substituted for a positive, and this is of more than philological importance. The negative idea of Unselfishness carries with it the suggestion not primarily of securing good things for others, but of going without them ourselves, as if our abstinence and not their happiness was the important point.
>
> (C.S. Lewis, *The Weight of Glory*)

When Jesus was asked what he thought to be the greatest commandment, he didn't begin by quoting one of the many "Thou shalt not's" that were available—and you had better believe that the Jewish religion had no shortage of them from which to choose. No, he began by saying something positive; he began in fact by saying the most positive thing imaginable, for he began his greatest commandment with an invitation to the best thing that the universe has to offer. For the command he spoke was: "*Love.*"

Now, I realize that we have all been subject to a certain amount of that religious climate that says: *"Renunciation is an absolute Good for the fallen race of Men. We are, in this condition, so thoroughly corrupt that any natural pleasure or delight (any of the things that humans universally tends to enjoy separate from strictly religious activities) must be wholly mistaken; must in fact be evil and contrary to the will of God."*

This point of view might be summed up by saying: "Everything that isn't God is *bad.*" Negation. Emptying. A glorification of renouncing things simply for the sake of renouncing them, in part perhaps stemming from a central misunderstanding of the words written by the apostle John, "Do not love the world, or anything in the world. If anyone loves the world, love for the Father is not in them." (I John 2:15) A common misunderstanding that leads many to think that the world (that is, the created order, the material universe) is intrinsically bad, and must be rejected in the pursuit of true holiness.

But I don't believe that this was meant to be the Christian viewpoint at all. You may find it in the Greek philosophers of the pre-Christian Mediterranean world, who thought all physical matter was bad, and only spirit was good. Or you might discern it in the more historically recent Buddhist teaching that Nirvana is achieved by the process of emptying yourself of all worldly interest or desire. In both the Eastern religion and the Greek philosophy escape out of the

created world is the goal. But the expressly Judeo-Christian viewpoint is that Creation is Good, as we looked at in detail in the
previous chapter.

> There are particular aspects of His love and joy which can be
> communicated to a created being only by sensuous experience.
> Something of God which the Seraphim can never quite understand
> flows into us from the blue of the sky, the taste of honey, the delicious
> embrace of water whether cold or hot, and even from sleep itself.
>
> (C.S. Lewis, *God in the Dock*)

If we look with unbiased, open eyes to the full counsel of
Scripture, I don't think our conclusion can be one of 'negative'
spirituality. What we find woven throughout the history of God's
working with and through the creation will not lead us to cry out,
"Everything that isn't God is bad!" No. Instead we will hear the voice
of God Himself exulting from the mountaintops the joyous cry:
   "Everything that isn't sin is Good!"
   This is not just mere wordplay, friends.
   It can change *everything*.
   Everything that isn't sin is good because God has made everything, and is only responsible for the existence of evil by the fact that
He loved us too much to make us anything but free creatures, with
the power to either trust, obey, and choose the Right, or walk with
head held high down a dark and willful path of disobedience and
rebellion—a destructive path of our own choosing. This choice and
this choice alone could drain the Goodness out of the wondrous
world God had joyfully intended for the sons of Adam and the
daughters of Eve. Only the impatience and distrust of a theft could
turn the good gift that was waiting to be unwrapped *in fellowship
with the Giver Himself* into a dark and horrid thing. A cold glass of
water on a hot day is an innocent sort of good, so long as we have

not cut in line or snatched it out of the hands of another whose rightful glass it was. Strawberries are good. The sweet smell of flowering jasmine, honeysuckle and roses are good—a lavish, extravagant good. Kisses are good, so long as they are not stolen kisses. Apples are good, and the pleasure of tasting one is a holy pleasure because the artistry and goodness of God is on display with each bite. So long, of course, as it is not a *forbidden* apple. Sunsets are good; and our delight in them is the highest fulfillment of, if not their purpose, certainly their meaning. Nor does one need to attend a religious service to enjoy a sunset in a 'spiritually appropriate' manner. Unless indeed the sanctuary of your church has very large windows with an expansive western view, a religious service might be the very *worst* place for enjoying the beauty of God's sunsets.

Now, that is not to say that we leave God out of our enjoyment of the sunset. Far from it. If we are of a certain sort of people—no doubt the sort of people that we hope to be—we will recognize simply in terms of the basic rules of good manners that when one receives a gift one ought to show gratitude. And so, for people like ourselves, the good gift well received becomes an immediate, present reminder of the expansive goodness of God, and of his Love. We, in turn, responsively grow in our love towards Him, for "we love because He first loved us." (I John 4:19)

And now I think we had better return to the original question at last: *"Just what exactly are God's desires towards us?"*

And still, I am hesitant to give the answer that has been so central to the last fifteen years of my life, knowing that my words will fall short, and fearing that the deep impact of what I want to get across will be lost. So do epiphanies always mock those who hold them dear—for an epiphany, when wild wonder drives us to speak it aloud, sinks immediately back into the mire of mere familiar propositional truth. Describe as we like with tears and sighs and all the passionate skill of the poets of old, no man can experience *our* epiphany. That being the case, I am aware that what has changed everything for me, the idea that has synthesized and made sense of the whole, giving to both my philosophy and my theology an internal cohesion and consistency, may yet miss the mark entirely for you. So let me just say that what we are after here is the shifting of something inside us at the deep level of our entire worldview, our overall approach to life, something that impacts everything.

"Just what exactly are God's desires for us?"

> If God is for us, who can be against us? He who did not spare his own Son, but gave him up for us all—how will he not also, along with him, graciously give us all things?   (Romans 8:32)

Don't let familiarity blunt the impact of these precious words, dear friends. Is it possible, we wonder? His intention for us is to graciously give us *all* things? The implication is stunning. And the *complete* antithesis to the religious mindset that the holier we become, the narrower we can expect our life to become: the narrower our passions; the narrower our interests; the narrower our desires. He wants to give us *all* things. He *intends* to give us *all* things. That is why I call it the Expansive Goodness of God. It broadens—not shrinks—our experience, our humanity, our personality, the dazzling array of possible wonders and delights that await. It infuses all. "Every good and perfect gift is from above, coming down from the Father..." (James 1:17) Or, as MacDonald put it:

> Such a creature knows the life of the infinite Father as the very flame of his life, and joys that nothing is done or will be done in the universe in which the Father will not make him all of a sharer that it is possible for perfect generosity to make him. If you say this is irreverent, I doubt if you have seen the God manifest in Jesus.
>
> (George MacDonald, *Unspoken Sermons, Volume 3*)

There is a reason that even the sinners, the losers, the outcasts, and the religious rebels of his day were magnetically drawn to the lodestone that was the winsome, desirable presence of Jesus: they had been witnesses to the most complete expression of the good intentions of God towards Mankind that the world had ever known...or dared to dream of. For the first time they saw that the deep ache in their souls for a fulfillment and happiness "east of the sun and west of the moon" was precisely what awaited the obedient children of the Father in the coming Kingdom of Joy Immeasurable.

The Coming Kingdom of Joy Immeasurable.

Can we just pause and let that sink in for a moment? Not as one truth among many, but as the End of All Things?

I wish with all my heart that I could do this one central truth justice, that I could communicate it in a fashion that would color your entire perspective on God's intentions towards you, on why He created you, and for what ultimate end. I am almost convinced that it is for this one thing alone that God has called me into His service: to live as an evangelist of His Goodness, of this one most ignored of His eternal attributes, that rightly understood, changes everything.

THE REHABILITATION

Now, I realize the last two chapters have been a *really* long way around to building a foundation for a treatise on the importance of friendship in a Christian worldview. But as C.S. Lewis wrote more than sixty years ago (and it has only become more true in the intervening years of cultural change), "...if a man believes (as I do) that the old estimate of Friendship was the correct one, he can hardly write a chapter on it except as a rehabilitation."

A rehabilitation indeed. We are talking about a structure so ravaged by the sands of time that major excavation is required to even find its foundations. An archaeological dig would be an appropriate mental picture. So, if the last few chapters have felt a bit like heavy spadework...well that's the reason why.

But even if a rehabilitation of our valuation of friendship in present day society is truly what we need, is it our business to seek it? That is the question I hope the last two chapters have begun to answer. Because I'm sure many in the Christian world are asking themselves, *With so many more 'spiritual' concerns to focus on, is the significance of something so natural, so earthly, as deep, lasting friendships really a topic for Christian reflection?*

And what of the question with which we began this chapter—the question that also began my own lifelong quest to understand God's intentions for human relationships? *Would* it have been more pleasing to God, after all, for two thirteen-year-old Christian boys in the summer of 1983 to submit to 'mature' authority and accept that the hazy concept of 'the general good of the group' was more important than the much firmer reality of the experiential goodness of their own flourishing friendship? Or were we somehow, in our simple innocence, yet able to recognize the great goodness of God when we tasted it? Even though it was an unexpectedly 'natural' good that at first blush had no perceivable connection to the spiritual' lessons we were being taught by our religious teachers? Were we, in fact, already tottering forward on the first feeble steps of an upward journey that would lead at last to the iconoclastic discovery that God's intentions towards us were full of a magnificent Goodness so great that it towered as high above our small religious sensibilities as the heavens hang above the vaulted ceilings of Mankind's tallest cathedrals?

FOUR

THE CROWN
OF LIFE

Friendship is unnecessary, like philosophy, like art, like the universe
itself (for God did not need to create). It has no survival value; rather it is
one of those things which gives value to survival.

- C. S. Lewis, *The Four Loves*

We've come a long way around, but hopefully at this point we
have made some progress towards establishing some important foundational premises. The fact that *society* was God's
intention for Mankind. That it was not good for Man to be alone.
We are, without shame or need for justification, intrinsically 'social
animals'. Our craving for connection of a deep and satisfying
nature is intentional: God made us this way on purpose. And so, as
a lone wolf in the animal kingdom is a broken wolf—a mal-
functioning wolf who is rebelling against the very nature of it's
wolfish heart—so a son of Adam or daughter of Eve who makes
the "vow of the lone wolf" does so out of deep hurt and deep

brokenness, to their own loss and the lessening of the good that
God longs to give them.

Then, in regards to that very good God desires to bring us, we
attempted to lay a foundation for the *expansive* goodness of God—
the truth that, when we are in a right relationship with Him, all
the created order and every 'natural' delight becomes a vehicle
through which we receive His blessing of abundant life. To God
'religious activity' was never meant to be a compartment separated
from the rest of human experience. Every moment of every day has
the potential to be full of God—*without being emptied of itself.* He
does not imperiously demand that we ignore the delights around
us so as to narrow our focus solely upon Him. He created us to
know Him, to walk with Him, to be in intimate association with
Him—all within the very intentional context of this material
realm we find ourselves in. Our human existence is not an exile;
these bodies that feel the warmth of the sun and delight in a cool
drink of water are not prisons from which we must escape.

> ...to receive (a pleasure) and to recognize its divine source are a single
> experience. This heavenly fruit is instantly redolent of the orchard where
> it grew. This sweet air whispers of the country from which it blows. It is a
> message. We know we are being touched by a finger of that right hand at
> which there are pleasures forevermore. There need be no question of
> thanks or praise as a separate event, something done afterwards. To
> experience the tiny theophany is itself to adore...If I could always be what
> I aim at being, no pleasure would be too ordinary or too usual for such
> reception.   (C.S. Lewis, *Letters to Malcolm*)

Now, these two truths have demanded our attention as necessary
steps in the rehabilitation of the idea that friendship is truly an
important topic, one falling under the umbrella of "the sorts of
things Christians ought to write books about". To the best of my

knowledge, these books haven't been written—at least over the last hundred years anyway—or if they have, they certainly haven't gained much traction. Certainly, we've got shelves and shelves dedicated to the marriage relationship. The Church has decided it was its mission to defend that border assiduously. Family relationships too, to some extent. *Boundaries*, by Cloud and Townsend. *Love and Respect* by Eggerich. *Love and War* by John and Stasi Eldredge. A whole library of books by marriage experts like Les and Leslie Parrott. All big sellers for the most part. And there must be hundreds more at this point—I don't pretend to keep up with them all. But clearly we can't get enough of it. I guess that's because we are stuck in these family relationships, and we know it would change our lives dramatically to find any rule, trick, gimmick, or advice that might help move those relationships closer to being healthy. Healthy? Heck, many of us would be dancing in the streets just to learn how to move into a place where those family relationships weren't downright toxic.

But books, sermons—whole ministries—dedicated to the topic of friendship? Times may be changing, but up until this point this just hasn't been the case. There is a reason, you know, in approaching this topic that we must rely so heavily on the witness of the last century's great Oxford don and cherished author, C.S. Lewis: in Christian circles very little has been written about friendship over the past sixty years. I even considered including his name in the subtitle of the book, as nearly half of what I have written is merely an elaboration of his chapter on 'Friendship' in his incredible book *The Four Loves*. It was only the half that I have not borrowed directly from his train of thought that compelled me to not risk deceiving my readers into thinking they were in for something different than what I was giving them.

But why this scarcity of relevant material for our subject? When did this marginalizing of non-familial relationships begin? And what does it say of a culture's relational priorities when that culture only takes the time to deal with those relationships that one simply *must* deal with: family, marriage, children—the inescapable ones? It begins to sound like we almost wished we *weren't* relational creatures, but since we have these familial situations we can't extricate ourselves from, we might as well see what we can do about making them bearable.

It wasn't always this way, you know. Friendship hasn't always been marginalized like it is today.

> To the Ancients, Friendship seemed the happiest and most fully human of all loves; the crown of life and the school of virtue. The modern world, in comparison, ignores it. We admit of course that beside a wife and family a man needs a few "friends". But the very tone of the admission, and the sort of acquaintanceships which those who make it would describe as "friendships," show clearly that what they are talking about has very little to do with that Philia which Aristotle classified among the virtues, or that Amicitia on which Cicero wrote a book. It is something quite marginal; not a main course in life's banquet; a diversion; something that fills up the chinks of one's time. How has this come about?
>
> (C.S. Lewis, *The Four Loves*)

How indeed?

NO TIME FOR FRIENDSHIP

Lewis wrote those words more than sixty years ago, near the end of his life. No doubt his verdict on the state of friendship in the modern world was based on experiences and observations from a lifetime that spanned most of the first half of the twentieth century. The early 1900's were a much simpler, slower time than the one you and I live in today. When you think about where 'the modern world' has come since then—well, I don't think Lewis in his wildest dreams could've imagined how much further into disregard the old Greek virtue of Friendship had yet to fall. "Something that fills up the chinks of one's time"? Good grief: I don't even think it's *that* anymore. I mean, maybe we still think that's where friendship belongs, 'in the chinks'—but who even *has* 'chinks' in their overbooked, non-stop, dawn-to-dusk mad dash to get life 'done'? No, since the days of Lewis' world our valuation of Friendship, at least here in modern western culture, has reached an all time low. Forget friendship being 'marginal'. Adult lives being lived devoid of anything remotely resembling true friendship —this is pretty much the norm, the reality that is now sweeping our society at pandemic proportions.

One of my favorite questions to ask men (yes, and women) of all ages that I run across in the course of life and ministry is this: "Who do you have in your life that knows *everything* about you? Who knows the inner story of your heart's journey? Who hears all the daily details of your struggles and your triumphs *(because our lives unfold in a specifically daily sort of way that the 'yearly synopsis catch-up phone call' just doesn't satisfy)*, the unseen adventures of your constantly changing walk with God?"

I ask the question, but for the most part it has become something of a rhetorical question, a futile question, merely the sad confirmation of a growing conviction. I know the answer before I even hear it, and the answer, without fail, is: *"No one."* None of the people I have put this question to have had a person in their life that satisfied those requirements. *None of them.* For goodness sake, I know *pastors*—spiritual leaders of whole communities of God's people—who by their own admission are living virtually friendless lives. Some of them feel the lack of meaningful friendships, like a successful youth pastor I know who admitted with disappointment that when he left his last church after seven years' loyal service, he left without having formed one single friendship from among his many coworkers on staff. Apparently helping to develop bonds that went beyond a 'friendly' working relationship wasn't on this 'task-oriented' church's priority list at all. Still other pastors I've known have seemed completely oblivious to their own friendlessness, like one head pastor I worked under for a few years who never invested a moment's time into a relationship unless he knew he could gain some personal or financial advantage 'for the greater mission' from doing so.

LONELY MEN

Just recently I was listening to an acquaintance's podcast. This guy has built a great ministry to men, meeting them outside the accepted religious context by putting on his events in microbreweries of all places. He offers these men a beer, a real-life story of brokenness and redemption they can relate to, and the gospel. It's brilliant. I love his courage and his passion and his willingness to live and work outside the box—even though I personally could never stand the taste of beer myself. I know, I know. Yes, I was brought up in a teetotaler family, but that's not my problem. I've tried, and I just can't convince my palate to enjoy it. But that's neither here nor there: it turns out you don't have to like the taste of beer to be a real man after all. And my waistline is grateful for it.

Now on this particular podcast I tuned into, my acquaintance was interviewing a small groups pastor from a large and growing church on the other side of the state from where I live. In passing (it wasn't the point of the podcast, unfortunately) the pastor mentioned a recent season of life where he had been struggling with some things personally and felt the need to seek out some professional counseling. He recounted telling the counselor that his struggles centered around two things. First, he was feeling tired and discouraged. No surprise there. The "ministry" as a profession is an exacting and emotionally draining line of work, fraught with great personal danger at the level of the soul. Of course, like most things in life, the blessings and rewards are directly proportional to the difficulty of the work.

But it was the second half of this pastor's lament that caught my attention. After admitting to the counselor that he was discouraged and worn out, he paused for a moment, and then added: "And, I'm lonely."

Lonely.

This pastor was lonely. Not just *any* pastor, mind. The *small groups* pastor, for goodness sake. The man tasked with leading a church of several thousand people into finding the best sort of 'community' that modern Christianity has to offer.

And he was lonely.

Don't get me wrong—I don't think there was anything especially 'wrong' with this guy. Based on his choice of job, I expect he probably was a healthier than average, relationally-minded, godly man. I only single him out precisely because we all sort of expect that if anyone knew how to find and maintain satisfying relationships, it would be a spiritual leader whose full time job was convincing other Christians of the importance of community.

No, by all normal standards, I don't think this guy was 'blowing it'. Not at all. This is just how deep the friendlessness in our culture runs. For whatever reason—for a great many reasons—most adults in society today simply don't bother to make, cultivate, or maintain deep, satisfying relationships. Or do I exaggerate? Have I just had the ill luck to be entirely surrounded by the few friendless people that don't truly represent the current state of affairs?

Okay. I *don't* know everyone, and what they experience. So you tell me then: how much time in the last few years have *you* invested in pursuing or maintaining a real honest-to-goodness friendship of the good old kind—the highly-valued, fought-for and prioritized kind that once were such a significant part of your younger days? *Okay*, you say, *so maybe it hasn't been at the top of my priority list lately*. Be honest with me though: does Friendship even make it onto the list at all? Sure, you agree that it would be nice to have great friends and all—just like it would be nice to spend your winters in the south of France, sipping wine from the fabled Loire Valley and reclining on a sun-soaked Mediterranean beach. But then, who really has the time to lament all the 'luxuries' in life that haven't fallen to our lot?

GRAVEYARD OF BROKEN FRIENDSHIPS

I was on my way to a ministry event a few weeks ago and I passed by the local high school just as a football game was ending. It was raining a bit, and as I slowed down for a stop sign I saw a group of people walking huddled close under an umbrella. They were laughing, engaged. They looked happy in one another's company; there was an implied affection in the way they walked, the way they leaned into the small canopy of protection the shared umbrella afforded. I paused to take another look, but even before I did, I knew that the people half-hidden beneath the umbrella were almost certainly high school students, and not a group of teachers, parents, or random adults from the community who happened to support the local high school sports programs. I was poignantly reminded of many a similar scene from my college days. Nothing would have been a more common sight than that of a tightly knit group of friends walking back from the football stadium to the cafeteria on a Saturday afternoon in the Fall, snuggled down close to one another in a physical intimacy that spoke of the deeper kind of intimacy they most certainly also shared.

As I continued on my way past the high school, I found myself wondering, *why is it that you don't ever see adults act like that: so close, so intimate, having that much fun in one another's company?* What changes so dramatically after our school years end? Why is it that college graduation has effectively proven time and again to be the graveyard of broken friendships, just as my brother knew it was going to be for him, and I had feared that it would be for me?

THE SILENT PANDEMIC

Granted, as modern citizens of today's lightning-paced world we certainly *know* more people than any of our ancestors did. Just look at our Facebook pages. Surely that counts for something? We know *loads* of people. We even dare the blasphemy of calling them 'friends'; and whenever we want to add to this dazzling array of shoestring acquaintances, the digital invitation we send out is even called a 'friend' request. (Although at least the LinkedIn app is honest enough to call them by their more appropriate title: *connections.* Because that's the real truth of it, isn't it? Knowing people isn't really about knowing people. As a culture obsessed with efficiency and functionality, it's really much more about how 'knowing' people can help *you*, how they might turn out to be useful connections to further your own ambitions.)

The dangerously unhealthy pace of twenty-first century life carries us forward into dizzying, ever increasing levels of busyness, and through our incessant activity it's possible that we may cross paths with thousands of people in any given day. At every traffic inter-section, in every grocery store, at the gym, the office, the mega-church we are so proud to attend simply because of its raw size and impressive attendance—at every turn we are treated to the most incredible parade of the most valuable and wondrous beings ever to set foot on the stage of this material universe. And yet, amidst this crowd, this throng, this mass of humanity, every statistic out there (not to mention the witness of our own hearts) practically shouts of our deepest truth: our unshakeable sense of loneliness. "Water, water everywhere, but never a drop to drink."

Drowning in a sea of people, and yet never in all the ages of Mankind have we lived out the days of our lives more Alone.

Or, I will ask again: do I exaggerate?

It has been said that we are living in the age of the Friendless American Male. (Women, being graced by God with an instinctive gift for relational thinking, still tend to stay a step ahead of the desolation covering the friendship landscape among us men; but in a culture like ours, it may be only a matter of time...) Like the proverbial frog in the kettle, this loss has been coming on so silently, handed down now to a third and fourth generation of friendless men—(did your father model to you a lifestyle that was deeply committed to life-long intimate male friendships? Fathers today, is this what your children have seen in your example?)—that we now have reached a point where we simply embrace the reality that, outside of family relationships, being alone is just what it means to be an adult.

Career, wife, children, God. Maybe add organized religious institutional involvement. Maybe move God higher up the list. Perhaps struggle with the fact that career tops the list, and try to bring it back to a place below those family relationships. But honestly, I've got to focus on our financial security, pay the bills, care for our immaculate yard and provide protection for our ever increasing piles of possessions.

You seriously think I chose this life of a 'lone wolf', cut off from the rest of the pack, forced to navigate the anxieties and insufficiencies of making adult life 'work' all alone, with no one to turn to, no relationships that don't depend on me being the responsible one, the one with the answers, always having to come through for everyone else? Is there even another way to live?

Yes, thank God, there is.

PANNING FOR GOLD

> Those are the golden sessions; when four or five of us after a hard's day
> walking have come to our inn; when our slippers are on, our feet spread
> out towards the blaze and our drinks at our elbows; when the whole
> world, and something beyond the world, opens itself to our minds as
> we talk; and no one has any claim on or any responsibility for another,
> but all are free men and equals as if we had first met an hour ago, while
> at the same time an Affection mellowed by the years enfolds us.
> Life—natural life—has no better gift to give. Who could have deserved
> it?   (C.S. Lewis, *The Four Loves*)

Times have changed much since Lewis painted this iconic, alluring picture of what the "golden sessions" looked like in his own life. I
expect none of us have experienced quite the same unique pleasures
of a three-day walking tour over the English countryside shared with
a few of our dearest and oldest friends. And although our own vision
of what such "golden sessions" might look like will vary in the small
details (if we can envision them at all), the beauty of his poignant
description yet has the power to fill each of us with the longing to
enter into a similar fellowship of our own—a fellowship of cherished
friendships full of shared memories and adventures.

Now, in contrast to our family of origin, which we have all been
blessed (or cursed) with through no effort or merit of our own,
there is no promise, no guarantee that we will ever experience deep
and lasting friendships of this kind. I'd go so far as to say that in
today's world it's an extremely rare gift that very few find. And when
we don't find it, how do most of us escape one, or either, of the
prevailing lies thrown in our faces that, a)God is somehow to blame
for not sending us soul-mates because, after all, our particular brand
of theology has taught us that we are helpless victims of fate, or
b)that we have so little to offer it's no wonder no one has chosen us

from out of the seven billion people on the planet to be their "particular friend", as the Victorian authors would have called it?

I'm aware that this is a tender subject for a whole lot of people, guys especially; but I'm positive we can include the women in this as well—at least a vast majority of the women I've known personally. It's tender because everyone *wants* friends, but not everyone *finds* them. And having found them, it is rarer still to keep them. You don't just get allocated tickets at birth you can then redeem later in life that read "Good for One Life-long Bestie". Friendships in a fallen world—friendships between broken and hurting people—prove all too often to be fragile and temporary things. And that's a cold fact even before we take into account that we're living in a society that places almost every priority higher than the making, developing, and preserving of deep friendships.

For above all else, aren't we are all seeking to find the fast track towards "the fulfillment of our dreams"? Perhaps we call it pursuing "our career goals", "our need to succeed", or our "thirst for advancement". Whatever term we use, I cannot begin to tell you how deeply the centrality of this pursuit has been ingrained in us.

We are, it would appear, now even seeking the fast track to personal success in the arena of full-time ministry, believe it or not. I've seen this personally; I know it's true. You see, I've subscribed for many years to what is pretty much *the* job placement website for people in church ministry. Sometimes keeping one eye on the "job market" can feel a little faithless to the parachurch ministry David and I began nearly twelve years ago; but then, a family of six must eat somehow: thus my uneasy, long-running relationship with this job placement website. Recently there has been one of those annoying little pop-up windows appearing on the screen each time I visit the website: a pop-up that I can only assume is meant to drive you towards considering some of their premium services. It reads: *"Are you looking for the church job that you deserve?"* And no matter how many times it has popped up, I continue to be taken aback, shocked and deeply saddened. If there was any place left in our world for people who wanted to devote their lives to the welfare of others and not themselves, I always figured it was in the Church. When did a life of servanthood and ministry become about putting myself on the fast track to what *I* 'deserve'?

The culture runs deep, friends.

DISPOSABLE RELATIONSHIPS

Call it Rugged Individualism or the American Way if you are in a favorable mood; call it self-absorbed narcissism if you are not. In our defense, at least some of us have the human decency not to intentionally step all over other people as we claw our way to the top. Not that you'll see many such gentler souls portrayed on reality television shows, but I'll assume for the sake of the dignity of the race that we aren't *all* as power-obsessed as the entertainment industry would imply through the personalities most often displayed there. And yet, even given that we are not as far gone as all that, the sad truth remains that in our society we have been taught to see the other characters on the stage with us in any given scene of our lives as, well, as pretty much incidental to the main plot. They are, to the modern mind almost a piece of the landscape—more *props* than persons.

Understand this, my friends: we are living in the age of disposable relationships.

Disposable. Functional. Convenient. Temporary.

There is no longer *any* relationship whose authority rises higher than our right to pursue personal independence and the greener grass that lies just beyond the borders of our own picket fence. We divorce our spouses when we fall out of love; when maintaining a healthy relationship becomes an uphill battle; when their presence in our lives becomes more hard work than we really want to have to deal with. We throw them over like yesterday's carry-out leftovers soon after we come to grips with the fact that the overall impact they are having on *our* pursuit of happiness has become, on the whole, a negative one.

We ship our aging parents off to "care facilities" when we decide that honoring the oldest, most deeply planted relationships in our lives is no longer worth the frustration or toil. We must, after all, think about what is best for *us*, and an old albatross hanging about our necks is just one more thing than we need to be dealing with right now. (Notice the cultural priority here: we *are* dealing with things—many of them, maybe even too many to bear—but it is all those *other* things that we deem unavoidable, whereas a devotion to our family we do not.)

We even throw parties when "we get our lives back" the day our children head off to college. We have raised them, prepared them for the world, and released them into it—just like the culture has told us we ought to. Let me tell you, none of our attitude towards "temporary" relationships guts me the way this one does. I am deeply distressed every time I hear a seemingly God-honoring, well-meaning Christian friend—who unquestioningly takes his cues from the prevailing spirit of the age—say something along the lines of, *"Well, my work is pretty much done. They are adults now. My job was to prepare them to succeed in the world all on their own, and now they must find their own path."* Yes, we have taught them how to succeed in the world. And in the very act of our teaching we must accept a certain culpability, even as the old Roman Cardinal confessed at the end of the moving film *The Mission: "Thus have we made the world. Thus have I made it."* We ourselves have perpetuated the ideas once passed on to us of what makes that world, and the definitions of what success by such standards must look like. Rest assured that our children have learned their lessons well: for it is they who will walk out on the next generation of unsatisfying marriages (or opt for less committed variations of romantic involvement and avoid marriage completely); they who will disengage with the following generation of sons and daughters, setting them adrift as soon as society permits; they who, at the first whiff of our approaching senility will, without thought or compassion, ship us off to the nursing homes that were always our destiny from the moment we taught them to think just like us.

Now, I realize we've been talking about relationships that are outside the central scope of our specific discussion on friendship, and it is not really my intent to mount a full assault on our society's relational failings. But it was necessary to highlight the prevailing malaise that hangs over even our closest familial relationships, in order to unmask the universally accepted but mostly unspoken notion that all relationships big and small, short or long, are ultimately temporary and disposable. We live in a broken society full of broken people, where studied observation would lead one to the conclusion that *relationships don't last*. It is a short leap from there to the assumption that relationships *weren't meant* to last. Even those dear ones we care for the most must be surrendered sooner or later on the altar of either their ambitions, or ours. Thus is the world.

GHOSTS OF FRIENDSHIPS PAST

Now, everyone who knows me knows that I consider one of the most unique things about my life to be the blessing of having had a deep, lasting, *daily active* friendship (not talking about old friends who we connect with once a year when we send out our Christmas cards), a friendship that has stood the test of time and distance, and proven to be the source of certainly half of all my worldly joy, not to mention the most important spiritual influence in my life.

But the fact is that this rare experience is far more *gift* than it is *reward* for some relational skill of my own. It certainly doesn't qualify me as some sort of relational guru. Far from it. The one great success has not preserved me from the pain and disappointment of countless other relationships that faded away through the years— many for which I share much of the blame. Like the society that nurtured me, I have mostly lived with the tacit acceptance that friendships were 'things for the moment'. Even in those seasons when they came close to being at the very center of all the present joy of our lives, yet we could not come to see that they *were* our lives. Always there was still the inexorable call of 'destiny' propelling us forward into a future that, though it cost us every last friend in the world, yet called to us with an imperious command not within our perceived power to refuse.

The Proverbs tell us that "there is a friend that sticks closer than a brother" (Proverbs 18:24), but in a world like ours, driven by personal career goals and self-interest, we simply aren't very good at doing "sticky" friendships, are we?

I know I keep coming back to tell stories about my college years, but I don't think that is a coincidence, considering our topic. Those were the "golden years," when friendship was King. Rather than a thing on the margins, it was, for a one golden season, truly a main course in life's banquet.

Do *you* remember that golden season? Did *you* ever know such a time?

Looking back, I would say that I had extremely close friendships with at least half a dozen guys, and pretty deep ones (especially by the standards of adult life since then) with at least a dozen more. During my four undergraduate years, though the group expanded over time, my core of roommates, my dearest friends, remained the same: Doug Allen, he of the extreme intelligence, the late night study sessions, and the besetting sin of being intrinsically incapable of passing up the chance for a bad pun or a bit of dry humor. Then there was David Wilkinson, of the soft heart and tough exterior, the quick laugh, the incessant conversation and the irrepressible penchant for anecdotal story-telling (always full of names, places and events that we had never heard of—and never quite knew if they were real or fictitious). And finally, Bryan Shoe, of the ever-changing fads, hair-cuts, hobbies, new gadgets, and equally new and dizzying array of exotically named girlfriends (although he was on occasion known to forgo his principles and pursue girls with even plain names like Mary or Kate, so long as the girl herself was not equally plain). Doug walked with his head wrapped in the clouds like an absent-minded professor-in-training—a role he was destined to play in later years; Wilkie was as solid and dependable as the earth beneath your feet—and twenty-five years serving, and then running, the same small, out-of-the-way Christian summer camp on the forgotten shores of Maine proves the truth of that solidity; Shoe, as changeable and as wild as the wind—as once more played out in the wild ride of great successes and heart-breaking sorrows his life has seen in the years since.

As for myself? Only they could tell you what addition I offered, if any, to the wide array of extreme and delightful characters they presented to the world around them. Perhaps, if anything, it was my romantic vision that yet believed, even in today's world, that the bond of friendship was worth pursuing, worth cherishing. For whatever reason, together we formed a fellowship of good-natured knuckleheads as close in spirit to the Three Musketeers of old as you could hope to find in the last decade of the twentieth century. Wilkie, who consistently failed to get a passing grade in his Math course, probably thought we *were* the Three Musketeers, in spite of the fact that the smallest child who saw us tromping across campus arm-in-arm could readily count that we were in fact a fellowship of four. For the better part of four years we were practically insep-arable. It was a rare thing to see one of us around campus not in the company of at least one, if not all, of the others. Naturally romantic entanglements proved to be an exception to that rule, but not always even then: for we quickly learned that double dating was the perfect way to have our cake and eat it too. Besides, if it were Friday night and we had no plans of our own, most of us had no problem playing the role of the somewhat awkward 'third wheel', invited...or otherwise.

Oh, the stories I could tell! (But then, you have them too, don't you—each one dearer and sweeter to you than mine could ever be?) Most of those stories would hardly come off as 'epic' to the casual observer. We weren't constantly engaged in uproarious pranks or newsworthy shenanigans. Oh, there were some, even if they don't read like a Christian version of "Animal House". Breaking into the abandoned Ovaltine factory and finding signs of recent satanic rituals. Running from Russian security when we accidentally produced a scare during a performance on campus by a famed Soviet symphony. Pranking the Resident Assistant on our floor...constantly. Cramming twelve friends into a spring break condo in Florida that only slept six. Getting a philosophy prof. and the college president himself to guest star on our pathetically inept intramural basketball team. Oh yes. We had our moments of glory.

THE SUMMER OF '69

Naturally, as four guys of varying temperaments and varying levels of commitment to things like hygiene, cleanliness, and order, living in the same cramped quarters engendered its share of mild ups and downs, much as could be said for every friendship. Our relationships were far from perfect. But on the whole the times we shared together were four golden years—years that, looking back, came and went with the heartbreaking swiftness of fleeting youth. Graduation came to us too, just as it had come to my brother and his friends two years prior, and in like manner our fellowship too was broken. It was much like what Bryan Adams sang in "*The Summer of '69*":

> Jimmy quit, Jodie got married.
> We should've known we'd never get far.
> Oh, when I look back now
> That summer seemed to last forever
> And if I had the choice
> Yeah, I'd always wanna be there
> Those were the best days of my life

With us it was Doug and Ruthie who got married—the very same week we graduated, if you can believe it. Talk about a mad frenzy to get on into the next season of life as quickly as possible. Next Shoe returned to his home in Reading, Pennsylvania to take a job as a youth pastor, and within eighteen months to meet and marry a wife of his own, as he too sought to follow the accepted times and seasons for such things as laid down by the unspoken rules of 'growing up'. Wilkie also left for the summer with the others, but lack of direction and a broken romance brought him back to the area for one more happy season—an unexpected gift for both of us. And I, who had been forewarned by my brother's experience two years earlier, chose to remain and pursue a graduate degree—if for no other reason than to extend that 'golden season' for just a little longer.

My gamble paid off: other relationships did grow up in those extra years, in their own way as strong and as precious as the old ones I had lost: Graham, my new roommate with whom I spent a wonderful summer travelling to Vancouver, England and India; Scotty, the missionary kid from Africa who perhaps had the greatest impact on my thinking and my faith that anyone else has ever had; Scotty's little brother Cedric and the fellowship that centered around his off-campus home, a fellowship with whom I became perhaps more inseparable than even my original four roommates. "Steve-O", Billy, Dawn and Dave, Tracey, Jill, Meridee: so many other dear friends, I am bound to leave someone out that I do not wish to forget. It was undoubtably the most relationally robust time of my life.

But even a two-year reprieve could provide only a brief stay of execution. Ultimately it was my turn to follow the offer of employment on a path that drew me away from these new friends, even as the old 'set' had left our golden years behind them as they set off on their own journeys, even as my brother's housemates had done at the end of their sojourn together. Granted, being who I am, the decision and the move were made against much of what my heart was telling me at the time. And yet in the end, unwilling though I was, I too was convinced that this was 'how it had to be.'

And now? Being the extremely 'relationship-oriented' guy that I am, what became of all these precious friendships? I am almost too ashamed to confess. The sad truth is that now I can go *five years at a stretch* without seeing even the dearest of them—to say nothing of some of the others that I haven't seen in upwards of *twenty* years.

Do you think I wanted those blessed friendships, those happy times, to end? Was I walking through those glorious college years with the constant thought, *"Now Derrick, this is all a transitory pleasure. These people that fill your days with laughter, conversation, and happy companionship won't even matter to you ten years from now. Don't invest too much, don't give too much, don't care too much. In a few years these people will be no more than ghosts of the past?"*

Hardly. What sort of friendship can you throw yourself headlong into if you are thinking of it as a short-term affair? And we *don't* think of them that way, do we? At least not usually. It's hardly a healthy approach to take. Okay, so my high school girlfriend did announce six-months prior to heading off to college that we should plan on breaking up when the day of our departure came (even though we were actually headed to the same college!)—and let me just tell you what a hopeless spirit *that* brought over the whole relationship. But mostly we know better than to do that sort of thing. And I think there's more of a reason than simply because it's a depressing way to approach life. I think it's because something deep inside our soul knows that relationships weren't designed to fizzle out and come to nothing. People are just too valuable to make a constant habit of leaving them in the past.

> So what's the glory in living?
> Doesn't anybody ever stay
> Together anymore?
> And if love never lasts forever
> Tell me, what's forever for?
>> (B.J. Thomas, "What's Forever For?")

ALL GOOD THINGS

What a seismic shift it would be in the landscape of our lives if we could just reorient our thinking around this one simple possibility: *What if God's original plan was for relationships not to end?*

Stick with me for a moment. Let us come at this remembering that the Christian Idea is ultimately the idea of Final Restoration: the Return of a Golden Summer glory lost before it had hardly begun, a glory beyond our collective memory, beyond our boldest dreams and our wildest imagination. A glory, by all human expectations, that is 'too good to be true.' But then, as Frederick Buechner reminds us, "Too good to be true implies a view of Truth, of course." (*Telling the Truth*) The story of the Cross and the Resurrection are part of a larger story: a meta-narrative that makes sense of not just our current fallen condition but something older and truer, and most importantly of all, something that's coming again, coming on the wings of a new Day yet to dawn.

Like the symmetry of a Shakespearean Comedy, or the perfect shape of Fortune's Wheel, we are told that the death of God was neither a random act of violence nor a cold theological necessity, but the very turning point of history, the bottom point on the dramatic circle where all seems utterly and irrevocably lost. For in that moment (who would've dared to write the story?), the downward fall of Mankind that began in the Garden at the Dawn of Time is suddenly arrested; the tide is turned, the movement reversed. The power of Life that dwells in Jesus proves to be stronger than the grave. The Resurrection of Jesus is a single historical event; but resurrection itself—and along with it, redemption and restoration—are more than just that single event. Through that event they have now become perpetual themes that begin to weave themselves into the very heart of the fabric of all things.

The story of the Incarnation is the story of a descent and resurrection. When I say 'resurrection' here, I am not referring simply to the first few hours, or the first few weeks of the Resurrection. I am talking of this whole, huge pattern of descent, down, down, and then up again. What we ordinarily call the Resurrection being just, so to speak, the point at which it turns...One has a picture of a strong man trying to lift a very big, complicated burden. He stoops down and gets himself right under it so that he himself disappears; and then he straightens his back and moves off with the whole thing swaying on his shoulders...this thing is human nature...I believe that God really has dived down into the bottom of creation, and has come up bringing the whole redeemed nature on His shoulder. The miracles that have already happened are...the first fruits of that cosmic summer which is presently coming on...to be sure, it feels wintry enough still: but often in the very early spring it feels like that. The spring comes slowly down this way; but the great thing is that corner has been turned.

(C.S. Lewis, *The Grand Miracle*)

"The corner has been turned." Friends, how deeply does that theme run through your own approach to life at this point in history, at this point in God's redemptive story? I suppose it is probably because of how *wintry* it does still feel here most of the time that we find it so hard to internalize a more epic, more robust message of redemption and restoration rather than settling for a gospel merely of forgiveness for sin and the promise of Heaven some day. "If anyone is in Christ, he is a new creation. Behold; the old has passed away, the new has come!" (2 Corinithians 5:17) Yes, we cling to this truth of radical change permeating everything about our life and our world...*in theory*. But doing so demands of us a constant battle against disappointment; at times even a blind and willful ignorance to the glaring similarities between our old selves and our 'new' selves. *"The spring comes slowly down this way."* Isn't that a gracious posture to take towards God's promise of restoration? It sure beats coming to the resigned conclusion that it simply doesn't work, or that God never really meant what He said.

Now back to these ideas about relationships we've all tacitly accepted as 'the way things are'. We've bought into this leap from the observable fact that 'relationships don't last' to the conclusion that this is nothing to lament or sorrow or grieve over because *this is how it must be. This is how it should be.*

> Something awful has happened; something terrible. Something worse, even, than the fall of man. For in that greatest of all tragedies, we merely lost Paradise—and with it, everything that made life worth living. What has happened since is unthinkable: we've gotten used to it. We're broken into the idea that this is just the way things are.
>
> (John Eldredge, *The Journey of Desire*)

Friends, for a new creation in Christ—one who is in the process of being restored to Edenic glory, who is being trained to receive the

inheritance of the Kingdom as an adopted son and daughter, who
has been promised that the whole of creation groans in anticipation
for the day they will come into that inheritance—there are very few
places in this world where such a one should be resigning themselves
to the idea that 'the way things are' must be one and the same to 'the
way things should be.'

> To the orthodox there must always be a case for revolution, for in the
> hearts of men God has been put under the feet of Satan. In the upper
> world hell once rebelled against heaven. But in this world heaven is
> rebelling against hell. For the orthodox there can always be a revolution;
> for a revolution is a restoration. At any instant you may strike a blow for
> the perfection which no man has seen since Adam.
>
> (G.K. Chesterton, *Orthodoxy*)

Yes, no doubt we have wintry conditions enough still to face in
this sphere of human relationships. Actually that's putting it mildly.
Right now I'd say we're plowed under ten foot snow drifts with no
expectation of a thaw on the near horizon. I don't think most of us
can even imagine what a springtime in the realm of human relationships might even look like; we certainly don't spend much energy
thinking how we might participate in bringing it about.

But we *could*. As Lewis reminds us, "We have the power either of
withstanding the spring, and sinking back into the cosmic winter, or
of going on into those 'high mid-summer pomps' in which our Leader, the Son of Man, already dwells, and to which He is calling us."

SOMETHING MUST CHANGE

Relationships *can* last. Relationships *should* last. Relationships, in
the good and perfect will of God, were *meant* to last. Grab ahold of
that idea, let it permeate your approach to life—and watch how it

changes everything for you.

Friends, we were created and designed to need deep and lasting relationships. But we live in a society that, while admitting this (to some small extent) in theory, remains deeply individualistic in every significant, practical way. And in the end, life consists ultimately not of our ideas but of our choices, doesn't it? And the choices we are consistently making belie our weakly held belief in the importance of relationships. Our supposed 'need' for relationships is constantly subjugated to a higher priority: self-sufficiency. How badly we 'need' our friends is mitigated by the overwhelming strength of another 'need', call it our Master Need: the overarching, inexorable need for Independence. For Autonomy. Our most important choices in life are driven, above all, by our need to never be truly needy. Something within the fabric of our culture yet continues to draw us, enrapture us, wind us round with velvet cords of whispering enchantments towards the wild, strong, independence that is the life of the Lone Wolf.

But this is no happy spell we are under now, and we have all paid the price for it. Just look around you at the people you know. For goodness sake, we don't even have to look beyond our own lives. Look at the choices you have made, the guiding philosophy that has been behind your choices, and the resultant life you are living now. Can you honestly deny that the life of a Lone Wolf, for all its external bravado, is, at the deeper level of the heart, really little more than the life of a *Lonely* Wolf?

For all of society's recent advances in technology, medicine, standard of living, etc., we are living in a time characterized more than anything by its prevailing sense of extreme Loneliness. Did you know that? The advertising agencies tasked with selling us everything under the sun certainly know about our loneliness. Every social media platform, every cell phone provider, every new technology knows that they can twist the very soul of a person into wanting what they are selling simply by promising them the 'greater connectivity' that every human longs for. We are assured that this technology will soothe the unbearable weight of our existential angst, bridge the gap between us and the world around us, protect us from the horrors of our soul's insufferable isolation.

But can I just ask: how has that really been working out for you? Has the promise of 'connectivity' had any significant impact on your life? Besides increasing your frantic sense of continual activity, exacerbating the depth of your loneliness whenever that constant digital activity is interrupted for any reason (what happens in your soul when you unexpectedly find yourself 'off the grid' and unable to access your 'cyber connectivity'?), and making it harder and harder for you to remain solidly present in the moment when actually spending real time with real people? Honestly, doesn't it seem like all this 'greater connectivity' hasn't delivered on its promise? That we, on the whole, feel *more* lonely than ever?

Is there some better way than what the digital world is offering to combat this growing inability we find in ourselves to connect in a satisfying way with those around us? To build the kind of relationships that might truly be described as the 'crown of life'? If you could find that better way, would it be worth its price in gold to you? Can you imagine how different your world would be right now if you were walking through life's joys and sorrows, its struggles and griefs and seemingly insurmountable challenges in the daily company of cherished, lifelong friends that knew every twist in the winding story of your heart's journey, and whose stories you knew almost as well as your own—brothers, kindred spirits whom you loved and trusted and delighted in above almost everything else in your life?

I can answer that question for you.

For all of us.

It would be...*incredible.*

FIVE

THE FELLOWSHIP
OF THE KING

They seemed to be a terror one to the other, for that they could not see that glory each one on herself which they could see in each other. Now therefore they began to esteem each other better than themselves. For you are fairer than I am, said one; and you are more comely than I am, said another.   (John Bunyon, *The Pilgrim's Progress*)

"Have I not chosen you?"
- Jesus of Nazareth

The last stage of their journey to Orodruin came and it was a torment greater than Sam had ever thought that he could bear. He was in pain, and so parched that he could no longer swallow even a mouthful of food...

With a gasp Frodo cast himself on the ground. Sam sat by him...At last he groped for Frodo's hand. It was cold and trembling. His master was shivering.

"I didn't ought to have left my blanket behind,' muttered Sam; and lying down he tried to comfort Frodo with his arms and body. Then

sleep took him, and the dim light of the last day of their quest found
‘   them side by side.

'Now for it! Now for the last gasp!' said Sam as he struggled to his feet.
He bent over Frodo, rousing him gently. Frodo groaned; but with a great
effort of will he staggered up; and then he fell upon his knees again. He
raised his eyes with difficulty to the dark slopes of Mount Doom
towering above him, and pitifully he began to crawl forward on his
hands.

Sam looked at him and wept in his heart, but no tears came to his dry
and stinging eyes. 'I said I'd carry him, if it broke my back' he muttered,
'and I will!'

'Come, Mr. Frodo!' he cried. 'I can't carry it for you, but I can carry
you and it as well. So up you get! Come on, Mr. Frodo dear! Sam will
give you a ride. Just tell him where to go, and he'll go.'

(J.R.R Tolkien, *The Return of the King*)

ONE WORD, TWO MEANINGS

If you grew up attending a church that had been built anytime
before the turn of the millennium you no doubt have memories of
a gymnasium or similar gathering space that was called the 'Fellowship Hall'. To the best of my knowledge, they were a requirement
for having a bona fide church building, at least one worth its salt in
the eyes of those religious folk who knew all about the worth of
salt, being the salt of the earth themselves. In fact one of the most
common activities taking place in these omnipresent 'Rooms of
Requirement' (a reference for you *Harry Potter* fans) across our
fair nation was the passing *of* the salt. For these Fellowship Halls
were often the site of sunrise pancake breakfasts and Wednesday
night dinners. But also the home of many a youth group relay race
and the occasional Christian concert. Sunday school classes and
Tuesday night basketball practices. Visiting missionary slideshows

and wedding rehearsal dinners. It was here, in the images that became associated with the Fellowship Hall, that I came to ascribe a certain ultra-specific meaning to the word 'fellowship': *the gathering of Christians for religious activities that contained something (no matter how minute) of a social element about them.*

Imagine my confusion then, when as a twelve year old I was first introduced to Tolkien's epic fantasy, *The Lord of the Rings*, the first portion of which was entitled, oddly enough, *The Fellowship of the Ring*. Here was that word again, 'fellowship', but in a very surprising context indeed. Apparently it could be used both as a verb *and* a noun. Even more curious, the verb form that I was used to hearing about at church made far more sense when it described the natural activities flowing out of the noun form. People who belonged *to* a Fellowship (noun form) were most properly described as actively participating *in* 'fellowship' (verb form).

This simple fact was, to my church-culture-soaked twelve year old mind, nothing short of a revelation. For one thing, the epic story I was drinking in like a Lost Boy dying of thirst in a desert had none of the tang or familiar flavor of what I understood as 'religious activity'—certainly not the kind that I had come to expect to be taking place in Fellowship Halls across the land. And one thing was immediately clear: that it was into Tolkien's sort of 'fellowship' that I longed to be caught up, drawn into, invited to share. For his brand of fellowship was the Fellowship of both Hall and Wilderness; it was the Fellowship of the Road and of the Journey and of the Quest. It was the kind of Fellowship that could stir the heart of a man, that could awaken in him heroic and adventurous longings—longings buried so deep he hardly remembered the last time he had even noticed they were there. The very thought of Tolkien's brand of fellowship acted upon me with the same alluring power that he depicted flowing into Bilbo's heart through the song of the dwarves the night of the fateful 'unexpected party' that began his adventures:

> As they sang the hobbit felt the love of beautiful things made by hands
> and by cunning and by magic moving through him, a fierce and a jealous
> love, the desire of the hearts of dwarves. Then something Tookish woke
> up inside him, and he wished to go and see the great mountains, and hear
> the pine-trees and the waterfalls, and explore the caves, and wear a sword
> instead of a walking-stick.   (Tolkien, *The Hobbit*)

My baptism into this new definition of fellowship was, in a sense, a baptism of fire—for a fire awoke in me and my heart burned to experience such a fellowship myself. And it was also like a kind of Pentecost, for the baptism included spirit and wind as well: enlivening spirit and rushing wind, and my first instinct was to be rushing like that wind myself—rushing as far from the Fellowship Halls of my religious upbringing as The Road outside my door could sweep me off to. And despite the subsequent cry of the religious hounds calling me back to their door, I have always since found myself ill at ease in their halls of fellowship, and at peace in the company of the road-weary pilgrims one meets wandering the greenwood in search of adventure.

> Every step of the common journey tests his metal; and the tests are tests
> we fully understand because we are undergoing them ourselves...You will
> not find the warrior, the poet, the philosopher or the Christian by
> staring in his eyes as if he were your mistress: better fight beside him,
> read with him, argue with him, pray with him.
>
> (Lewis, *The Four Loves*)

Yes, like many another young boy, Tolkien's fantasy tales had stung me wide awake and opened my eyes to see that the 'real' thing I had been offered through organized religious programming contained nothing but the shadow of a goodness it did not understand, while the make-believe world actually held more of the solid, living Truth that my heart hungered to know and experience.

INCARNATION AND DEEP MAGIC

Before proceeding, I want to go back to my previous premises and say once again that I believe we were intentionally and purposefully designed by our Creator for deep relationships, and that those relationships were intended to grow and increase, lasting throughout all the days of our lives, and beyond. They are God's intended antidote to the loneliness we all face as individual souls often adrift in a wide, wide world. At their best they are truly the crown of life, the greatest natural gift any person could receive, as Lewis claimed. Nor, in the light of both the Genesis creation account and the expansive goodness of God, does their position as a 'natural' gift lessen the weight of their significance.

With all those assumptions as background, it's time to turn and have a look at the life of Jesus Himself. If we take an open-minded look at how our Lord lived his earthly life, I believe we'll discover a few more startling and hopeful things about human relationships— more specifically, about Friendship itself. The first thing we'll discover is that when God chose to write Himself into the human story as one of the characters *in* the story, *he comes as a man who treats friendships with a priority and a dignity and a necessity unlike almost anything the world has ever seen before.*

Or did you never notice that detail?

Of course we may wonder, just how important is this little plot detail? This is Jesus we are looking at, remember: God the Son taking on human form. No, that sounds misleading. Not just 'taking on human form', like playing dress-up, or putting on a disguise: becoming human. Fully human. "In the beginning was the Word, and the Word was with God, and the Word was God...The Word became flesh and dwelt among us. We have seen his glory, the glory of the one and only Son, who came from the Father full of grace and truth." (I John 1:1, 1:14)

I use the metaphor that God is here 'writing Himself into the play as a character in the play', but I do not agree with those who think the details of Jesus' life were insignificant because he was, for the most part, play-acting. John Eldredge makes this point well:

> The heroic actions and miraculous powers of Jesus' life attest to it (the fact that he is God). So, when we read what we would call the more human moments, we feel that Jesus was sort of... cheating. With a wink and a nod we know what's really happening is that Einstein has dropped in to take the first grade math quiz. Mozart is playing a measure in the kindergarten song flute choir. After all, we're talking about Jesus here. The guy who walked on water, raised Lazarus from the dead. He never broke a sweat, right?
>
> But, then, what do you make of the terrible sweat in Gethsemane?...
>
> Gethsemane was the most terrible farce if Jesus was faking it.
>
> He was human. Really.   (John Eldredge, *Beautiful Outlaw*)

Now, with that in mind, obviously everything about this colossal and unparalleled event, this unimaginable Incarnation, is going to be significant. (What a terrible sorrow it is that half the world doesn't believe it and the other half of the world is no longer in speechless wonder at the thought of it.) But despite our lack of perspective, we need to wake up to the fact that this is huge, friends. Deep magic, so to speak. Something beyond words, beyond the mind of man to comprehend. Way beyond.

(Just as an aside—but an important aside—let's be honest about the fact that one of the things that acts as a real turn-off to our non-believing friends when it comes to our faith is this attitude we project that we *do* comprehend all this, that it all makes perfect sense to us, (and why for goodness sake doesn't it to them?) From their perspective it all feels like a wild flight of fancy too gigantic to swallow, (and why for goodness sake do we act like it's the most obvious thing in the world?) this idea that the pre-existent Being that fills the whole universe with His Presence, that holds all of Reality together by the voice of His command, was both *willing* and *able* to condescend to somehow becoming one of His own extremely limited physical creatures. It would behoove us to admit that there is no small amount of unsearchable mystery woven into the fabric of the Christian story. You might be surprised what a breath of fresh air this can be in a world that is swiftly becoming bored to death with mere scientific 'facts'. A little mystery is what the world is lacking, and if we'd just accept that, we'd notice that mystery is one thing we've got in spades. This is deep magic, friends. Remember that. Deep Magic.)

Now, one of the many ways to view the Incarnation—this event of indescribable wonder—is to see that God is, from one perspective, stepping in to human history and saying, *"Look, this whole human experiment has been off the rails for so long nobody can even remember what my original design even looked like. So I'm going to show you what it means to be a human. In fact, I am going to show you how to do it perfectly: so pay very close attention."*

And yes, certainly there were more purposes to the Incarnation than just modeling a perfect life. As important as that is, the broken, fallen thing within us simply doesn't have the capacity to imitate the perfection modeled by Jesus merely by trying harder. I don't want to give the impression that I am diminishing the mission that brought Jesus among us by giving sole attention to the details of the human life that He lived along the way to fulfilling that mission. Without question this was also the chosen path through which there could come to all who chose to receive it: rescue from a dark enslavement to an imperfect life; rebirth of the dead thing within that was necessary if we were to live differently (and eternally); and, reconciliation to the One from which all goodness and perfection emanates, not to mention the promise that the goodness of Jesus himself was now working within us, making the impossible possible. But none of these theological truths diminish the mythic, romantic significance of the fact that we are watching the author of humanity stepping onto the stage to take a turn at being human Himself.

And handed the leading role on the stage, what sort of a Man does He become? Pay close attention here:

When God becomes a man, He becomes a man who loves a good Fellowship.

Do you see it?

Really, the most startling thing of all about Jesus' personal commitment to deep, intimate friendships is the fact that you almost *never* hear anyone acting startled by his personal commitment to deep, intimate friendships. Which is because you almost never hear anyone talking about it *at all*. It's like we've been staring at the most important story in the history of, well...history, for most of our lives, and yet we have remained completely blind to some of the most curious details. Here we have the Son of God stepping onto the stage, and one of the first things he does as a public figure preparing for the great mission that he has come to accomplish, is to invite a dozen guys to get in on the ground floor of that mission with him.

> As Jesus walked beside the Sea of Galilee, he saw Simon and his brother Andrew casting a net into the lake, for they were fishermen. "Come, follow me," Jesus said, "and I will make you fishers of men." At once they left their nets and followed him. When they had gone a little farther, he saw James son of Zebedee and his brother John in a boat, preparing their nets. Without delay he called them and they left their father Zebedee in the boat with the hired men and followed him. (Mark 1:16-20)

Jesus went up on a mountainside and called to him those he wanted, and they came to him. He appointed twelve—designating them apostles— that they might be with him...   (Mark 3:13-14)

THE CULTURAL INFLUENCE

Oh, I know, we are so broken in our relational understanding that all we can see in 'the calling of the Twelve' is something organizational, something official, something we can fit into one of those compartments we are obsessed with dissecting our world into for easier management. Somehow we've got Jesus, the first-century, small-town Mediterranean Jew, plotting and scheming precisely the way we would expect from a twenty-first century American businessman. He is leveraging the 'having of disciples'—a mildly popular teaching method of the day used by some Greek philosophers and a few Jewish rabbis—against the long term value it will bring to his 'business plan': the propagation of His message. He figures this is the most effective way to get the news about the Kingdom of God to the world. He is, in fact, much like a modern man, thinking *functionally*. This has nothing to do with friendship. No way. Jesus is way too busy saving the world for that. This is about getting the job done, pure and simple.

You see? This is how we think. This is how the religious leaders who have *taught* us how to think about these things think. Because they are false teachers, bent on distorting the truth? No, mostly they are just the product of the culture, even as we are. More of our collective modes of thinking are products of the culture than any of us care to realize. Culture, you see, is a medium—like air and water are mediums—in which we are immersed to the point of complete saturation. We are not experientially aware of swimming our way through the oxygen and other gases that form the earth's atmosphere every moment of our existence. Nor is the fish aware that it is 'in' water, as if it had ever been in something else. It has no frame of reference that allows it to speak of 'being wet': it has been what we would call 'wet' its entire fishy life. This is precisely how culture impacts us: as a medium that we breathe in and out with every breath we take. And therefore, it should be plain to see that whenever the Church is not infused with a dynamic, combative spirit of revolution and rebellion (which, let's be honest, we've rarely witnessed in recent years) it will passively and subconsciously receive into itself many—if not all—of the aspects of the surrounding culture. Which is why what you experience when you walk into the average local church is not so much specifically 'Christian' as it really is just twenty-first century American culture, modified by varying degrees of Christian influence.

And yes, those degrees of Christian influence certainly do vary from church to church. But it is the larger culture of society as a whole that is informing the majority of our attitudes and approaches to the way things ought to be, even in the way we 'do' church. In many ways the church you attend on Sunday morning has more in common with the shopping mall you visit on Saturday afternoon than it does another church you might visit on any day of the week, so long as that week dates from the year 1850.

Now, being that we live in a culture like ours that mostly doesn't view the world from a relational paradigm, do you think it's too shocking of a surprise that we're prone to overlook, or misinterpret, the beauty of Jesus' deep personal commitment to friendship? To not notice how significant his little band of brothers was to the way his entire adult life played itself out? He spent more than three years—the only three years in Jesus' life we have much record of mind you—living moment by moment in intimate proximity with The Twelve. Everything he did, they did. They shared everything together. Jesus himself claimed that he had kept nothing from them; it was he who dared call them 'friends'.

> I no longer call you slaves, because a master doesn't confide in his slaves.
> Now you are my friends, since I have told you everything the Father told
> me.   (John 15:15)

Endless miles of dusty roads. Nights spent camped out on the hard ground under a star-studded sky in the most out-of-the-way corners of the kingdom. Risks, dangers, threats—physical and supernatural—around every turn: awaiting them in every remote village, brewing in the council chambers and throne rooms of the mighty. Intrigue and adventure along the Road towards the greatest rescue mission in the world. In any world. Friendships growing ever more intimate with each threat, each miracle, each late night conversation around the campfire.

Forget your Sunday School lessons, your flannel board Jesus. This fellowship of the hidden King—no matter what else it was, my friends—was *absolutely epic*. More epic than even your fondest childhood visions of what you thought the world's greatest, most alluring friendships must look like.

THE INSEPARABLES

> "If you are in haste, monsieur," said D'Artagnan, with the same simplicity
> with which a moment before he had proposed to him to put off the duel
> for three days, "if you are in haste, and if it be your will to dispatch me at
> once, do not inconvenience yourself—I am ready."
> "Well, that is again well said," cried Athos, with a gracious nod to
> D'Artagnan, that did not come from a man without brains, and certainly
> not from a man without a heart. "Monsieur, I love men of your kidney,
> and I foresee plainly that, if we don't kill each other, I shall hereafter have
> much pleasure in your conversation. We will wait for these gentlemen, if
> you please; I have plenty of time and it will be more correct. Ah! Here is
> one of them, I think."

In fact, at the end of the Rue Vanguard, the gigantic form of Porthos began to appear.

"What!" cried D'Artagnan, "is your first second M. Porthos?"

"Yes. Is that unpleasant to you?"

"Oh, not at all."

"And here comes the other."

D'Artagnan turned in the direction pointed to by Athos, and perceived Aramis.

"What!" cried he, in an accent of greater astonishment than before, "is your second witness M. Aramis?"

"Doubtless he is. Are you not aware that we are never seen one without the others, and that we are called in the musketeers and the guards, at court and in the city, Athos, Porthos, and Aramis, or the three inseparables?"

(Alexander Dumas, *The Three Musketeers*)

The Inseparables indeed. I love these guys. I always have. I can't remember a time even in childhood when I didn't know what it meant to be a Musketeer; or know that the main glory in being *one* of them was the necessity of there being *three* of them. What young boy doesn't imagine how wonderful his life would be if he could be part of a legendary fellowship of heroic souls like the noble and virtuous Athos, the extravagant and boisterous Porthos, and the amorous man of quiet dignity and high intrigue Aramis? These men, these heroes, these demi-gods: oh, to be welcomed as a brother into such high and noble company! To be caught up in their kingdom-saving adventures, striding with an almost cheerful heedlessness into dark and deadly dangers, arm-in-arm and brimming with the devil-may-care nonchalance that comes from knowing whether you live or die, you will live or die One for All, and All for One! There are few other myths that capture the very heart of this latent desire slumbering deep within us to share in this rarest of gifts heaven can bestow: an epic friendship so great, so powerful, that the world would resound with the rumour of its telling in story and in song.

MERRY MEN

For nearly two hours they kept at it, exchanging many a hit, while the wood rang with the blows of staff on staff.

'Come, hold your hand,' panted Robin at last. 'Let us end the quarrel. For neither of us will gain much by threshing the others' bones into a bran-mash.'

'I hunger still for my five hundred pounds,' gasped Arthur. 'Indeed, I must earn them, or I cannot pay the hundred which I owe to you!'

'Come and join my merry band in Sherwood,' said Robin. 'I'll promise that you'll earn much more than five hundred pounds there—though I'll see to it that you pay me your debt!

Arthur-a-Bland hesitated...

Robin then blew his horn, and before long Little John and several others appeared among the trees.

'By the Mass!' exclaimed Arthur, 'Is that not John Little whom I see coming over yonder?'

'That was his name,' answered Robin, 'before he suffered a forest change and became my dearest friend and most faithful follower as Little John.'

'Then I am with you indeed,' cried Arthur. 'John is my own cousin, our mothers being sisters, and I have ever loved him like a brother. And I have been seeking him these several years.'

'What is the matter, good master?' called Little John as he drew near and saw the blood on Robin's face.

'This fine tanner has been tanning my hide for me!' answered Robin with a grin.

'He is to be commended,' said Little John gravely, 'for few can do that. But if he is so stout a fellow let me have a bout with him and see if he can tan my hide also!'

'Hold your hand, good John,' said Robin, 'Here has been fighting enough. This our new companion is called Arthur-a-Bland...I believe that you know him!'

Then Arthur and Little John flung their staffs away and clasped one another, almost weeping with joy. And when Arthur had sworn to be loyal and true in all his dealings with Robin Hood and the rest of the Sherwood outlaws, Robin took an arm of each and led them away towards the secret glade to eat, drink, and make merry over their new alliance. And as they went through the tuneful woods they sang gaily:

Oh ever hereafter as long as we live
We three will be as one:
The wood it shall ring and the minstrel shall sing
Of Robin Hood, Arthur, and John!

(Roger Lancelyn Green, *Robin Hood*)

"*We three will be as one.*" This, my friends, is what a fellowship looks like. This is the beautiful thing that, as modern citizens of a modern world, we have resigned ourselves to living without. And yet, our hearts dare to ask: *Why? Why must we live without it?* What rich and beautiful facets of human experience have we surrendered without a fight?

"Though one may be overpowered, two can defend themselves. A cord of three strands is not quickly broken."   (Ecclesiastes 4:12)

JESUS AND EPIC FRIENDSHIPS

So let me just confess to you that one of the core assumptions about the life of Jesus that has been growing in me over the years is a distinctly *relational* assumption. It's based on my experience of our relational God, a core belief about the reason for which we were created, and my deep convictions regarding the nature of love. The assumption I am making is this:

Jesus 'did' heroic, deep, satisfying male friendship better than anyone else ever has.

I don't even think that any of those most famous, most iconic of all literary friendships we've grown up with have anything on Jesus and his band of wandering buddies. I'm serious about that. I believe it—believe it with all my heart. I know: that may sound like wishful thinking, like a major leap in logic on my part based on the actual accounts of Jesus' life that we have available for study and reference. But I believe that the ancient writing style in which the life of Jesus is told, our own cultural expectations, and a persistent religious haze that often sucks the human element right out of the gospel stories have all combined to keep us from seeing the epic adventure these men actually embarked on together, this incredible Fellowship of the Man who would be King.

But let's go back and look more closely at the gospel accounts again. Notice how Jesus gets up before dawn to go spend time alone with the Father: "Early in the morning, while it was still dark, Jesus got up and slipped out to a solitary place to pray." (Mark 1:35)

Now I know we've taken this insight into Jesus' pre-dawn prayer life and turned it into a template for what good spiritual disciplines look like. I grew up on stories of great men of the Christian faith who woke hours before sunrise to pray and read their Bible. The earlier they woke, the holier they appeared to be to my youthful imagination. Unfortunately, it turns out I'm not much of a morning person myself. In my early twenties I discovered that my ability to focus my mind, engage my heart, and receive willing participation from my body was far stronger at night than it was in the morning. I could have some really great prayer times, and yet I was still haunted by the popular understanding that truly holy people have their 'quiet time' first thing in the morning, and there was clearly something amiss with my relationship with God in the quirk that I wanted to have mine at night. Because that wasn't the clear example we got from Jesus, right? I mean, this passage about him slipping away before sunrise to pray, that's where most of this pressure is coming from, isn't it?

Now, don't get me wrong. I think the biggest spiritual problem in the Church today is that the majority of us don't spend very much time at all alone with God. So please don't hear me saying that sitting with God first thing in the morning isn't the very best way to begin your day. It absolutely is. But I also think we need to recognize that there was actually something deeply practical and *specific to his situation* in Jesus' pre-dawn hikes into lonely places. Something deeply practical that I think we've missed, something driving Jesus to get away and talk to God at what many might call an ungodly hour of the morning. The simple truth was this: *the wee hours of the morning were the only time in Jesus' entire day that he could steal away and be alone without someone noticing.* Without someone interrupting. Without someone asking if they might tag along. Unless he picked a time so early that he could count on all twelve of his band of merry men being fast asleep, he wouldn't have had the unbroken solitude he needed to spend uninterrupted time alone with Abba. That's just how relationally intertwined our Master's life was. Get away early, or don't get away at all.

> "Early in the morning, while it was still dark, Jesus got up and slipped
> out to a solitary place to pray. Simon and his companions went to look
> for him, and when they found him they said 'Everyone is looking for
> you.'"   (Mark 1:35-37)

Sounds like he got away just in time. Another hour of sleep and his entire day would have been swallowed up, given over to the needs of the relationships around him, not to mention the crowds that were already gathering outside the city, coming in search of the Healing Rabbi who might just yet turn out to be their long awaited Chosen One. Certainly Jesus' mission, and his choice to fulfill that mission while simultaneously creating—and living from within the context of—the greatest Fellowship the world had ever known, came with certain costs and sacrifices.

Clearly they were costs he thought worth paying. Still, I can't help but wonder if all things being equal, he wouldn't have enjoyed an extra hour or two of sleep every now and then...

And yet, I'll say again: because of how we've been trained to view the world, we mostly dismiss his whole stunning choice of living arrangements by chalking it up to cultural differences between his day and ours, don't we? Like it was all the rage in Jesus' day to share a tent with twelve of your closest buddies, and no more worth our consideration than the fact that they dressed in robes, grew long beards, and ate their meals sitting on the floor. As we are all prone to the vanity that C.S. Lewis called "chronological snobbery", we assume that if only those first century Palestinians were as wise and advanced as we are, they would have known how much better it is to dress in expensive name-brand jeans, shave the majority of their body hair, and eat their meals at an approved distance of forty-eight inches above floor level. And, let us not fail to add, they would have known how simply *gauche*, how *archaic*, how behind the times, it is to attempt to share a tent—or a flat, a condo, an old Victorian house just off the edge of campus—with twelve, or any number whatsoever, of your closest friends.

Jesus could have done things differently, you know. He didn't *have* to take disciples; having taken them, he didn't *have* to invite them to come and "be" with him, every blessed hour of the day: nights, weekends, and bank holidays. But he did. And we say, "Wow, what a Saint to put up with *that*," because here's the sad thing: thanks to our cultural training in an individualistic mindset, we are far more likely to think about what Jesus *gave up* by this move than about what he *gained*. Am I right? Do you notice that in yourself? Do you find yourself instinctively thinking how hard that must have been for Jesus, rather than thinking how amazingly, wonderfully fun it must have been for him? For *all* of them?

I think I understand where a little bit of our problem stems from, why we tend to cringe and shrink and add the 'babysitting of the Twelve' to the list of our Lord's 'sufferings' rather than to see it as one of the deep joys of his earthly life. It stems from the fact that most sermons which attack 'individualism' and preach 'community' almost always approach the subject along the lines of telling us our moral duty. It's all 'shoulds' and 'shouldn'ts' and guilt and duty and the whole litany of usual suspects we have come to expect from our somber-toned guardians of the moral compass. I never once heard a sermon on the importance of rejecting my American individualism that spoke directly to my own deep desire to experience a life that was *better* than the one my American individualism could offer. No, they always made the denial of our Individualism sound merely like one more way to carry one's cross. I never once heard a preacher say, *"Hey, folks, remember how much fun it was living in a college dorm, or in a college apartment with all your buddies? Wouldn't it be great if life could be like that again?"* I don't know about you, but that sure would've caught my attention, and probably given me a much more open mind to the ideas being presented. *Wait, the stodgy, religious sounding word "koinonia" really just meant spending tons of time with your closest, dearest friends? And this is something that matters to God? He wants this for me? Well, now you're talking! I'm down for a lifetime of that!*

It's a pretty obvious psychological fact that you can spoil the fun of just about anything by making it mandatory. A sport you loved until daily, intense, non-optional practices killed all sense that it was, in fact, a game. A college chapel or religious event where missing it meant negative consequences, marks against your record. A love for writing or any art, spoiled by a deadline and the subsequent pressure to make it happen *right now*. Any job doing a thing that you used to like doing, until it became your job and you had to do it every day...or else.

It seems to me that this is the sort of thing that the Church has done to our desire for fellowship, for I have never heard a sermon on fellowship, community, or interpersonal relationships that awakened in me a desire for *any* of those things, despite the fact that I do in fact greatly desire them already.

Whoa. Did you hear what I just said? It sounds absolutely crazy, doesn't it? But I'm gonna stick by it, and repeat it for those of you that never like to go back and reread the previous paragraph: I have *never* heard a sermon on friendship or fellowship (the noun form) that appealed to my deep, innate desire to experience those very things. Even though I already *do* desire them. *Greatly.* Almost more than anything else this world has to offer. So how exactly could the modern preacher seem determined to miss that? Talk about mishandling the full weight of an argument, overlooking the latent power inherent in your case! It's like having a sanctuary full of people wearing jet powered backpacks and trying to get them up out of their seats by resorting to used car salesman tactics, begging and cajoling them into buying super expensive bottles of Wonka's Fizzy Lifting Drink at the over-priced snack bar in the church lobby. The disconnect really is inexplicable. Why not just remind us how deeply we naturally desire this? Are we back to a disbelief in the expansive goodness of God? Are we still convinced that there can't possibly be anything good or virtuous or pleasing to God in an activity that we happen to also find deeply pleasing at the level of the human heart? Did God create us as humans simply to insist that we deny our humanity? Is this what we've come to think of Him, how we continue to perceive our Heavenly Abba?

Before the jaded sense set in that life is merely one long, drawn-out survival act, behind the resigned acquiescence to "suffer the slings and arrows of outrageous fortune"—somewhere deep in our past we hold the faint memory of a time when we knew that we longed for friends, soulmates, a brotherhood with which we can journey through life, do great things, overcome impossible challenges, storm the very Gates of Hell if necessary (and something stirring within us almost hopes it *will* be.) Even now when we meet such a Band of Brothers in the pages of history or fiction, when we see it portrayed in film or story, we are inexorably drawn to it with a deep yearning and hunger that aches to experience a similar heroic bond in our own lives. And when we look carefully at the life of Jesus we discover—oh, could it be?—that the fulfillment of this yearning is in fact the unique and indivisible possession of the Church, for no 'band of brothers' has ever existed that was more epic, more heroic, more glorious than the one that stands at the very heart of the Christian story.

The kind of fellowship you thought only existed in the pages of fiction or the annals of history from a friendlier time, a time when "All for One, and One for All!" was actually a thing? This, my friends, is a precious portion of that "life to the full" which Jesus came to offer.

We were meant to have it.

It is our birthright.

SIX

THE FELLOWSHIP
OF THE KING

PART II - HOW TO SAVE A WORLD

"By this all men will know that you are my disciples: that you love one another." (John 13:35)

"The Quest stands upon the edge of a knife. Stray but a little, and it will fail, to the ruin of all. Yet hope remains, while all the Company is True."

(J.R.R. Tolkien, *The Fellowship of the Ring*)

Having turned our attention to the life of Jesus, the first thing that becomes clear is that when God took the stage as one of us, He came as a man who valued friendship to the highest degree: embraced it fully and remained deeply and shockingly committed to it throughout his adult lifetime. Though the gospel writers—with the fate of the world hanging on their careful and deliberate witness to what they have seen, (and so must be forgiven their brevity)—are able to give only the briefest, tantalizing glimpses into the more human activities of daily life with Jesus, they yet take time to illustrate that His commitment to friendship was firm, steadfast, and formidable. So formidable in fact that He was willing to challenge the accepted cultural understanding of His times—that family was the ultimate relationship to which one owed their highest allegiance.

> While Jesus was still talking to the crowd, his mother and brothers stood outside, wanting to speak to him. Someone told him, "Your mother and brothers are standing outside, wanting to speak to you." He replied to him, "Who is my mother, and who are my brothers?" Pointing to his disciples, he said, "Here are my mother and my brothers. For whoever does the will of my Father in heaven is my brother and sister and mother."
>
> (Matthew 12:46-50)

Now, I realize that this passage is about a lot of things besides just how important friendships were to Jesus. As John Eldredge points out in his book *Beautiful Outlaw*, one thing we are witnessing is our Lord's absolute freedom from the power of family ties—that imperious power that so often is wielded in a manipulative style that keeps us from doing the will of the Father, the very work of the Kingdom we are most suited for, the thing that is ours and ours alone to do. In these last few generations of fear-driven, safety first, extremely cautious living, of 'wise financial planning' and 'serious adult decision making', I can't even begin to imagine how many eager young disciples of Jesus have had their radical zeal and faith deflated by the cautious, worldly wisdom of a well-meaning parent, now long jaded in their own journey by the wearying impact of the many 'cares of this world'. Or by a sibling who traded their own 'save-the-world-for-Jesus' dreams for the daily grind of the work-a-day world, then comes to your door, as Jesus' own siblings did, insisting you give up this foolishness and come home before the whole family is brought to ruin.

We have been raised in a society that is instinctively opposed to the wisdom Tolkien placed in the mouth of the wizard Gandalf, when the small hobbit Pippin had rashly offered his life in the service of The Steward of Gondor: "Noble deeds should not be checked by cold counsel." The adult world that I have known has consistently shown an unwavering commitment to the simplistic truth that all good counsel *must be cold counsel*. How few of us hear words of affirmation from the family members whom we so deeply want to please in that moment when our hearts draw us toward unconventional paths in pursuit of God's Kingdom purposes. To see how Jesus fared under similar misunderstanding, to know that He doesn't want any of His disciples to miss the adventure He is calling them into under the weight of coercive family pressure—that in itself is wealth enough to glean from this one story from the life of Jesus.

And yet, I don't think we can overlook the other element that is on display here—not just the pulling down of the family from a dangerously high pedestal, but in contrast the lifting up of the deep significance of non-familial relationships. That is to say, the *importance of friendship*. Remember the context here—Who it is that's speaking, and what sort of life choices He's been making since he came onto the world stage. This guy has already raised the significance of journeying through life with "the boys" to an unprecedented level. With that in mind, I don't think that when He points everyone's attention to the disciples and declares that *they* are His family we are merely seeing a Jewish flair for dramatic hyperbole as He gets a point across concerning the oft-felt tyranny of family ties. I think He really does value His little fellowship of followers to the same level of intensity most people feel towards their dearest family members. He lives with them. He travels with them. He eats His meals with them. He invites them to share in His 'business' (the Father's business). He invites them to share in His secret power

(Matthew 10:1). He calls them His friends (John 15:15). He beseeches in prayer for their safety, their protection (John 17:6-19). He promises them thrones and glory for all time in the Kingdom to come (Matt. 24:45-47; Matt. 25:34; Luke 12:32-33; Luke 22:28-30). Knuckleheads or not, I think it's safe to say that Jesus really did love these guys.

FRIENDSHIP FOLLOWS FUNCTION?

Now, I mentioned earlier how we have been trained by our individualistic worldview to mostly judge the importance—and subsequent longevity—of our relationships based on their use-fulness to us: based on their functionality. (Which, mind you, is much of the reason we don't *have* deep friendships, isn't it? The really great ones, for the most part, refuse to germinate and grow under the conditions created by those who are merely *using* friend-ships to further some other end.)

And it really *is* an awful approach to take—that should be made clear. This one facet of modern culture—that relationships last only as long as their formal function remains intact—is having a colossal impact on our lives, though we rarely give much attention to that fact. It certainly has left its indelible mark on my life. Most especially so because I have spent almost my entire adult life working in the 'formal' (function-based) relational arena. Whether it was through youth ministry, coaching youth sports, or substitute teaching, I found myself invested in a constant stream of signif-icant relationships—all of which depended upon me holding an 'official' position that defined my reason for those relationships. Understand, the young men and women in my ministries and on the teams I coached were always deeply important to me—as they needed to be in order for me to do my job well. I know that for many of them I was an equally important character in their lives:

for a brief season of life anyway—a *surprisingly* brief moment in time. While each of those roles lasted I found myself investing in the relationships that were at the center of those roles as if they were going to go on to be a permanent part of my life. I thought that the depth of the friendships I had built would last beyond the 'formal' role, would continue to grow and deepen in the years ahead.

But invariably the story always turned out the same. Soon after the 'formal' role I performed in their life ended, so did the relationship. My 'usefulness' to them had come to an end. The matrix for our 'forced' involvement with one another on a weekly basis was eliminated—and without that, what 'reason' was there for us to spend time together? I wasn't family, and I didn't have an 'official' role in their life. The swift current of life moved them on, mostly without so much as a backward glance. Now, looking back over the years I can tell you that I hear from—perhaps once-a-year at the most—only a handful of these people I was so deeply invested in. And I can only count *one* out of them all that has remained on my short list of present-day, active, growing friendships. *One*. Over twenty-nine years of investment in four churches, four high schools, and more soccer teams than I can remember. *One*. It would be heartbreaking, if we weren't resigned to it all by this point.

Of course, you've experienced something similar. Maybe not to the same extreme, unless you also work in a profession built around interpersonal relationships. But we've all been affected by this, because we've all been raised in a society that doesn't know much else besides 'formal' relationships. In today's world we spend time with people because it is our job, because we have a formal role—a position and a title—that explains and justifies our relationship with those people. (Or else we know what it's like to be on the other end of this, and people have spent time with *us* because it was *their* job.) When the formal role ends, so does most of the time and effort invested into the relationship. This just seem to be the unspoken rule we live by. And even while the formal role does last, we still are only comfortable within the formal *framework* of that role—our access to relationships is constantly limited by our ability to explain our actions based around some type of functionality.

At the last church I was on staff at, I used to eat lunch every week with a kid named Kenny—a long-haired rocker with little ambition in school and in life, but with a strong need for a listening ear, for someone to take an interest in his teenage struggles. Giving him a few hours over lunch every week was an easy, natural choice, and while getting him to open up could be a chore, for the most part I really enjoyed hanging out with him. But the pastor I worked under didn't like it one bit. "Why are you wasting time with Kenny?" he asked me one day during a monthly ministry review. "He's not an influencer at the local high school. He can't further your ministry. Spending time with him just isn't *a strategic* use of your time."

It's a pretty sad commentary on how we think, but it's a true story. It happened. I'm guessing it happens a lot actually: relationally minded youth pastors being diminished for not seeing the world through the same lens that their task-oriented supervisors do. Jesus may have told us that His personal passion was for search-and-rescue missions, for leaving the ninety-nine to go after the one, but our current church culture is looking for people eager to baby-sit the ninety-nine that remain neatly grouped in the choir loft awaiting instructions, and not people who would rather exert themselves by relentlessly chasing after the one.

As a society we've come to a place where we're only comfortable within the formal roles, and even then only as they help execute the task-oriented vision of the world that we can understand. And it's as true in the Church as it is in the world. We consider it odd when someone who used to be the local youth pastor—but no longer is—suddenly shows up to cheer on some of 'his kids' at a cross country meet or a Battle of the Bands. We question their social maturity, their motives, their inability to 'move on'. *No one's paying him to care about these kids. Why is he still hanging around?* In our pessimism we go so far as to question their intentions, their integrity, their very character.

I remember back in college my first boss in youth ministry questioned *my* interest in spending time with middle schoolers out-side of programmed events. "These kids aren't your friends," he stated flatly to me one day during my junior year. "It's not like you're going to call them up on a Friday night and ask if they want to go to the movies."

Problem was, that's *exactly* what I had been doing. That's how several of *my* youth group leaders had treated *me* when I was in junior high. As testimony of what that had meant in my own life, for nearly twenty years I carried in my wallet a ticket stub from the night a college-aged Chip Hardy took me and David, two goofy thirteen year olds, to see a James Bond movie at the cheap, second-run theatre in our hometown.

Chip didn't spend his Friday night with us because he was *supposed* to.

He did it because he *wanted* to.

And that meant the world to us.

Moments like that were probably the main reason I had loved my junior high church experience so much. The main reason I had wanted to go into youth ministry myself. I was keenly aware that in order to impact lives, there needed to be no question in the minds of the students in my ministry that I cared for them beyond the 'requirements' of my formal role in their lives.

Now, I hope we've established by this point the fact that Jesus chose to live in a deeply relational fellowship primarily because he was acting out of His perfect humanity, showing the world what it meant to be truly human—to be a deeply, intimately, relational being even in a fallen world. First and foremost it was, all 'functionality' aside, a very satisfying way to journey through the world: the grandeur and delight of a shared adventure. This foundational truth *cannot* be overlooked (especially since it *is* almost entirely overlooked *all* the time.)

At the same time, the way Jesus lived His life was also a display of the deeply intimate, relational nature of God Himself—for remember, Jesus life was no play-act, and from His own mouth we are told that He "only did the things He saw His Father in heaven doing" (John 5:12). We are told, in fact, that He was the exact representation of His (The Father's) being.(Hebrews 1:3) God Himself, we must realize, is at His core, a relationship-oriented Being. Jesus' incarnation merely brought that truth down to our level, 'put the cookies on the bottom shelf', so to speak, in an attempt to bring that truth home in a way we couldn't help but understand.

What an awful irony it is then, after all that effort, that for most people the hardest part of the Christian faith to fully embrace and accept is this idea that God truly *wants* to be intimately, relationally involved in our lives! Apparently we can't even find the cookies when they *are* on the bottom shelf. This is perhaps the greatest tragedy of all—the highest price that we end up paying as a people who do not see the world through a relational lens. For when we misinterpret God's intentions towards us, we miss out on the central purpose of our existence: intimacy with our Creator.

Now, all that being said, in spite of our relational deprivation I think there *is* something about the relational choices of Jesus that can *also* appeal to those of us who are so entrenched in our culture that we simply *can't* stop thinking of relationships in terms of functionality. Understand, I'm not going to suggest that 'using' relationships to some end was anywhere near one of His primary motives—so very unlike the way we tend to do relationships today. But for arguments sake, let's allow our 'task-oriented' worldview back into play for a minute and see what there is to learn even for relationally challenged people like ourselves.

HISTORIC DISCIPLESHIP

Up until this point I'm sure that some of you have been doubting the truth of all this, arguing instead that the guys I've been referring to as Jesus' 'friends' were really just his *students*—what the gospels called His 'disciples'—and that their interaction with Jesus was really defined by a formal, culturally accepted matrix for relationship, just like so many of ours have been. But I hope you are beginning to see that this was not the true case, that the master/disciple relationship was merely the *context* from which something much deeper and more lasting was destined to blossom. Remember, we just saw that Jesus wasn't afraid to deflect His family's prior right to His time by going so far as to call his disciples "my brother and sister and mother". (Matt. 12:49) Then He made it clear to those same disciples that he considered them His friends (John 15:15), that He loved them (John 13:34), and most tellingly of all, that their relationship was not contingent on any usefulness, promising instead that their friendship was neverending—that He was going to be with them to the very End (Matt. 28:20).

Yes, clearly Jesus utilized the master/disciple relational construct that was familiar to the people of His day. And yes, I could go on and on about how we've clearly struggled as a Church to follow His example, how we've come to label so many different things 'discipleship' that completely miss the deeply relational, life-on-life transference of experiential truth that was required in the original master/disciple teaching paradigm. But I will leave that for another time. Suffice it here to say that our current task-oriented approach to life doesn't even have the *capacity* to do true discipleship the way that Jesus did it. In fact, you'll notice that, being the kind of relationally challenged people that we are, the whole idea of 'discipleship' can only be packaged and sold to the modern American Church by emphasizing its functional merits: *Clearly Jesus had been able to change the world with just a small band of disciples, so maybe this small, slow, deeply relational approach might 'work' for us as well!*

It sounds crazy, but it's true. Just try to find a discipling philosophy today that doesn't try to sell itself on its merits for 'getting the job done'. I don't think you can. The only selling point we understand is functionality.

In stark contrast, people in certain cultures down through history certainly have chosen the master/disciple teaching style simply because that format actually appealed to them: for they had been trained to view the world with an inherently relational mindset, even as we have been trained with an inherently individualistic mindset. And thus the pace, the intensity, the small numbers and the close proximity of the master/disciple method: it all meant that you were not only teaching and training, you were also at the same time increasing the circle of significant people in your—by our standards —extremely limited world.

Now, it is true that besides its natural appeal to such relationally minded people, there always has been a basic *functional* goal of the master/disciple relationship: to mold the craftsmanship, the performance, the teaching—whatever the matrix for that particular master/disciple relationship happened to be—of the learner until it became identical to that of the teacher. A disciple, once fully trained, could carry on the work of the master with unbroken continuity into the next generation.

Now, ultimately this is the goal of Christian discipleship. To have no recognizable difference between the disciple and the Master is truly the end of all ends.

In the same way the Church exists for nothing else but to draw men into Christ, to make them little Christs. If they are not doing that, all the cathedrals, clergy, missions, sermons, even the Bible itself, are simply a waste of time. God became Man for no other purpose. It is even doubtful, you know, whether the whole universe was created for any other purpose.

- (C.S. Lewis, *Mere Christianity*)

THIS IS PERSONAL

Jesus definitely believed in the power of the master/disciple relationship. He didn't *have* to operate that way you know. He could have remained more aloof, more mysterious; He could have saved all His teaching for the crowds, the synagogues, even the Temple courts themselves. Who knows? Maybe He could have booked a speaking tour across the great ampitheatres of the Roman Empire. Isn't that pretty much how most 'celebrities' in the Church today do things? Surely Jesus could have made sure He had a few 'handlers' to keep the riffraff out of His hair, so He could focus more on really bringing the thunder at the remaining stops on 'the Sermon on the Mount Reunion Tour'. But that's not the choice Jesus made. He never let the crowds become more important than His disciples, the guys that He was living out the adventure of everyday life with. And remember, the choices Jesus made in His lifetime were intentional and significant. Eternally significant. It was no accident of history that He stumbled into the particular cultural milieu where the discipleship model existed among everyday artisans, esoteric Greek philosophers, and highly acclaimed Jewish rabbis.

But now, here's the really curious thing. As time went on I began to notice that Jesus didn't actually *put* all his emphasis there—the way we claim He did—didn't make a point of the discipleship method alone actually *being* the center of his secret plan for spreading the good news of the advancing Kingdom. Believe it or not, it turns out he's got an even bigger plan: one most of us have never heard even mentioned.

Look with me at what we find in the latter part of the gospel of John, chapters 13-17. Here we are getting a rare extended glimpse into Jesus' interaction behind closed doors with 'the boys', and our sneak peek finds Him unloading a treasure trove of priceless information to his Inner Circle. From the way the 'beloved Apostle' John recounts the story, this scene takes place on the very eve of the crucifixion, in the final hours leading up to the arrest in Gethsemane. It's their last night together, and Jesus has a lot on His heart. Or maybe John has his ears pricked and he's paying closer attention than usual. Probably a bit of both. There's a lot to say, and if possible for one so inherently overflowing with Light and Life, there's perhaps an extra note of passion and urgency in the words of the Master as he looks lovingly around the room, carefully choosing the last words of counsel he has time to offer the men who have walked through this turning point of History as his inseparable companions.

Now, if you know anything at all about dramatic storytelling, you realize that the scene is set for something special—for parting words that will be remembered for all the generations to come. Like the moment near the end of the film *Braveheart*, when all the crowd grows silent to hear the last confession, or perhaps desperate entreaty for mercy, from the condemned Scottish freedom fighter William Wallace. But begging for mercy is the last thing on Wallace's heart. Instead the crowd stands in stunned silence as the music swells and the dying warrior roars with his very last breath the defiant cry that sums up all he has lived and died for: "Freedom!" Now, this moment in the gospel of John is one of those climactic moments that all good storytelling lives to express, and I think it's safe to say Jesus does know a thing or two about storytelling, considering His Father is the Storyteller, the Great Author of...well, of everything. Listen with fresh ears to what the Son of the Great Storyteller does with this dramatic moment:

> My children, I will be with you only a little longer. You will look for me, and just as I told the Jews, so I tell you now: Where I am going you cannot come. A new command I give you: Love one another. As I have loved you, so you must love one another. *By this all men will know that you are my disciples*, if you love one another.
>
> John 13:33-35 (italics added)

Now, I understand that we have been trained to see the words of Jesus here as a universal statement directed towards *all* Christians in *all* the generations to come. Because, again, we have learned to approach the Scriptures as a textbook of theology even in the places where it is clearly presented to the reader as a narrative—a captivating story in which the context informs, *and is inseparable to*, the meaning. But I know, I know. We've been trained so differently. No matter what significant, *in the moment* meaning Jesus' words carry, isn't the most important thing for us to do is to receive them directly? As if we were there? As if He were speaking them personally and intentionally to us now today, two thousand years later?

Well, yes. Assuming that by doing so the original message is not sacrificed entirely, overlooked, or ultimately lost through its universal application. But that's *exactly* what we are in danger of doing here by choosing to see the universal application first and foremost. Because this command is absolutely loaded with context. And when we step back and look at Jesus' words within that original context, I think we will notice that there is something *deeply relational* in what He is saying. Yes, we *can* extrapolate the command given here to his close Fellowship of disciples and dear friends to "love one another" (as you'll notice we *always* do) to mean that all Christians everywhere throughout time and history ought to love everyone in the

whole world. But then, there's also a real problem with this univer-
salizing of Jesus' words, besides just the obvious problem of ignoring
the vitally important context of what he actually said and thus
missing a huge plot point in the unfolding drama of Mankind's
redemption. The other problem is in a mistaken, but wildly popular
religious idea about the very nature of love: the idea that a finite
human being like ourselves could love "everyone".

Friends, here's a spoiler alert for you:

We can't really love everyone.

We can't love everyone because real, deep, genuine love can only
exist within the context of a relationship.

LOVE IS MORE THAN AN ACTION

Stick with me for a minute before we return to the original message of Jesus' words to his dear, beloved intimate disciples and
friends. In our attempt to revive a vibrant and healthy appreciation
for intimate relationships, we need to clear away some of the fog and
confusion first.

So let me say again: in spite of the pop culture Christian-speak of
our day, *we can't love everyone because real, deep, genuine love can only
exist with the context of a relationship.*

Yes, we can, and ought, to treat others—even strangers we've never
met—in a loving manner. We can show them lovingkindness. We
can show them 'Charity', as this sort of 'love your neighbor as
yourself' way of treating others used to be called in the old lists of
virtues. And all these things are certainly good things, don't get me
wrong. It is imperative that we are transformed by the life of Jesus
into the kind of people so overflowing with joy and strength and
virtue that we instinctively and effortlessly treat everyone with all
the kindness and deference an eternal soul created in the image of
God deserves.

But kindness is *not* Love. Kindness is only one of the *fruits* of Love, something that naturally flows from Love, but something that we also can offer to those around us when it *doesn't* flow, when it is a hard-fought, intentional act of the will. But this sometimes painful act of the will, this treating people in a loving manner when we don't in fact feel very much like doing so, is not True Love, for God is Love and a similar reluctance has no place in His heart. When the Christian preachers say, *"You don't have to like the person, you just have to love them,"* we must assume that they are using a sort of shorthand, reminding us that we ought to treat those we don't love very much at all as if we did in fact love them. We must hope and pray that they aren't so confused about the true nature of Love that they think we are in fact loving those we do not even like.

I know, I know: you've heard it a hundred times in the Church, that Love is not a feeling, but an action. And it's true that any love that is true love *will* result in action. If it doesn't work towards the happiness of the beloved, it can hardly be considered love. If the sheer, unstoppable desire to give the beloved every possible good and perfect gift for their enjoyment isn't part of the equation, then it probably isn't love. But actions alone—well, I can tell from a lifetime of experience that good actions can be mimicked, or can flow from well-trained habits that have nothing to do with the heart. And True Love, whatever else it may be, is always also a matter of the heart. Or how else do you explain the clear command: "You shall love the Lord your God with all your *heart*..."? (Matthew 22:37)

And yet somehow in this age of cold reason we've come to view truly heartfelt, passionate love as sort a bonus. Like extra credit: a non-essential that's a nice surprise if we happen to experience it on rare occasions. But mostly we read in I Corinthians 13 the list of qualities that true love possesses and we say to ourselves, *'I can discipline myself to be kind. I can teach myself to be patient. I can learn not to envy. I can imitate all the virtues of True Love.'* Yes, because these virtues *are* virtues. They *can* exist without True Love being the empowering force behind them. As one with loads of personal experience, can I just point out how easy it is to slip into the insidious trap of serving people—of treating them with the sacrificial acts that externally appear as lovingkindness—long after Love itself has given way to resentment, bitterness, and frustration?

THE LOVE OF GOD IS CENTRAL

Remember: God is love (I John 3:16), and when we are commanded to love our brothers (I John 3:21) we are in essence being told to have for them the same heart, the same interest, the same affection that God does. Deep love can only grow from deep caring, and deep caring requires deep knowing. Make no mistake: God has never loved a Stranger, and True Love is not blind. That's why His love matters. That's why it means Something. Why it means everything. *Because it is the One who knows us most that is the One who loves us best.*

Love—true becoming like God as He is in His deepest nature kind of Love—by its very essence *must* be a relational thing. There's really no way around it: you've actually got to *know* someone to truly love them, not just the idea of them, or the species in general. The deeper the knowing, the greater capacity for love. Love that can be tested. Love that doesn't just claim to be 'unconditional', but has already seen us for everything we are and yet loves us still.

Understand friends, the Love of God is no mere curiosity.

"Why do I exist?" This is the question that every soul who has ever wandered the paths of the living beneath the changeless stars of high heaven has cried out into the void, bending all the powers of their being to faintly understand; and it can truly be said that the only answer that has offered the slightest hope of satiating the eternal mystery of Being is this:

"I exist because of Love."

Because of love.

It all boils down to love. As author Gerald May put it, "We are created by love, to live in love, for the sake of love." Our creation was an act of love. We exist so that we might live a life defined by love—first the love we receive, then the love we give back responsively. *Love, Love, Love.* Believe it or not, the Beatles got that one right.

So you see why it's so important not to sell love short, not to call 'love' that which is unfit to even touch the dirty, trailing hem of Real Love's garments? For in this one little word the very nature of the foundation of All Things is at stake. The meaning of life and the purpose of our existence. Which is why it matters very much what we mean by 'love'. It needs to be more than mere kindness or even pity. As John Eldredge wrote, "We don't want to be someone's project, we want to be the desire of their heart." *(Waking the Dead)*

Does it make a difference to *you* to know if God loves you because you are the desire of His heart, or simply because He is a Being so marked by love that He loves you as a matter of personal principle, simply to remain true to His own Nature? *Could* the consolation of your heart's deepest longings be found in the idea that somewhere in the Great Beyond there sits some benign, gracious King who pities you, but cares nothing for your company? Is a little disgusted by you if you must know the unspoken truth lurking behind the benevolent but condescending smile? Yet has chosen to "love" you nonetheless (by which we must mean act towards you with lovingkindness and charity) out of the goodness of His own heart? No delight. No longing. No passion. No "reckless, raging fury," as Chesterton once described the Love of God. Could this be the fabric from which the universe has been woven, the Story which God is telling? Is this what True Love looks like? If it be so, then I daresay that a great many mortal men have dreamed fairer dreams and imagined happier worlds than the present one—the world that such a belief would imply that

God was able to come up with. Against such a belief I echo the sentiment of the Narnian Marshwiggle, Puddleglum:

> "One word, Ma'am" Puddleglum said, coming back from the fire; limping, because of the pain. "One word. All you've been saying is quite right, I shouldn't wonder. I'm a chap who always liked to know the worst and then put the best face I can on it. So I won't deny any of what you said. But there's one thing more to be said, even so. Suppose we have only dreamed, or made up, all those things—trees and grass and sun and moon and stars and Aslan himself. Suppose we have. Then all I can say is that, in that case, the made-up things seem a good deal more important than the real ones. Suppose this black pit of a kingdom of yours is the only world. Well it strikes me as a pretty poor one. And that's a funny thing, when you come to think of it. We're just babies making up a game, if you're right. But four babies playing a game can make a play-world which licks your real world hollow. That's why I'm going to stand by the play world. I'm on Aslan's side even if there isn't any Aslan to lead it.
>
> (C.S. Lewis, *The Silver Chair*)

I don't know about you, but I'm squarely on the side of God's Love—and on the side of that Love being more, not less, intimate, passionate, and wonderful than all the greatest human manifestations of love we have all tasted, given and received throughout the swiftly running days of our lives. Romantic love (Eros), brotherly love (Phileo), deep affection (Storge)—all the old distinctions and differentiations made between the human loves—all the most glorious and powerful components of these must find their root and their fulfillment in the Agape love that moved God to create the Universe—and then, in individual moments too intimate for words to convey, specifically and carefully create each and every one of us. The idea that the love of God is less wonderful, less passionate, less magnificent than these other human loves when at their brightest and best—that it is simply incomprehensible to me. Which is why I stand with Puddleglum. With Aslan. With the love of God being better than we've dared to hope...better than we've ever imagined.

THE MASTER PLAN

Now, returning to the passage from John that got us thinking about the truth and nature of love, here's why we get it all wrong when we jump forward in time and try to universalize Jesus' words to his disciples on the night of His betrayal. When we underplay the very personal nature of His command that they love each other, and His promise that this above all else would be the mark and the sign that He had been among them, and that the Spirit of the coming Kingdom of Joy yet rested upon them. Here's where we've been wrong even in our best attempts at glorifying the teaching style called 'discipleship', our best attempts to return to the style modeled for us in the earthly adventures of our Lord.

Are you ready for it?

Pay close attention now.

Here it is:

Jesus didn't individually disciple a dozen separate, unique, independent pupils, as the modern copies of His efforts tend to imply. He didn't gamble the fate of the gospel message on merely the merits of the master/disciple relationship alone. Despite what we teach in even the best Christian Ed. circles, getting back to genuine discipleship is only going to recreate half of Jesus' method, at best. There's something else our individualistic worldview has totally missed.

Jesus simply didn't leave the fate of the world in the hands of a dozen random, unassociated, individual disciples.

He left the fate of the world in the hands of a Fellowship.

That was the essential idea, the *in the moment* primary meaning of those now famous and much misunderstood words, "By this all men will know you are my disciples, if you love another" (John 13:35). Or, if you could permit me to paraphrase: *It's not enough for all of you to run off on your own, trying to love the world back to me. Your first task is to love one another, and the world will come running to you. The world will see the Fellowship of the King and know that the restoration of mankind has begun.*

Do you see it?

I'll confess that I missed it for years. In spite of my own quite instinctive reaction of pleasure and delight whenever I met such epic fellowships in fiction, myth or art, somehow I couldn't see this for what it was, right there staring back at me out of the heart of our own Christian story. Somehow I had missed the fact that the Son of God had placed deeply intimate human relationships at the center of His plans to reconcile and restore fallen Mankind to Himself, and to its intended glory.

Let me repeat that: *He placed deeply intimate human relationships at the center of His plan to reconcile and restore Mankind to Himself, and to its intended glory.*

Friends, I had to say that twice because even now I'm not sure that the full weight of this truth is settling into even my *own* heart, not sure if I'm letting it unite the habitually divergent streams of religious thought and epic longing into one cohesive picture of a Reality beyond my wildest hopes and dreams. Is it possible, we must ask, that a fantasy writer like J.R.R. Tolkien, when he enchants us into dreaming that we ourselves might live within a fellowship like the Nine Companions tasked with the saving of Middle Earth—is it possible that he actually *hasn't invented anything*, but only borrowed from God's Story, only opened our eyes to what has been being offered to us all along?

We have looked at the beginning of the story of humanity and seen that God fashioned His chosen people's written record of the

Creation to specifically highlight the fact that "it is not good for man to be alone." As G.K. Chesterton pointed out, in the doctrine of the Trinity we have, to some mysterious degree, come to also see that "it was not good *for God* to be alone." Then, in the way that Jesus Himself chose to walk in His mission through the recorded years of His ministry, we have seen that, even here—as true for Heaven's King as for Earth's lowliest shepherds and fishermen—it was not good for the Son of Man to be alone. (see John 6:67; Matthew 26:37-38) And now, here, at the pinnacle, at the turning of history's tide, we see that to be a disciple of Jesus tasked with the mission of spreading the glad tidings that Mankind's winter is passing at last—that for such a one of these 'disciples', it was just as delightfully true as ever that God never intended for them to hazard that adventure alone.

Dare I say it?

Dare I write the words that seem far too good to be true?

I must. It *has* to be said:

The Epic Fellowships of myth and legend rightly belongs to neither myth *nor* legend: they are God's true desire for His people and do in fact stand at the very center of His Kingdom work on this Earth.

There it is: the expansive goodness of God breaking through our old religious doubts yet again. Every good and perfect gift is to be ours, for it is His good pleasure to freely give us *all* things. Who dared to imagine that in His perfect creativity, our greatest happiness and the fulfilling of His Kingdom work would be indivisible one from another?

This is a Goodness beyond words.

And it just keeps getting better.

SEVEN

THE ANCHOR
OF YOUTH

Playing, playing with the boys
I'll be staying, playing with the boys
After chasing sunsets
One of life's simple joys
Is playin' with the boys
-Kenny Loggins, *Playing with the Boys*

This has been a wonderful day,' said Mole. as the Rat shoved off and took to the sculls again. 'Do you know, I've never been in a boat before in all my life.'

'What?' cried the Rat, open-mouthed. 'Never been in a—you never—well, I—what have you been doing then?'

'Is it so nice as all that?' asked the Mole shyly, though he was quite prepared to believe it as he leant back in his seat and surveyed the cushions, the oars, the rowlocks, and all the fascinating fittings, and felt the boat sway lightly under him.   'Nice? It's the *only* thing,' said the Water Rat solemnly as he leant forward for his stroke. 'Believe me, my young friend, there is nothing—absolutely nothing—half so much worth doing as simply messing about in boats. Simply messing,' he went on dreamily: 'messing —about—in—boats; messing -'

'Look ahead, Rat!' cried the Mole suddenly.

It was too late. The boat struck the bank full tilt. The dreamer, the joyous oarsman, lay on his back at the bottom of the boat, his heels in the air.

'—about in boats—or with boats,' the Rat went on composedly, picking himself up with a pleasant laugh. 'In or out of 'em, it doesn't matter. Nothing seems really to matter, that's the charm of it. Whether you get away, or whether you don't; whether you arrive at your destination or whether you reach somewhere else, or whether you never get anywhere at all, you're always busy, and you never do anything in particular; and when you've done it there's always something else to do, and you can do it if you like, but you'd much better not. Look here! If you've really nothing else on hand this morning, supposing we drop down the river together, and have a long day of it?'

The Mole waggled his toes from sheer happiness, spread his chest with a sigh of full contentment, and leaned back blissfully into the soft cushions. 'What a day I'm having!' he said. 'Let us start at once!'

(Kenneth Grahame, *The Wind in the Willows*)

I love this story. It's one of my all-time favorites, for so many reasons—more with each new reading. C.S. Lewis often said that he couldn't understand how a person could claim to love books and yet be satisfied with reading their favorite stories only once; as an adult he himself made an effort to read *The Wind in the Willows* again every year. Following in his footsteps, I have adopted a similar habit of re-reading Kenneth Grahame's enduring classic on almost a yearly basis. I'll pull it off the shelf in the early spring, when Mole's response in the opening chapter to Nature's imperious call as it reawakens around him strikes so very close to home for those of us who have endured a long Midwestern winter:

Spring was moving in the earth above and the ground below and around
him, penetrating even his dark and lowly little house with its spirit of
divine discontent and longing...The sunshine struck hot on his fur, soft
breezes caressed his heated brow, and after the seclusion of the cellarage
he had lived in so long the carol of happy birds fell on his dulled hearing
almost like a shout. Jumping off all his four legs at once, in the joy of
living and the delight of spring without its cleaning, he pursued his way
across the meadow...

In the past few years I have become more consciously aware of
why I am delighted, fascinated and drawn repeatedly to return out
of my adult world back into the one found in *The Wind in the
Willows*. Part of that attraction is its ability to usher you into a
world (perhaps only possible by almost entirely eliminating the
'human' element?) in which all the characters seem to be constrained by no responsibilities whatsoever beyond the pleasant
demands made by the laws of Friendship: no higher priority than
the happy enjoyment of one another's company. If you've read it
yourself lately, perhaps you noticed the same rare, carefree quality
about each of their episodes and adventures. It's so alluring...and,
sadly, so unlike the world that we know. Maybe you've noticed that
too? Honestly now: I've got to confess that I have hardly *any* real
life experiences to compare with the sensation one gets from
reading about Mole and Rat's lazy summer days (they seem to last
for years at a time) upon the River; their hastily planned yet
nevertheless opulent picnic lunches with Otter; their contented
hearthside chats with Badger, pipes in mouth, slipper-shod feet
resting on the fender; their sudden freedom to embark on a many
days journey with Toad in his canary yellow gypsy cart at the drop
of a hat—or more literally in their case, at the drop of a hint from
the most persistent, stubborn, and lovingly irascible lord of Toad
Hall.

The world that Grahame's charming characters inhabit seems to be a world where *vacation* is the norm. For us as readers it is a window into a place that is so far removed from our familiar 'task-oriented' world that we might suspect we are seeing what a purely 'relationship oriented' existence looks like for the very first time in our lives. Their whole life together is portrayed very much like what one might feel on a never-ending holiday spent with one's oldest and dearest friends. It reminds me of what I have only ever felt on a few tantalizingly brief occasions: the ten glorious days David and I spent travelling Britain by rail; the three unforgettable weeks he and I spent in Hong Kong in the summer of '89; the multiple seven day cruises lazing our way around the Caribbean in high pomp; the many mad dash weekend road trips to Maine, to Florida, to San Antonio, to the Rocky Mountains, etc. Beautiful, wonderful adventures all—but always just a fleeting escape from 'reality'.

Oh, so very fleeting.

But things are not so here along Grahame's Riverbank. The magical world inhabited by Ratty and Mole and Badger and Toad is a world where the kingly experience that is mutually-chosen intimates going about the 'serious business' of simply enjoying life together is allowed to blossom, expand, run wild and free—free of any of the heavy burdens of duty and necessity that take up the lion's share of our time and attention here in the 'real world'. There, no one has a job, much less a career. Money is available, but where it came from, or why they are at liberty to spend it without giving a thought to earning more, no one bothers to explain. Which again brings to mind the life we have experienced only in our long-lost childhood, or, if as an adult, only on our all-to-rare and always brief escapes from our work-a-day world—that world characterized, defined, and dominated by the heavy weight of all that is expected of us.

IS CAREFREE STILL AN OPTION?

And let's be honest: once we become responsible 'family men' we may not even experience this sort of thing when we *do* try to escape for a few days. Frankly there's a world of difference between going on vacation with your family and getting that supremely rare 'escape' weekend with the old gang. Or am I alone in feeling that way?

My own family gets exactly one vacation a year—something we can only afford to do because it's an all-expense-paid time away with my dad at his one-week-a-year spot near Daytona Beach, Florida. It's not extravagant by any means, but it's an incredible blessing for a sun lover like myself to get out of the long, cold winter and soak up some much needed Vitamin D. And Heaven forbid that I complain. It's a true Godsend, one that I start counting down to starting, oh...around about the day after Christmas.

But I find it a little ironic that so many people remark about what a great 'vacation' I must be having when I'm down there. Usually I reply that as the responsible figure in a family of six it really feels less like a vacation and more like 'trading being responsible at home for being responsible at the seashore.' When the welfare and happiness of everyone else is something you have to constantly be looking out for, it feels a lot more like being a full time Cruise Director than it does like being Rat and Mole lazing on the sun-drenched river, "simply messing about in boats".

As I'm writing this, we've actually just got home from this year's trip, and although the golden, backward-falling glow that our imagination so often sheds upon our memories is already growing stronger, it is not yet so strong that I have forgotten what an ordeal the vacation actually was. Yes, I said it: it was *an ordeal*. We were seven people crammed into a living space suited for four: no privacy, no time to oneself, no moment of the day that didn't require something of me. Our youngest son Cody is five now, and let me tell you: this little tiger is a handful. Constantly in trouble, constantly in need of affection. Right now he's a full-time job all in himself. Add our fifteen month-old daughter Gwendolyn to the mix, and this was by far the most challenging family vacation yet. Without the requisite space or time for reading, rest and conversation with God, I spent the entire trip losing ground in the deeper things of the soul. A *very* unhealthy way to live. By the end of the trip, I knew that I might look tanned and refreshed on the outside, but the true reality was anything but. I returned home in desperate need of a vacation...from my vacation.

I'm sure those of you with families of your own can relate to some of that feeling. And yes, I'll say again, it would be sulky and utterly thankless for any of us to whine about how things are at this season in life. These days are going to race past like a fleeting shadow on the mountainside; disappear like a morning mist on the Southern California coastline. Sure, a big part of me misses those old carefree days of the past. But I really do love that now I get to provide happy, carefree vacations for my family. Sometimes I even find myself driven with some manic, subconscious urge to make the trip as fairy-tale perfect as it can possibly be from their perspective, even if it means more work, more effort, more time switched "on" for me. Perhaps because I know how brief those years of innocent childhood are going to be for them. Perhaps because I figure if I'm not getting to have a true 'vacation', the sacrifice had better be for something—after all, what a waste it would be if no-one got to live a Willows-type existence. Perhaps, as the metaphorical stand-in for God—as the father figure in my small corner of His universe—I want to live up to His example and shower them with "every good and perfect gift", and I figure moments like this are at the top of that list. Perhaps I do it simply because I love them.

Whatever the case, I think my experience is a fairly universal one among men that have now entered the stage of fatherhood. Vacations are different here. *Life* is different here. This stage of life pretty much demands that we are always hyper alert, always responsible, living almost every moment 'switched on'. And you can only carry the responsibility for all those that depend on you for so long before you get permanently stuck in the 'on' mode, before you forget how to ever switch back 'off'. At some point you stop and ask yourself: *Do I even remember what it feels like to be carefree? Even in my 'off' moments, have I lost the capacity to rebound to such a lighthearted place? When I actually have permission to be 'off', do I remember how to switch 'off'?*

THE BEST MEDICINE

Carefree. It's a quality that I've been thinking about a lot lately. And the first thing I'm noticing is how foreign the very *idea* of it strikes me at this point. Like it's pretty pointless to give it much thought. "Crying for the moon", so to speak. But the more I think about it, the stronger my longing becomes to recapture some of that carefree quality again. And in odd contrast to those longings, the next thing I'm noticing is that no one in Christian circles is talking about finding some of that carefree life as if it was a thing 'mature' adults bothered much about. (Much like I noticed my own first reaction to be.) Sort of along the lines of sharing aloud in your church small group about your secret desire to learn to fly like Peter Pan to Neverland, or how you still dream of becoming a professional athlete or an Olympic medal winner in middle age. In other words, wasting your breath sharing about things that fall squarely into the category of 'just ain't gonna happen'.

But then I saw this question on the back cover of John Eldredge's most recent book, *Get Your Life Back*, and my heart leapt:

"When was the last time you felt carefree?"

And I thought, *Okay, good. I'm not crazy. I'm not the only one who's missing that lost part of himself, or the only one who's noticed that it's gone. It's probably a pretty common struggle, actually.*

A few years ago I was enjoying one of those brief escapes from living life constantly 'switched on', taking a rare weekend away to visit David at his place in Colorado. Since he moved there in 2001, his home on the skirts of the foothills of the Rocky Mountains has always been a haven of hospitality and refreshment, very much like the Rivendell of Tolkien's Middle Earth. But in recent years these rare holidays have required an ever-increasing period of 'detox' from all the heaviness, responsibility and worry that I mostly live under at this stage of life on a daily basis. Every year it seems that the transition to feeling lighthearted and carefree is more difficult to make, takes that much longer to get to that place. Sooner or later I do get there, but not without a struggle. (What's wrong with that picture? I'm so stuck in the 'switched on' position that I have to struggle to find my way through to a place where I can relax and have fun?)

Anyway, part way through this particular trip I finally began to unwind a bit. After a longer than usual struggle I was able to toggle the switch to 'off', stop feeling guilty about being away from the family, and just enjoy myself. Finally I started to catch a glimmer of that all-to-rare feeling of lightheartedness. I remember on the second night of the trip David and I ducked into a Walmart to get something—I don't remember what—and we were by then acting about as lighthearted as a couple of college freshmen. Everything we saw, everything we did, was somehow a source of a fresh wave of laughter. At one point we were both on the floor laughing until the tears flowed over some joke or another that had brought us to our knees. There we were, two grown men lying on the floor at Walmart gasping for breath, our laughter echoing through the cavernous expanse of the nearly empty superstore. I'm a little surprised someone from security didn't rush over to ask us to quiet down, stop making a scene, act more our age. If they had I reckon we would've sprayed them with a can of shaving cream or whatever was handy and made a run for the exits.

As we left the store I remember wondering aloud to David why we just never see people our age 'cutting up' in public? What's wrong with the human race? *Kids* act like that all the time. Why don't most adults? Because it's 'immature'? Well, if by 'maturity' we mean a stodgy, dour-faced surrender to the heaviness of adult life then I don't think I have much interest in being 'mature'. I'm pretty sure that part of the reason we don't see old friends enjoying themselves like this in public is that whole loss of carefree lightheartedness thing—that sad loss of even the capacity to go there when the situation allows. But another part of the reason we don't see old friends 'cutting up' in public, I'm beginning to realize, is even more obvious. We don't see it because *most adults rarely make time for friends*—for those old, intimate friends anyway, the ones who alone possess the power to return us to a time and place when 'our hearts were young and gay', when carefree lightheartedness was still within our reach, still a mode of living we had the capacity to experience with ease.

A PLACE FREE OF DUTY

In a circle of true Friends each man is simply what he is: stands for nothing but himself...That is the kingliness of Friendship. We meet like sovereign princes of independent states, abroad, on neutral ground, freed from our contexts. This love (essentially) ignores not only our physical bodies but that whole embodiment which consists of our family, job, past and connections. At home, besides being Peter or Jane, we also bear a general character; husband or wife, brother or sister, chief, colleague or subordinate. Not among our Friends...Hence (if you

will not misunderstand me) the exquisite arbitrariness and
irresponsibility of this love. I have no duty to be anyone's Friend and
no man in the world has a duty to be mine. No claims, no shadow of
necessity.   (Lewis, *The Four Loves*)

As a man grows through the stages of his life, entering into ever-increasing levels of responsibility that come with being an employee or business owner, perhaps a ministry leader, a husband, a father, a devoted son to aging parents—now more than ever he is going to be in desperate need of some respite from all the burden of these responsibilities. We rush from one 'duty' to the next at a dizzying pace all day long, and even still we often fall into bed haunted by the spectre of all the things we should've done and simply couldn't fit into the travelling circus that was our day. This insanely paced life is precisely why a man is going to need to be "freed from all context", free to enjoy the "exquisite irrespon-sibility" of being amongst his friends as a "sovereign prince" among freely chosen peers. Perhaps one who has never felt their life sinking beneath a flood of ever-increasing duties and requirements will not fully understand just how 'exquisite' a little irrespon-sibility would be at this point. It's also possible that one who lacks deep and intimate friendships of the type Lewis is talking about won't really understand the power they possess to free us—if only for an evening—from the tyranny of our seemingly endless list of responsibilities.

But they can.

They really can.

Now, this is not to say that as fathers and husbands it would be a good and healthy thing for us to discover that we are 'growing desperate' to escape our family. The whole thrust of much of the ministry directed towards men in recent times has been laboring to convince them not to bail—physically or emotionally—on their

families, and I'm not about to contradict that, even if it seems to
me to be an approach that focuses on fixing a symptom rather than
dealing with the root causes. But that's not the kind of 'escape' I'm
talking about. Notice the difference here, because it's far more than
just semantics, and may help some of you who are feeling a little
guilty about this desire for 'escape', worrying that, given the
circumstances and the commitments you have made, this longing
must at its core be an unholy one. So let me be clear that it is the
role that is demanded of us—and the fact that the role itself is the
most demanding one imaginable—that we need some respite from,
some healthy form of escape. Not the people. We *love* the people
—or would remember that we have forgotten how much we love
them—if only the weight of our cares wasn't resting so heavily on
our burdened shoulders that our eyes no longer rise to look into
those of the ones for whom we sweat and toil.

I DON'T WANT TO MISS THIS

This morning my son Nathaniel, who just turned ten, shuffled
half-awake out of the bedroom, and snuggled up to where I was
sitting on the couch enjoying some all-too-brief alone time talking
with God ahead of the new day's responsibilities. In a minute he
had fallen asleep again, and as I looked down on his peaceful face I
was pierced with sudden remorse. An inner voice whispered:
*When is the last time you simply stopped to look, to really look? To
study the lines and shape of this sweet boy's face? You've been running
yourself ragged to care for his every need, but if you keep this pace up,
isn't it going to be obvious to him—to them all—that their overall
impact on you is mostly just...weariness? Like the most true thing
about themselves is that they are a burden? And wasn't your deepest
desire when you became a father the exact opposite: to make your boys
daily aware that you delighted in them, that they were the Beloved*

Son you wished you had been to your father at that age?

I felt totally caught. Busted. I knew that I was hearing something about my heart's recent posture that was both painful and true. Recently my attitude towards my family has taken on an edge. "Service with a Smile", the old ad used to boast: I was now to the weary and distracted point of offering "*Service with a Sigh*".

Now don't get me wrong: nothing on this planet matters to me more than my sons. Nothing on God's green earth. And yet...and yet sometimes I know that *I am missing this*. Some of the most blessed years of my life, and yet at some deep experiential level, I'm missing them. So distracted, so overwhelmed. So caught up in the neverending list of responsibilities that come with this life that I'm not even experiencing the joy *in this very moment* that all those responsibilities exist to protect and nurture. All the work, none of the joy. Oh, it's there to be had. But because of the perpetual worry and planning and doing, I know I'm missing way too much of it.

A family I am close to went through a recent divorce, and one statement from the teenage children that surfaced during the painful separation was, "Dad was always so busy with work and stuff that needed to be done that even when he was here, he wasn't here. He'd be right there next to you, but he wasn't fully there." Ouch. It's a painful indictment, one we all hope never to hear spoken of us. Personally, I used to think that could never be me. Never. I mean, if I don't know how to do relationships well...then what *am* I good at? And yet, when I'm honest with myself I know that I'm not as fully present with people as I used to be. Having the same requisite 'free brain space' that I used to have—the space required to really be present to someone else's story—is not a given at this stage of life. With each passing year the burdens just continue to grow, the to-do list continues to get longer, my thoughts race swifter than flight from one demand to the next, and the reservoir of strength and joy feels like it just isn't large enough to meet the increasing demands (my own demands, let alone other people's). Before I know it I find myself staring blankly at one of my sons wondering what vitally important—at least to his child's world—thing he has been telling me for the past two minutes without me having heard a single word of it.

When the mythological Atlas places the whole world on his shoulders, by the very nature of logic we understand that he can no longer see the thing he carries: the task itself requires that he turn his back towards the very thing he loves.

We cannot afford to do the same.

TAKE IT ON THE RUN

Look, you say, *we already know that adult responsibility in today's world can be overwhelming. We don't think we really need any more reminders of that, don't need anyone pouring fuel on the fire of our secret sense that, like Frodo struggling over the last leg of his journey to destroy the One Ring, we too are just a day's march away from being borne down beneath the burdens we carry. No: best not to talk of it, stir up any more of the slumbering existential angst than absolutely necessary. After all, isn't it from this same desperate desire to escape these burdens that so many men choose to walk away—opt to up stakes and bail on their problems entirely?*

Sometimes, yes.

The youth pastor at my home church did that very thing just a few years after I had graduated from youth group and headed off to college: abandoned his family, his job, his calling to ministry, everything. Gave the whole kit and caboodle the middle finger and ran off to Vegas, where he ended up dealing cards at a blackjack table. Now, my natural inclination is to not be too quick to judge people. After experiencing a little bit of life's woes myself, I tend to give people the benefit of the doubt. Life can be brutal. I like to think this guy was essentially a good man who just got so overwhelmed with the adult demands placed upon him that he finally broke beneath the strain and ran for the hills. But regardless of my empathy for what might have drove him to it, and despite the grace that flows so easily from me when I consider my own glaring imperfections, the fact is that this man's actions really hurt a lot of people, let down countless more, and permanently impacted the spiritual journeys of a whole generation of students in our one small corner of the world.

Granted, most men don't run, don't do anything nearly so dramatic. It's possible that very honorable reasons keep them from bolting—although I think many of them stay put just because they have lost the strength and courage to do anything extreme in an attempt to break out of the life they've fallen into. (Even if the radical course of action would turn out to morally be the wrong choice, I know that for many men today that's not really what's driving their decisions. On the surface maybe, but not deep down.) These men no longer live with the passion or intensity to choose a radical path, be it for good or for evil. Instead they lose themselves in addictions to alcohol, pornography, food, sports, entertainment—anything that takes the edge off, lets them check out and forget their troubles for a time. Many of these addictions are especially insidious, because they don't overthrow our ability to carry on an outer demeanor that suggests all is well with our soul—even when nothing could be further from the truth.

And let's not forget that there is a third group of men—equally struggling with where the current of their life has swept them off to, but who fight both the urge to run and the temptation to hide behind addictions. What of these so-called 'faithful' men? These dutiful, servant-hearted men who slog on under the weight of their responsibilities in Atlas-like determination? Those men who persevere, but at the cost of growing ever more defeated, ever less like the men they might have been at their best, stripped of the joie de vivre that once marked their hopeful rise to manhood? These are the Resigned Men: the men who have made an uneasy peace with the fact that Life is hard and Life is serious, and there's really no reason to hope for anything different at this point because this resignation is actually a very appropriate response to the situation they find themselves in at this season of life. They are summed up by the statement once made to me by a close friend stuck in an empty, loveless marriage: "There's nothing to look forward to but Heaven now."

Resigned Men. Hopeless men. Truly these are the walking dead. Sure, in terms of external behavior, they are the "promise keepers" that some branches of Christian thinking consider to be the pinnacle of masculine discipleship. But are these the kind of men that you look up to? The kind of men that fill you with hope and courage and belief in the goodness of God? Is this the life you always dreamed of for yourself?

The Running Men. The Addicted Men. The Resigned Men. All too often these are the end results of the burden of "adulthood" that we have placed upon ourselves. Not a very pretty picture, is it? What other options are there, we find ourselves wondering? Isn't there some help to ease the often heavy burdens of this season in life that doesn't culminate in running away like a coward, seeking refuge in dangerous addictions, or resigning oneself to a slow death of the heart?

THERE IS HELP

Yes, thank God, there is help. And no, I don't want to understate the importance of how God *Himself* can directly impact the equation through our intimate, personal relationship with Him. *Of course* it is primarily in Him that we can find the necessary resources we need to renew our strength:

He gives strength to the weary and increases the power of the weak..those who hope in the Lord that waits upon the Lord will renew their strength. They will soar on wings like eagles. They will run and not grow weary, they will walk and not faint.

(Isaiah 40:29,31)

find a reservoir of joy:

Do not grieve, for the joy of the Lord is your strength. (Nehemiah 8:10)
Ask and you will receive, and your joy will be complete. (John 16:24)

lay down our heavy burdens:

Come to me, all who labor and are heavy laden, and I will give you rest. Take my yoke upon you..For my yoke is easy, and my burden is light.

(Matthew 11:28-30)

and experience fullness of life:

I have come that you might have life, and have it to the full.

(John 10:10)

There's plenty of reason to take heart, much that God has had to say over the years about the toils and heartaches of this world, much that He has promised. Certainly we'd all be doing a lot better if we were consistently taking all this to Him, trusting those promises, seeking our life and our joy from the very fountainhead from whence it all flows. Our relationship with our heavenly Father is intended to be the deep root of our lives, our strongest weapon in the battle against loneliness and loss of heart. Without a very real, very present intimacy with God Himself, our lives become cut off from the very source of...well...Life.

I remember watching the wildly popular Tom Hanks film *Cast-away* (I saw it on t.v. many years after everyone else had already seen it) and I remember thinking, *"Oh, so this is what it would look like for a person who has no relationship with God to be stranded on a deserted island."* It was fascinating, and more than a little saddening, really. I'm glad I was at a place in my walk with God at the time to actually feel confused, and more than a little pitying, at the manner in which Hank's character responded to his time away from human inter-action. Do you remember how desperate he became for another person to bounce his thoughts off of? No doubt the key enduring image that the movie added to our general fund of pop-culture references was "Wilson", the volleyball that out of overwhelming loneliness Hanks' character turns to for companionship. Separated from the ground of his being, without a clue of the potential companionship that was only a whispered prayer away, he tried to fill the emptiness with dead things, things that never could possibly meet his inherent need for connection, for relationship—for intimacy.

It was actually a powerfully moving message, when viewed from a Christian perspective. When we do not walk in daily, satisfying relational intimacy with our Abba Father, we ourselves can become little better than castaways, seeking counsel and companionship from things as foolishly inadequate to our need as a lifeless piece of mutilated sporting equipment.

THE DELEGATING GOD

But then, we aren't here in these pages talking so much about what God can do for us *directly*, but about some of the *mediums* through which He has deliberately chosen to share His life and His love with us. Yes, it is from His hand that we will receive relief from our burdens, renewed strength to man-up to our responsibilities, and even deep draughts from those reservoirs of joy that do not so easily run dry. But we need to understand something. We need to understand that so much of what God has to give us, is *able* to give us, or has *chosen* to give us, on this plane of existence is going to come to us indirectly *through the material world that He specifically created as the setting and backdrop for our journey.*

We must not forget the core beliefs I have taken such care to affirm up to this point: Creation is *good*, and our life on this planet is *not* an exile. Broken and deformed though it is, there yet remains much material good through which God is capable, and eager, to meet with us. "I see his face in every flower" goes the old poem, and if He is meeting us in such simple organisms as the flowers of the field, surely the vessels that He is most able to fill, the vehicles He is most able to use, are those complex creatures made in His own likeness.

Which is why I believe that one of the *key* pathways through which He can bring us into these very places of freedom and relief that we are desperately seeking is through others. Specifically through the company of dear friends, through the "exquisite irresponsibility" of "sovereign princes" gathering together for the sheer pleasure of one another's company, entirely freed from all "shadow of necessity".

You might say that we've now come to the central point, the whole thesis of this book. And it is this: that God, who "seems to do nothing of Himself that he could possibly delegate to one of His creatures" (C.S. Lewis) has ordained that much of what He wants to give us must come through other people. Most specifically to our point: *through the healing beauty of dear friendships.* Refusing to receive the good that God is giving because it is an indirect good, because it is a 'natural' good, because it most often is experienced outside the walls of normal religious programming—refusing it for these reasons is not a higher form of holiness. It is simply a misunderstanding of our situation, a refusal to accept that the Author has constructed His scenes well, that He is bringing His Word and

His Life to us through both the props and the fellow actors He has chosen to share the stage with us in our appointed hour.

Let me say that again: *much of the good that God desires to bring into our lives is going to come to us through the material world, and especially through other people.*

Now, I know this willingness to accept that much of God's goodness will come to us through indirect channels can be really difficult for a person raised in an individualistic society. Mostly we aren't even aware how deeply this runs in all of us. I know I wasn't aware of it in myself. But I remember how strongly I reacted when someone first suggested to me that perhaps the answers I was seeking in prayer might actually come to me through the ministry of other people speaking into my life, instead of directly from that 'still, small voice' I was waiting for. *"It's called a personal relationship with God, because it's personal!"* I ranted. *"Anything He's got to say, He can say directly to me, understand? We don't need you!"* I really had no clue how much my American spirit of individualism was informing my understanding of spiritual laws, no idea how much I was missing by insisting that God meet me directly, or not at all. How many sunsets had He sent me to close another wearisome day with a healing burst of delightfully inefficient, extravagant beauty? How many warm breezes did He send to caress my face with soothing whispers of comfort and love and Home? How many powerful words of encouragement and affirmation did dear friends speak to me acting as the mouthpiece of the Almighty, only I couldn't receive them as such, because it was only His voice that I thought had permission to speak into that old ache in a genuinely transformative way?

Of course, the history of the Church has always stood against our own national rugged individualism. The Church has always—or almost always—known that spiritual gifts had been divided and meted out by the hand of the Father in a fashion that swept the 'lone wolf' option off the table, that required His children learn to either cooperate, or miss something of the full joy intended in our adoption. "The eye cannot say to the hand, 'I don't need you!' And the head cannot say to the feet, 'I don't need you!'" (I Cor. 12:21). So says the Word of God. Alas, we beg to differ.

Delegation. That's just a big part of how things work. And it comprises much of how God has chosen to operate in the world around us, and in our personal lives. "Creation," Lewis reminds us, "is delegation through and through." That is why we are going to discover that so much of what God has for us—so much of the good that He's longing to shower on our lives—can be hindered, or even lost, when we cut ourselves off from any of the various mediums through which He wishes to work. When we disregard and deny one of those mediums (as vehicles through which God's grace enters our lives, do we go too far to call them sacraments?) such as Friendship, the place that it was intended to fill in our life must remain empty. The lost joys, adventures and experiences of intimate friendship can not be replicated in some other fashion. There is no like-for-like replacement for those particular delights, those unique conduits of Divine love. If we do not seek them there, we must go without them, and our lives be so much the poorer for it.

> "Are you not thirsty?" said the Lion.
>
> "I'm dying of thirst," said Jill.
>
> "Then drink," said the Lion
>
> ...The delicious rippling noise of the stream was driving her nearly frantic...
>
> "I daren't come and drink," said Jill
>
> "Then you will die of thirst," said the Lion.
>
> "Oh dear," said Jill, coming another step nearer. "I suppose I must go and look for another stream then."
>
> "There *is* no other stream," said the Lion.
>
> (C.S. Lewis, *The Silver Chair*)

For most modern American men, and for a great many modern American women, one of the key streams through which God meant to pour a steady flow of His love and goodness into our lives has been allowed to be dammed. Blocked. Cut off. If we continue to take our cues from the prevailing culture it is almost guaranteed that one seat at the banquet of Life's full delights will remain, for us, everlastingly empty. Jesus may have come that we might have abundant life (John 10:10), but we'll miss so much of this abundance He is offering if we refuse to see Him at work in the natural world. And the crazy thing about it is that we're doing it to ourselves, this limiting of His abundant goodness, this not valuing the gift He was giving for the exquisite prize that it is.

Dare I even ask you how highly you've been valuing the gift of Friendship in your life? Have you been treating it like the conduit of God's practical, tangible, here-and-now love for you that it is?

"Life—natural life," said Lewis speaking of True Friendship, "has no greater gift to give."

No greater gift.

How have we lost sight of this?

OUR DAILY NEED

Twice this very morning I had occasion to feel the weight of this truth again, to be reminded of just how blessed I am in this regard. They are just two examples from thousands—but the two that happened this very morning, in the midst of writing this chapter.

The first occasion was just a silly thing, really: a memory of something that happened back in junior high—something about a Sunday school class and a fermented bottle of apple cider. It made me smile, but it also made me want to share the memory with someone who had been there. In fact, the only thing that separated the memory from merely a bittersweet reminder of days long gone, the only thing that transformed it into a living source of re-enjoyable good humor, was the ability to speak of it with an old friend who possessed the same fond memory. Sharing the memory helped link me to my past again—made it feel like a solid, tangible thing that had actually happened once upon a time to me—just at a time when I was feeling a dangerous and unhealthy disconnect from the larger thread of the story of my life.

The second time this morning I found myself wanting the companionship of my oldest and closest friend makes for a less amusing anecdote, unfortunately. As background, let me just say that life has been pretty relentless lately in its demands. I'm guessing you might know a little bit about seasons of life like that too. Now, mostly I'm a pretty resilient guy. 'Long-suffering' is probably near the top of my all-too-short list of better qualities. But when you live under a constant state of tension and agitation it really doesn't take much to reach that point where you are completely fried. You know, that place where a good night's rest and even a healthy amount of time alone with God in the morning somehow isn't enough to reset the *fried-o-meter* and bring the needle back down to a healthy level. Now, on the whole I think I've actually been doing fairly well (for me, anyway) under the strain, 'rising above' as they say, by grounding my day—multiple times a day—in the love and goodness of God. But in spite of my best efforts to practice a healthy amount of 'benevolent detachment', sometimes I find that my patience, calm, and good humor are hanging on by an invisible thread. One that feels like it's about as thick as a spider's web, with the tensile strength of a strand of cotton candy. Days like these become a disheartening dance of 'one step forward and two steps back'. Like the straw that breaks the camel's back, it just takes one small thing to go wrong, and I'm ready to buckle.

That's what happened again this morning—I don't even remember what set it off (maybe I stepped on a sharp toy, made the mistake of checking the balance of my bank account, spilled a drink or burnt someone's toast)—but suddenly my day was swirling around the rim of the toilet bowl on the verge of going south with a flush. I was sinking fast, and knew I was in need of rescue. I wanted out of the noise, out of the mess, out of the house. I wanted to escape somewhere with God and get my perspective back, have a real tangible encounter with His goodness, and maybe, hopefully, His joy. But I also realized that the antidote in that moment to how I was struggling needed to be something that would draw my heart in the complete opposite direction to where it was headed—some experience that possessed the power to shepherd my soul towards lightheartedness again. Yes, I knew I needed some silence, some solitude, some time reconnecting with God. But while always the place we should look *first,* I think you can agree with me that sometimes our attempts to commune with God can usher us into an experience of childlike lightheartedness, and sometimes...well, sometimes, they just don't. Understand, that's *our* issue, not His. It's our inability to let go completely of our worries, our cares, our backlog of mounting frustration—perhaps even harbored bitterness at the turn our circumstances have taken—that is holding us back. God isn't the one who's withholding peace, joy, and childlike freedom from life's heavier burdens. We know what Jesus wants for us—his words could not have been clearer: "Do not let your hearts be troubled." (John 14:27) "Do not worry about tomorrow." (Matthew 6:34)

But as I said, for whatever reason, going into your prayer closet for a conversation with God doesn't always bring about tangible, immediate results—at least at the emotional level anyway. And in the moment I've been describing, I could think of at least one *tangible* medium through which God could shift my heart away from feeling burdened and towards feeling carefree. I knew what I desperately wanted: to taste that "exquisite irresponsibility" that can only be found in the presence of an old friend. I needed a counterweight to balance the scales a bit, something as opposite to my fried and frustrated 'responsible adult' self as could be found. In that moment I found myself dreaming of a weekend escape in the mountains with David. That would have been worth its weight in gold; obviously it was also a little out of reach. So a bit later, when an opportunity afforded itself, I picked up the phone instead. A twenty minute phone call and a few good laughs (I'm sure I hadn't had *any* good laughs in many days) turned out to be more than treasure enough. "Words aptly spoken are like apples of gold in settings of silver," as the Scriptures remind us (Proverbs 25:11).

Sure, when I returned back to my present situation everything hadn't magically turned rosy. All the crud was still there, threatening to pull me back under its dark influence. But my heart was just a bit lighter, enough to put me in a much better place to handle the day, to take it all in stride, to rise above.

Can I say it again?

"Life—natural life—has no greater gift to give."

ANCHORED TO A LIGHT HEART

Please hear this, friends: As adults, weighed down by the worries and cares of modern life in a sometimes dark and always deeply broken world, we desperately need our oldest and dearest friends. We need them like flowers need the sun, like grass needs the rain. We need them as often and as consistently as the time can be spared. Strike that: time *must* be made, as we usually do tend to make time for the things that matter most to us. And intimate friendship belongs near the very top of that list of things that ought to matter most to us. Nothing else in our lives, no tool, no weapon at our disposal has the power that those friendships do to turn back the clock, to beat back the ravages of Time, so that we might better be able to receive the Kingdom "like a little child." (Mark 10:15).

Old friends, in fact, are like a lifeline, a strong anchor that can bind us and return us—if ever so briefly—to the happy, carefree days of our youth. And, oh how we need to return there—as frequently as we can. For there were a great many things about life and faith and our hope in the goodness of God and in His good intentions for us personally that we have lost through the passing of many difficult years. Precious gems we have surrendered to the sands of time. Treasures of the past that desperately need to be excavated from the debris once again. It may feel like those memories, along with the people with whom we made them, were merely the gifts of a moment: a moment now long past, a moment forever lost and beyond recall.

But it need not be so.

Neither past joys nor old friends were meant to be wholly lost, or cease to be powerful mediums through which God's lavish love could flow into our lives.

You'll recall the story I related earlier in the chapter about David and I, two grown men on the floor of a suburban Denver Walmart late at night, gasping for breath, we were laughing so hard? I'm hoping you know from personal experience that feeling you get when you've laughed so hard your stomach muscles ache like you've just been through a really tough workout. But the thing I failed to mention about that scene is that it is actually *miles* away from my "normal". The truth is my abs *rarely* experience that ache that comes from prolonged hysterical laughter. I don't laugh like that very often; I don't create scenes like that everywhere I go. I might, if everywhere I went my best friend went with me. When we're together, the laughter comes easy—easy, and often. (So often that it can be dangerous to put us in a setting where too much seriousness is required.) There's so much history behind us and between us that we are always finding an inside joke, some allusion to another funny memory, a wordplay or a double meaning in just about every conversation. It's all great fun, and honestly I'd love to live a whole lot more of my life in such a lighthearted state.

But, as fun and as refreshing and desirable as all that is, I simply can't work myself up into that state of adolescent hilarity with just anyone. *Just anyone?* Talk about an understatement. There is *no one* among the remaining seven billion people on the planet with whom I enjoy that sort of relationship, even though this is the kind of lighthearted person that I long to be. But that kind of freedom to let down my guard and let loose doesn't come easy for me—or for a lot of people I suspect. It takes a certain depth of history with a friend, a history that hails back to younger, more carefree days to usher me into one of those truly heart-lifting "golden sessions".

Deep, well-aged, anchor-to-our-youth friendships really are such rare and deeply personal gifts. *Intentional* gifts from a loving, relational God; gifts no one should have to navigate adult life without. And yet, most people in our culture today—both inside and outside the Church—do, in fact, continue to make life choices that result in living without these cherished gifts. What madness is this? No one would argue that these years of adult responsibility wear much more heavily upon our harried souls than did our days of carefree youth: can anyone explain why we've turned away from the one lifeline that keeps our hearts anchored to what we knew better then, that friendship is responsible for more than half of all the happiness this world has to offer?

Did you know that, by the way, that there was something *intentional* about the people you have crossed paths with, that you have been blessed to call your friends throughout the different chapters of your life's story? It's true, and it's worth remembering. We may not have paid it any attention at the time, but it's worth going back in our memories and receiving now as the deliberate gifts they always were. I have such deep fondness for many of my college friends, as you've no doubt gathered by this point, and I can't tell you what deep joy and increased faith in God's love for me I experienced when, in later years, I came to see that those good times, those good people—they were *intended* to be mine. I was *meant* to have them. The happiness I felt in those days was not merely the random product of a random universe, but an intentional gift, the tangible wooing of a loving God displaying the height, width, and depth of His extravagant goodness. Perhaps if you look back on your own story, allowing God to open the eyes of your heart, you will see that He has done the same for you. Though, you like me may have been unaware at the time how precious and rare those seasons steeped in happy fellowship would turn out to be...how easily lost in the pursuit of our American Dream.

But what to do now? Those days are gone, and we've all been living more or less like a Lone Wolf ever since, having cynically left the sweet, healing company of our old friends somewhere deep in the pages of our past.

Can I just offer that perhaps it might not be too late to make a shift in our priorities? Why not take a chance and dust off those old friendships again? Make that phone call, throw out the invitation. God brought those people into your life for a reason, remember. Can you honestly say for sure that you have exhausted that gift completely, that you've drained every last drop of joy from that cup—that cup that God measured out for your deep pleasure? Is a lifetime even long enough to drink such a cup to the dregs?

Can I make another suggestion?

Do it *now*.

Track those old friends down today, before something else comes up, before the weight of your responsibilities drives it out of your mind. By God's mercy, perhaps you'll discover that it's not too late to reopen this precious conduit of God's goodness into your life once again.

It was for just such a hope that this book has been written...

EIGHT

IN SEARCH OF
AUTHENTICITY

Love must be sincere.
Hate what is evil. Cling to what is good.
Be devoted to one another in brotherly love.
(Romans 12:9)

God can testify how I long for all of you
with the affection of Christ Jesus.
(Philippians 1:8)

"'But I must go,' said Frodo. 'It cannot be helped, dear friends. It is wretched for us all, but it is no use your trying to keep me. Since you have guessed so much, please help me and do not try to hinder me.'

'You do not understand!' said Pippin. 'You must go—and therefore we must, too. Merry and I are coming with you. Sam is an excellent fellow, and would jump down a dragon's throat to save you, if he did not trip over his own feet; but you will need more than one companion in your dangerous adventure.'

'My dear and most beloved hobbits!' said Frodo, deeply moved. 'But I could not allow it. I decided that long ago, too. You speak of danger but you do not understand. This is no treasure-hunt, no there-and-back journey. I am flying from deadly peril into deadly peril.'

'Of course we understand,' said Merry firmly. 'That is why we have decided to come...'

...'But it does not seem that I can trust anyone,' said Frodo.

Sam looked at him unhappily. 'It all depends on what you want,' put in Merry. 'You can trust us to stick to you through thick and thin—to the bitter end. And you can trust us to keep any secret of yours—closer than you keep it yourself. But you cannot trust us to let you face trouble alone, and go off without a word. We are your friends, Frodo. Anyway, there it is. We know most of what Gandalf has told you. We know a good deal about the Ring. We are horribly afraid—but we are coming with you; or following you like hounds.'

'And after all sir, ' added Sam, 'you did ought to take the Elves' advice. Gildor said you should take them as was willing, and you can't deny it.

'I don't deny it,' said Frodo, looking at Sam, who was now grinning. 'I don't deny it, but I'll never believe you are sleeping again, whether you snore or not. I shall kick you hard to make sure. You are a set of deceitful scoundrels!' he said, turning to the others. 'But bless you!' he laughed, getting up and waving his arms. 'I give in. I will take Gildor's advice. If the danger were not so dark, I should dance for joy. Even so, I cannot help feeling happy, happier than I have felt for a long time...'

(J.R.R. Tolkien, *The Fellowship of the Ring*)

If you've ever read the original book version of *The Lord of the Rings* Trilogy, you'll remember the internal struggle little Frodo Baggins faced when the wizard Gandalf revealed to him the true nature of the magic Ring he had inherited from his Uncle Bilbo. Never in his wildest imagination did he suspect that he was now in possession of the fabled One Ring, the Ring of Power, forged by the Dark Lord Sauron in the fires of Mount Doom thousands of years prior. Never in his darkest nightmares had he imagined that he would become the subject of that selfsame Dark Lord's full, malicious attention. But now the poor, frightened hobbit knew that he could not remain in the Shire and place those that he loved in imminent danger; and still, he quailed at the thought of having to bear this secret burden and hazard this dangerous journey alone.

Luckily for Frodo, his friends were not as easily deceived as he believed, and had gathered enough information on their own to guess that Frodo was about to undertake just such a perilous journey fraught with dangers almost too terrible to imagine. Even more luckily for Frodo, he was blessed with the sort of friends who never considered letting him face those dangers alone. "We are your friends," explains Merry Brandybuck—as if nothing more needed to be said on the matter; as if, to these simplehearted hobbits, being someone's friend meant that being willing to "jump down a dragon's throat to save him" was simply an assumed part of the deal. *All for one and one for all* was the prerequisite attitude behind all true friendship, and deadly peril was a small price to pay for the pleasure of possessing such an unmerited gift at all.

Oh, if only it were so on Earth as it is in Middle Earth.

A CONFLICT OF DESIRES

Sadly, you and I were born into a time and culture where epic friendship is an ancient relic, one mostly found in the old stories of simpler times. In our Age it is defiant Individualism that rules supreme over the ways of Men. Although we may not say the words out loud, "*Every man for himself!*" is more the cry that sums up the prevailing mood of our time than that old cheer of the musketeer, "*One for All, and All for One!*"

Naturally, if this is in fact the situation we find ourselves in—if it is truly 'every man for himself'—then it is no wonder that we must scrape and scrap and study and train to become the most self-sufficient people possible in order to survive. If we have nothing to rely on but our own wits and skill and strength, we must carve out, and continuously maintain deep inner reservoirs of each of these qualities—these and many more. In a word, we have little choice but to train ourselves to survive the world by embracing the life of a Lone Wolf.

And granted, there *is* a strong romantic pull towards the seemingly ultra-masculine life of the Lone Wolf character—the cowboy, the secret agent, the unflappable, stoic 'army of one', the all-conquering hero. I admit it; I feel the pull towards all that macho stuff too, at times. Who wouldn't want to be a character like the 80's television hero MacGuyver? Who wouldn't want to be the guy who can solve any problem, build any contraption, escape the deadliest danger, with nothing but a paperclip, a stick of chewing gum, and a roll of duct tape? That sort of self-sufficiency is so attractive to us who were born and bred to worship without reservation at the twin altars of our nation's gods, Independence and Autonomy.

Yeah, there's a strong pull towards all that. But then, here's the thing—the thing that brings us right back to something I observed in the very first chapter, back when I was watching my older brother walk away from that old Victorian home where he and seven of his buddies had spent 'the best days of their lives'. As I said then, right there down in the same place that longs to be the self-sufficient MacGuyver type, I find in myself an even more powerful longing, a longing that can also be encapsulated best by another classic 80's television show: *The A-Team*. Remember that gem? Growing up, it had to be one of my top ten all-time top favorite shows. Plenty of excitement, lots of explosions, a constant stream of near-death escapes—and always someone in dire need of being rescued from a terrible situation they had no way of extricating themselves from without the help of the A-Team.

Personally, I was always far more into *The A-Team* than I ever was into *MacGuyver*. Here you had on display all the heroism, all the wits, skill, and strength you could ever hope to possess—only this time it came not in the context of one solitary individual standing alone against an unfriendly world, but rather in the context of an interdependent fellowship of friends and heroes fighting those same evils together: side-by-side and back-to-back. And what a fellowship it was! Templeton Peck, a.k.a.'Faceman', the irascible con-artist and ladies man. 'Howling Mad' Murdock, the reckless but fearless pilot who lived his whole life two sandwiches short of a picnic, like the escapee from the insane asylum that he in fact was. B.A. ('Bad Attitude') Baracus, the growling mountain of muscle no one dared to mess with. And Colonel John 'Hannibal' Smith, the unflappable cigar-smoking genius and mastermind who "loved it when a plan came together." Each with his own array of specific talents; each a unique and irreplaceable member of the team.

I suppose some Hollywood writers could have made separate television series about each of these heroic and entertaining characters—but those separate story lines wouldn't really have been nearly as good as *The A-Team*. The interplay of personalities, the shared adventure, the appeal to our desire to live in redemptive, purposeful community—this was the central beauty of the whole thing. If it was good to be a hero, how much better it must be to be but one hero among a fellowship of heroes! In The A-team my teenage heart was surprised to see a rare depiction of the fact that there was a way to be heroic without taking the path of the Lone Wolf after all: a way to enjoy being strong and yet also enjoy experiencing a need for others at the same time.

Looking back on those childhood longings, I suppose I've always been enamoured to some degree by the idea of 'the group', 'the team', 'the fellowship': the rare beauty of viewing life not merely as an adventure to be lived, but as an adventure to be shared. Yes, I think I've always believed in the power of 'groups'. I think I've always known that there was something central to experiencing fullness of life inherent within the idea of a True Fellowship.

And I've also always known that the westernized Church of our day did not know how to do such things well.

Oh, we think we do.

But we don't.

Not even close.

SMALL GROUPS, BIG PROBLEMS

This isn't the time or place to offer a full critique of the Church's use of formally organized groups in pursuit of accomplishing its mission. And yet, I don't see how we can avoid saying *something*, considering the nature of our topic on the forgotten significance of true Friendship. Now as a preemptive disclaimer, I'm the first to admit that of course it is easier to criticize than to exhort—to actually offer solutions and not merely point to the problems. But, here as elsewhere in life, things rarely change for the better until we have begun an honest dialogue about the status quo—about how things currently stand.

I'm guessing that some of you have been feeling a bit defensive throughout this whole conversation about our basic relational ineptness as a culture, wondering, *"What about the small group movement that has been transforming the ministry of the local church in America over the last twenty years or so? Aren't we as Christians already catching on to these relational ideas? Aren't we already displaying an exceptional commitment to the kinds of life changing relationships you are talking about?"*

Well, in a word...no.

No, we're not. In fact, I'd offer that the true situation is really quite the opposite. Stick with me here for a minute. I'm not trying to be unnecessarily negative, argumentative or deconstructive. But the honest truth is that for the most part the local church just *isn't* offering up life changing relationships. And judging by the way our ministries are built, I'm not remotely convinced that it is something we're even *trying* to do.

It's not just that we're bad at fostering meaningful Friendships .

It's that we haven't even set that as one of our goals.

If true, satisfying and lasting friendships blossom out of one of our small group programs, well...isn't that nice? What a happy and lucky coincidence! But ultimately, what business is that of the Church's, if such a deep bond of friendship happens to blossom between a few members of the congregation? We have holier fish to fry. After all, isn't the church's mission limited to the spiritual plane? To bringing people into a deeper relationship with God? Fostering a more intimate walk with Jesus? Opening up pathways for finding a fuller expression of the abundant life that Jesus came to show us and invite us into through his Spirit and his Life pulsating within us?

Okay, given that that's a good summation of the local church's priorities, there's still all that 'abundant life' stuff to be taken into account—if you're in agreement with me that it should be included in the general description of the church's mission. And that's a bit awkward, if we've just dismissed the importance of fostering one of life's great pleasures through our religious programming. 'Abundant life' sounds like it has more than just spiritual implications, doesn't it? The Good News after all, most would agree, was meant to be good news for the whole man—body, soul, and spirit. I know that in the Christian circles *I've* moved most happily in over the years, it has been generally understood that Christ came not just to 'save' us from Hell, but also to redeem and restore all that was broken and lost in our humanity. *(And remember the theme of the Creation account in Genesis, that it was not good for Man to journey through life alone. It would make sense that healing us of our loneliness would be some part of restoring God's plan for our lives, wouldn't it?)* What are we to do with the Church's role in this redemptive work of God? Is it really likely that He never intended any of the work of Christ (and thus the ongoing work of His Church) to spill over out of the merely 'religious sphere' and pour new life into our experience of human relationships?

> A new command I give you: love one another. As I have loved you, so you must love one another. By this all men will know that you are my disciples, if you love one another.   (John 13:34-35)

> If anyone says, "I love God," yet hates his brother, he is a liar. For anyone who does not love his brother, whom he has seen, cannot love God, whom he has not seen. And he has given us this command: Whoever loves God must also love his brother.   (I John 4:19-21

> ...I have said before that you have such a place in our hearts that we would live or die with you.   (II Corinthians 7:3)

Well, you say, *when you put it like that...*

But, then the stubborn argument continues, *this is the Church we are talking about here. Surely if we aren't concerned about fostering deep, satisfying friendships, it must be because we have even better relationships to offer than just mere natural friendship, right?*

Sure, okay.

Would someone mind pointing me in the direction of wherever we've been hiding these 'better' relationships?

No, only a person who has never enjoyed the rich, satisfying, deep intimacy of *true* friendship would dare suggest that our programs aimed at 'doing life together' (by sharing a meal and a curriculum led conversation at Deacon Rob's house twice a month with a few randomly chosen couples we barely know) are anything but an insipid imitation of what it looks like to *really* do life together.

To be fair, how *could* we expect our programmed groups to be anything more than what they generally turn out to be, when, as an organized institution we are mostly satisfied with taking our relational cues from our relationally inept society? With building whatever 'group ministry' we offer according to the larger culture's impoverished template of relational values?

FUNCTIONAL AND TEMPORARY

Here's just one example, one that could be drawn from many. As we've noted earlier, our culture trains us to believe that relationships have value directly proportionate to their usefulness. And so the local church unconsciously buys into that, and builds groups that are primarily *functional*: groups that are mostly about what they can *do*, what they can *accomplish*. If you look closely you'll notice that the local church's allegiance to small group ministry isn't really flowing from a commitment to the beauty, joy, and delight that can transform our lives through satisfying relationships. Really it's more a commitment to the idea that *people learn better under certain conditions*. It's a commitment to the belief that people learn better in conversation, in dialogue, and when a more interpersonal teaching style is utilized. Mostly we drive people towards our small group ministries because we believe such small groupings are more effective tools for growth and learning—not because we have any commitment to the idea that friendship is "the crown of life", that "life, natural life, has no greater gift to give."

Here's another example. The culture tells us that following our own personal ambitions means that relationships should never hold us back from pursuing our dreams, that those relationships must always be considered disposable at need. So the church buys right into 'disposable', temporary relationships—doesn't even hide behind any unspoken assumptions on this one—and literally *designs* small group ministries in which the group is specifically *programmed* to be terminal, designed to thwart any attempt at satisfying our need to be deeply known.

"Join our group for a year, and then next year you'll be ready to lead your own group for a year, and then those people will move on to lead their own group, etc., etc. ad infinitum."

We call it 'raising up leaders', or 'multiplying our ministry model' and then collectively pat ourselves on the back for creating a ministry that is 'all about relationships', when we have done anything but that. Our relational ineptness runs through everything we do in these groups like an overarching theme. Our endemic lack of relational skills lead us to create small group ministries that actually just dovetail into our cultural need to remain guarded and self-sufficient. We build groups that don't even *claim* to possess a robust philosophy concerning the importance of intimate friendships, or show any respect to the basic rules of how such friendships are formed, or how they are maintained. We aren't developing groups designed to draw us back into the pack: we're making groups that are little more than a gathering place for Lone Wolves. My goodness, we *cater* to the Lone Wolf, offer him just the amount of relationship his individualism can stomach without scaring him away. And without ever daring to suggest to him that there might be something better, some other path to take that would require the death of the Lone Wolf in him, but also the birth of a whole new world he can not now imagine.

So many of our group endeavors, lacking the priorities and vision needed to make them truly great, simply end up increasing our sense of loneliness, the chasm of separation that has dogged our steps all our adult lives. And it's true what they sometimes say you know: the most poignant kind of loneliness really *is* the loneliness that can only be felt in a crowd. The loneliness you experience when you are with other people, yet remain essentially unknown, uncherished, uncelebrated. When you are with people, but they all appear to be satisfied with a superficial connection, fine with not really getting to know you. Not the real you. Not in any deep, significant way that makes a difference. Not in a way that touches the loneliest places in your heart.

> ...most small groups are anything but redemptive powerhouses because, while the wineskin might be the right size, they don't have the right wine. You can do some study till you're blue in the face, and it won't heal the brokenhearted or set the captives free. We come; we learn; we leave. It is not enough. Those hearts remain buried, broken, untouched, unknown.   (John Eldredge, *Waking the Dead*)

The simple, unavoidable fact is this: individualistic people, steeped in an individualistic worldview, deeply task-oriented and lacking any epic vision of friendship simply *don't have the capacity* to offer to the people they serve the transformational relationships those people desperately need and desire.

Now hold on just a minute, you might be thinking. *How could you dare to claim to know what motivates the average small group ministry program in the American Church today?*

Well I'm glad you asked.

A GLIMPSE BEHIND THE CURTAIN

You'll recall my earlier confession that for the better part of my adult life I've maintained something of an uneasy relationship with certain church job search websites. Whether it was my lack of faith in the mission God had placed on my heart, or whether it was the desire to receive approval from friends and family for my career choices, or whether it was just the pressure to find "my place in this world" down some easier, more financially viable path: for all of these reasons and more, I kept one finger on the pulse of the "ministry marketplace' (what a terrible phrase) for the better part of fifteen years.

Oh, I'd go away for a few weeks—maybe even a few months if life was going smoothly, or I sensed God was asking me to rest more in His guidance and stop striving to fit a square peg (me) into a round hole (the average local church). But then I'd always circle back, and when I'd return there'd be hundreds of new openings to peruse from churches across the country. Many of them weren't of interest to me, but whenever an open Small Groups Pastor position flashed across the screen my heart would leap with excitement. *Maybe this one will be the perfect fit,* I would think, hope springing eternal. *Sure, I've never been a small groups pastor, so my resume can't back me up on this, but won't my passion for one-on-one relationships and my epic, romantic vision for true friendship and deeply intimate fellowship shine through to such an extent that any church would be dying to hire me?*

Well, as it turns out...no. No, they wouldn't. Through many years of casual-to-somewhat-serious searching, no one doing the actual hiring at any of these churches ever saw something deeper beyond my lack of like-for-like experience building a 'successful' small groups ministry. I've probably got about fifty rejection letters and emails—all sweetly worded of course—from church secretaries, search committees, and human resources departments as proof of the fact. A very painful fact—one that the Enemy has not overlooked in his assault on my heart. (Could it be that my adult appreciation for *The A-Team* series of my youth stems in part from the cold fact that no one ever has considered me worthy to be on their 'A' team?)

To be honest though, long before all those rejection letters arrived, I mostly knew they were coming. I knew because the job descriptions I had perused by the hundreds, and the phone interviews of which I had had just a handful, all warned me that an epic, romantic vision of true friendship and deeply intimate fellowship had nothing to do with leading a modern small group ministry in the churches of today. As one pastor said while interviewing me, "We don't really need a pastor so much as a program director, a facilitator." It was evident time and again that if a church had to choose between relational skills and type-A efficiency, well, they'd take the efficiency every time. At every step along the journey my spirit was being warned by God that these were not healthy or welcoming environments for someone who dreamt of relationships that might satisfy my glorious vision of all they had the potential to be.

And that vision *is* glorious. That vision is at the heart of my dissatisfaction, at the center of my unwillingness to jump into an unhealthy environment micro-managing someone's regulated but woefully insipid imitation of the Real Deal.

Because my friends, we *need* the Real Deal.

THE IMPOSSIBLE DREAM?

Okay, you say, *maybe you can tell us what it is you think a small group ministry should look like?*

A just question indeed.

Only...I'm not sure I can answer it.

And yes, with that statement I realize we are dangerously close to that whole 'run down the current regime without offering anything better' situation that I dislike as much as you do. But at the same time I don't want to get too sidetracked by this issue. To be fair though, let's be honest about the struggle inherent for anyone set with such a Herculean task: finding a way to package deeply mean-ingful relationships within the confining context of 'organized programming' can really feel like a hopeless endeavor. Nigh impos-sible. I would even propose that for a certain large percentage of the male population the inherent impossibility is assumed. Assumed and insurmountable. To them there could never be a marriage of 'institutionalized relationships' and True Friendship. Which is probably a big part of why they are so hard to 'corral' into your programs, your couple's groups, your men's ministries—whatever it is you're trying to steer them towards like so much stubborn cattle, whatever it is that you are asking them to buy into.

Now, if you could offer them the Real Deal, they might find a way to make time for *that*. But they've been to enough of your groups over the years to expect the Real Deal anymore. It doesn't take a lifelong job search in the area of pastoring small groups for the 'man in the pew' to recognize the functional, terminal, shallow, and non-transformational nature of most institutionalized groups. It doesn't take any study at all to sense that what you've been offered is radically different from the thing that you actually long for. And make no mistake friends: this passing off of a weak substitute for the Real Deal can have some pretty severe consequences.

There's always a danger of answering a question—filling a void in our lives that's crying out for attention—with a false solution. The danger is that now we've filled the void with something, and, our thirst satiated for the moment, we can easily give up on the quest for a better solution, for the true solution. Even if we have a deep sense that our situation has not been improved by the solution we've been offered, we may abandon our search for no other reason than simply because we've 'been there, tried that'. We went to church, we tried their groups, and we didn't even get the edge taken off our existential loneliness through those programmed group experiences. So what happens next? Well, some dutifully carry on, trying to teach themselves to get used to the disappointment. They keep going to the groups we create for them because, sad to say, even these weak imitations of true friendship are better than what they currently are being offered. It's not just the Church that struggles with this, remember: it's our whole society. That's why there are some guys still faithfully showing up. It beats having no relationships at all. But not for the majority of men. The majority end up going to the other extreme: throwing the baby out with the bath water, giving up on the whole thing as an exercise in futility. They jump to the conclusion (easily supported by their idolization of the Lone Wolf) that 'community' or 'friendship' or 'fellowship' or whatever you want to call it never did have the power to touch any of the deepest aches in their heart in any significant way.

Well, no, not when they're done like that they don't.

I admit that I don't really know where the solution to this conundrum lies—although I think it involves a radical shift in our philosophy of ministry in general, which we will consider in the next chapter. I'm not even one hundred percent sure we can talk about developing a better way of 'doing institutionalized relationships' and talk about what I'm calling the 'Real Deal' in the same conversation.

But we are trying. Believe me, we are trying.

WALKING A FINE LINE

In our own ministry, The Warrior's Path, this challenge is at the heart of everything we do. And yet we still face much of the same difficulty as any other ministry when it comes to getting past a lot of guy's natural 'BS detectors'. There's just no use pretending that there aren't inherent problems with having an organized ministry where one of the primary goals of the ministry is to eliminate the kind of forced, shallow, temporary relationships that most organized ministry creates. One key difference is that we enter the whole endeavor knowing the limits of what we are able to offer. We have the event, while never leaving anyone in doubt about what we want to foster through the event—and beyond. Running a retreat, a conference, a mission trip or a pilgrimage—all those are good things. But they are also the equivalent of giving a man a fish: he 'eats' for a weekend, for the length of the programmed experience. On the other hand, leading a man towards a soul mate, a fellowship, a band of brothers —that is more like teaching him to fish: he will 'eat' at life's banquet table for a lifetime.

And yet even with a clear vision of these new priorities to guide our efforts, the reality is that finding soul mates—lifelong companions willing to jump down a dragon's throat for you—is the rarest of gifts. Trying to manufacture such a meeting of hearts is like trying to capture lightning in a bottle, then advertising it for sale at your next scheduled men's event. You just can't promise that. You certainly can't *control* it, any more than you can make a specific man and a specific woman fall in love with each other just because they both have some general desire to fall in love with *someone*—or worse yet, because *you* desire them to fall in love with each other.

But we *do* want to be in control. Therein lies the rub. How could you advertise a 'ministry event' to today's businessminded world if your whole programming scheme is to put a dozen good men together in the woods and just see what develops? My goodness: *anything* might happen! If we don't 'control' the situation through programmed activity, who's to say that any of what *does* happen will even qualify as ministry? Where is the dividing line between a private escape with friends and a 'ministry retreat'? But then of course the big paradox you face is this: if you *don't* have a 'ministry' at all, then no one besides your own inner circle of friends will ever know about your next life-changing weekend away in the mountains. But the moment you put it on a calendar and title that weekend away 'a ministry event'—well, suddenly you are dealing with that extra layer of formality and awkwardness that can really put your relational intentions in doubt. Are we a Fellowship of freely chosen friends, looking forward to a weekend of deep joy, personal growth and renewed intimacy with some of our favorite people? Or are we merely participants at someone's event, consumers of a product, service, or experience that they are selling?

Can you have the necessity of the one, there merely to lay the faintest, most inconspicuous groundwork for the growing supremacy of the other? Oh, how we pray that it can be so.

ROADBLOCKS TO FRIENDSHIP

I think we are really faced with two questions here. The first is, *"How do we foster deep intimate friendship within the context of 'structured ministry' as it now exists?"*, and the second is, *"Is the attempted project so self-defeating in its very nature that the church ought to be rethinking its entire approach to fostering Christian community?"*. That is to say, we must ask if ultimately the power inherent in a fellowship of "freely chosen peers" is chopped down at the knees the moment it becomes clear to these selfsame 'peers' that they have not freely chosen one another at all, but have been brought together as the result of some church policymaker's basic need for regulation and control?

First, in response to the simpler question, let's look at a few things to keep in mind when working within the context of our existing vision of ministry—specifically our attempts at fostering 'community' through the usual, organized pathways. Just a few basic shifts towards developing a truly relationship-oriented approach to all this, if we plan to keep working within the current paradigm of how to 'do' church. Because let's face it: mostly we have remained deeply task-oriented, even when we're trying to 'do' relationships. (The fact that we insist on using a task-oriented phrase like 'doing relationships', or 'doing community' just proves how deep our current orientation runs, and how far we still have to go in this). Learning to think and act according to the basic principles of how great relationships are made and maintained is an obvious place to begin.

EVERYONE NEEDS DEEP CONNECTION

For starters, it is essential that we come to realize that *everyone* you
come into contact with needs deeper, better relationships than what
they're currently experiencing. *There are no exceptions.* I know it may
appear to the contrary. But we must look past the public image—the
false self—every one of us projects to the world in an attempt to
prove our high-functioning level of 'personal autonomy'. The door
to real relationships swings wide and welcoming only when our eyes
are opened and we can see that this public image is nothing but one
elaborately constructed lie. In spite of every external appearance to
the contrary we absolutely must keep in mind that *no one* has it all
together, *no one* is as self-sufficient as the image they project to the
world ("it is not good for the man to be alone" Gen. 2:18, remember?), and *everyone* experiences deep loneliness and isolation (it is a
universal condition of our fallen Race). We must keep this in mind
because the phony facade people project really has a way of deterring
us from even wanting to try, wanting to put ourselves out there
relationally at all. Looking past it is the essential first step towards
making meaningful connections, and, if other things align, may even
lead (dare we hope?) to true friendships. So take it as a basic fact: no
matter how it appears on the surface, everyone you know does have a
deeply unmet relational need.

Now, I'm aware that the moment you actually try to bring a group
of *actual* people together, immediately you will be tempted to
question the truth of this. Jason is a jokester, always the loudest one
at the table, lots of fun to be around. But you never get the sense that
he's ever going to let you in to see what's really going on inside.
Aaron is a master with words: he always sounds so sure of his
theology, so quick with the knowledgeable reply. But there never
seems to be a crack in the armor, a sense that you've ever heard a
word about his real life and his real struggles. Sean, on the other

hand, hardly speaks at all. He contributes nothing. You begin to wonder if he's thinking anything at all. Perhaps the lights are on, but nobody's home. Then there's Chris, the alpha dog: so much bravado pouring out of him that everyone at the table feels diminished in his presence. There's no way anyone's going to open up and get vulnerable while he's in the room. Certainly not about any sort of personal struggle, any sign of weakness. His mere presence has the ability to make our whole hope of intimacy suddenly seem...well...a little girly.

Every time you sit down with an actual group of people and try to get to know them, all of these roadblocks to your intentions are going to get thrown in your face. testing the strength of your resolve. Much of the doubt that will then rise, of course, comes from within ourselves—a result of our own perception. Because to some degree, deep down we still idolize and romanticize the masculinity and strength we think it takes to successfully play the Lone Wolf. And so, rather than looking beyond the surface when someone in our group projects an air of confidence and self-sufficiency, we recoil. Back off. Crawl back into our relational shell. Maybe even write them off as 'not into all this touchy-feely stuff' and drop the whole effort to make a meaningful connection. We are so easily deceived by the false image of guarded self-sufficiency they project, in large part because we haven't truly given up on the conviction that if only you are strong enough, it really *can* be done. Something deep inside of us has not fully let go of the idea that the life of the Lone Wolf is still a highly desirable option.

On top of our own confusion on the matter, you can't forget that almost everybody you meet has been working their whole lives to perfect that false image of self-sufficiency they're projecting. *Of course* you're going to be tempted to buy the deception.

But don't give in.

Hold to the truths that you know from analyzing your own heart, your own desires for relationships, and fight through the fog of lies.

These other guys are not somehow stronger than you, more capable, more self-sufficient in a way that should inspire your envy. They are isolated, alone, cut off from the pack and usually more vulnerable than they remotely realize. No matter what anyone pretends, remember God's first and final word on the matter: *"It is not good for man to be alone."*

YOU GET WHAT YOU PAY FOR

Secondly, we need to accept that true relational intimacy, while a treasure of greater worth than silver and gold, is a commodity both rare and costly—costly in time, in effort, and in personal vulnerability. You don't just get that sort of intimacy by asking relative strangers deeply personal questions because they happen to be in this week's small group curriculum. (The old joke floating around the Christian Ed. department back in grad school went like this, *"Hello Joe, welcome to the group. It's nice to meet you. Why don't you come and put your chair in the middle of the circle, and share with the group the worst sin you've ever committed?"* A caricature of course, but not too far off from how we do things far too often.)

We are after transparency, yes. Absolutely. Getting past the false image of self-sufficiency is key to everything good, as we just noted. But you also have to keep in mind something. That false image we run up against in everyone we meet is there for a very powerful reason. It's there—rightly or wrongly—to protect them from the criticism, judgement and rejection that the world is so quick to mete out. Even as ours has been expertly constructed for similar protection. And so it should be obvious that most of us would rather not cast our pearls—the treasure of our true selves—before...well, in a kinder paraphrase, before those who will treat them lightly or carelessly, before those who can't yet value how much the deep story of our heart's journey really matters. How deeply it matters to God.

To ourselves. To our true and faithful friends.

In this regard it's the same here as in romantic relationships: rushing into 'false intimacy' of any kind that isn't supported by depth of commitment will almost always end in grief. Look around you. Look back on your own life. You know this is true. True intimacy is a costly treasure that must be earned.

Sadly, far too many men's ministries have caught on to this idea of pushing past the false self in pursuit of genuine transparency, and while their vision is healthy, their methodology remains all wrong. In our impatient, instant-everything American style, this new wave of 'relationally minded' ministries are asking men to offer up the deep treasures of their secret heart: but at absolutely no cost to the people doing the asking. They offer shallow lip service to the promise of 'brotherhood' and deep friendship in exchange for the revealing of your truest, most vulnerable self. But all too often there's just no follow through on the promises. Mostly, I think, because their 'vision for ministry' never did take into account what life would actually look like for them if they really gave themselves in mutual friendship to the people in their ministry. After all, relationships are so time consuming, and they can't let anything bog them down or steer them off course: there are 'great works' to be done for the Kingdom! They'd rather get a hundred men to bare their deepest secrets through any method they can than commit themselves to the slow, natural unveiling that comes from walking through many years with just five men. Like a ruthless strip mining corporation, they raid the fertile soil for its treasures and then disappear overnight—on to the promising location of their next 'project'. All their best intentions are undone by their relationally insensitive methods, resulting in a form of spiritual abuse that makes most men that much less willing to open up the next time, less willing to ever believe that he is being offered true membership into a fellowship of peers. And ultimately, these ministries with the right words and the wrong execution are making it that much harder for the rest of us, because they have relegated to the realm of 'useful metaphors' something that we were created to experience as a living, breathing, attainable reality. The same-old dry, impersonal ministry that now refers to your same-old dry, impersonal small group as a 'Band of Brothers' is not doing the church any favors. *Not* helpful, dear friends. Not helpful in the least.

RELATIONSHIPS THAT MATTER

Finally and most importantly, we must realize that the kind of relationships everyone longs for are almost always those of the two-way-street variety. Which is to say, the only relationships that really possess the power to deeply impact people's lives are the kind of relationships that also deeply impact us.

I'll say that again:

The only relationships that really possess the power to deeply impact people's lives are the kind of relationships that also deeply impact us.

Now I know a lot of people in organized ministry may balk at this, because accepting this truth really puts a limit on the number of people we can hope to deeply impact, because we can only get to that place with as many people as we are willing to let into our own lives, into our own 'circle of trust'. Now I'm not just saying it's enough that we learn to consider people a 'priority', or to say that they 'matter' to us. That's certainly a good thing, and a step we need to take. Until we make some attempt at seeing people as of greater value than other things in our life, we won't progress very far along relational lines. All people matter to God, and therefore all people ought to 'matter' to us. But beyond that, deeper than a general appreciation for humanity, I'm talking about getting to that place where we can say that our *relationship* with very specific individuals matters *to us*, at a very personal level.

And yes, we will always be able to accomplish *some* good in our more large-scale, less intimate, ministry-driven interactions with larger numbers of people. And if that's the best we can do, well, of course it's better than not ministering at all. But it's time we were honest about just how deep these more surface level interactions can take us with others. We won't ever be able to truly touch that inconsolable ache in another person, the ache to be known, to be loved, to be chosen—not until they've been invited into that place inside ourselves that shares something of that same ache to also be known, loved, and chosen.

Don't look to your ministry philosophy—one that's been developed in some ivory tower, wholly unassociated to the real world —just look to the honest testimony of your own heart. If you exclude the world of organized religious programming that we've all been trained to accept as valid in spite of how we might feel, hasn't this always been true for you? Haven't you always been far more interested in pursuing those relationships that seem to be full of *mutual* affection, where both parties are more-or-less equally invested and equally desirous to see the friendship 'go the distance'?

In stark contrast to fostering genuine relationships that are undeniably based on mutual affection, I can promise you that almost no one—especially men—want to think of themselves as someone's charity work, their 'project', their 'assignment', their 'ministry', or the way that they hope to earn brownie points with God. Do *you* want someone to 'condescend' to build a relationship with *you* on those terms? It's a safe bet that you don't. So keep that one truth at the forefront of your mind as you develop your own ministry plans, and you will clear away much of the nonsense that passes for the institutional Church's present day attempt at 'meaningful community'.

WHAT WE CANNOT LIVE WITHOUT

Now, I'm aware that this last half of the chapter has been directed mostly towards people in ministry, people responsible for how organized religious programming in the local church and in other ministries 'do relationships' (their phrase, not mine). We've been asking how they can improve their approach to fostering genuine relationships. And it's an important question to be asked—even more important for it be answered. And answered well.

But what about the rest of us? While much of this is applicable to our own lives, when it comes to organized religious programming, well, let's be honest: our level of investment in making the church's programs 'work' is very different than that of our religious leaders, wouldn't you say? Because what really matters most to us is that we get the chance to experience the fullness of life that Jesus offered us, that we don't miss out on any of the conduits of grace and goodness that God has designed for our joy. So whether the small group ministry at First Church On The Corner lasts another twenty years or not isn't really a life changing issue to most of us—not if we've been loyal participants, yet continue to walk through life virtually alone, unknown, and separated from all the rich blessings that can only be found within the context of deep and lasting relationships.

Don't get me wrong. A small group ministry is a good thing, and most churches are better off with them than without them. But there is a deeper, more haunting question that we long to have answered:

Is there something more?

And I think you can guess the answer we've been drawing ever closer to throughout the pages of this book:

There can be, dear friends.

There can be.

NINE

THE LEAGUE
OF IRON

As iron sharpens iron, so one man sharpens another.
Proverbs 27:17

There are certain things we feel to be beautiful and good,
and we must hunger for them.
George Eliot

You're only as strong as the man on your right.
King Leonidas, *The 300*

For nearly three years now I've been inviting a few guys in their early thirties over to my house on a weekly basis to just 'hang out'. They are all creative types—musicians, actors, filmmakers— which really resonates with me as someone who gets deep pleasure from my own creative outlet: writing. We eat a lot of pizza and junk food, talk about surface life, talk about deeper stuff, and catch up on everyone's current projects. It's been a massive blessing to all of us, actually. Creativity is much harder work than most people realize, and no personality type benefits more from being encouraged in their work than the creative soul. Last summer we had an absolute blast collaborating on a project together. One of the guys had an idea for a movie, so I wrote the script and they went on to act in, direct, and produce the movie later that year.

Somewhere along this three year journey with these guys—in the spirit of our pleasure for the theatrical—I dubbed our little gathering 'The League of Stories'. And yes, our weekly hangout is very much an off-shoot of my organized, intentional ministry to young adults in our local area.

But in another way...it isn't.

Well, not anymore.

I say that because after three years of spending so much time together all of the stilted, awkward, structured components of the relationship have melted away to be replaced by a far better reality. I don't have to hunt them down, instigate everything, coerce them to make time to get together. We don't have to meet on a designated night of the week: any free day will do. Sometimes one of the guys will even just drop in when the rest of the group is busy.

I no longer have to worry about what they think of me, or worry that I might somehow deep-six the relationship by sharing too much about my own struggles, or graciously calling them out on theirs. Long past is the sense that either they, or I, am 'on trial'—testing the waters to see if we like each other or not, if we have the chemistry to 'go the distance'. As the Victorian author George Eliot said, "Friendship is the inexpressible comfort of feeling safe with a person, having neither to weigh thoughts or measure words." By that test, I can tell you these weekly hangouts certainly haven't felt like ministry in quite some time: *they just feel like friendship*. And, I should add, *as significant to my world as they are to theirs*. That's the true test. There aren't many things I look forward to more during the course of a week than Friday or Saturday night hanging out with 'the guys'.

Now, I'm not saying we do friendship perfectly. We've still got a ways to go. But you could say that in any friendship. Relationships have a neverending capacity for getting better, for going deeper.

But I sure can tell you this: the very worst thing I could do at this point would be to give 'the guys' any sense that I view the whole thing as 'my ministry'. Why would I *want* to? Yes, it looks better on a monthly 'ministry' newsletter, and so long as we are trying to justify ourselves in the eyes of our family, peers, and potential financial supporters, we will always be tempted to return to the formal roles and labels that the Christian world understands. But for me and 'the guys' those are hardly noble reasons for retreating back into the 'formal', and certainly not worth the damage it could do to our growing friendships. We have passed out of the world of organization, structure and control into something much deeper, stronger, and more satisfying.

AT ODDS WITH OUR WORLD

Which brings us to the tougher of the two questions we posed in the preceding chapter: Can a true relational orientation be applied to the modern Church's programmatic and task-oriented attempts at fostering satisfying relationships? And once applied, could the old 'programmatic' form survive the revolution that is sure to follow? Are the two approaches just too intrinsically at odds?

I confess that I don't really know the answer to this one. I do know that it's a question I've been haunted by for most of my adult life. I remember way back near the beginning, as a twenty-four-year-old grad student studying to go into full time ministry, terrified to find myself wondering at times: *Is all this stuff I'm learning about the nature of how people's lives are truly transformed talking me right out of my career?* Soon after, in my first full-time job as a youth pastor, the questions were back, only they weren't just theoretical anymore. A few months into the ministry I found myself being asked in no uncertain terms to 'spend less time with the kids' and focus my attention instead on just preparing the Sunday morning and Wednesday evening events. *Stick to the program, kid. That's what you were hired for.*

Truly relationally-oriented people don't survive long in our task-oriented driven society—or, for the most part, in our task-oriented churches either. Remember my earlier story about the youth pastor that tried to separate David and I by putting us in separate cabins at junior high summer camp? How she tried to convince us that our relationship, if left alone and allowed to flourish, would be a distraction to their 'program'? Well, thirty-some years on from that, and, in unbelievable irony, it all happened to me again yesterday.

I'm not kidding.

Yesterday.

This time it was my oldest boys, Tristan and Nathaniel, off to their first away-from-home experience with their youth group. As I've already noted, I've got a lot of fond memories from my own camp experiences, so I had really hyped it up to the boys when it came their turn to go to camp. But at the same time, I was worried. Sure there were golden memories of wonderful weeks of camp that David and I had spent together. But there were also memories of camps he did *not* attend—camps where *none* of my friends attended, and they were some of the hardest, loneliest weeks of my life. So I was keenly aware that relationships meant everything when it came to having an unforgettable camp experience. And knowing that my second son Nathaniel is younger at heart than his biological age, added to the fact that he was brand new to the youth group, I honestly wasn't sure how he would do away from home for the better part of a week. So he requested to room with his older brother. *I* spoke to their leaders and requested they be allowed to room together. In fact when I agreed to send them to camp I never imagined that they *wouldn't* be allowed to room together. But they are in different grades you see, and no one in leadership at the church seemed remotely interested in messing with 'the program' for the sake of fostering a family relationship.

Now, you've got to understand that I've poured twelve years into doing everything in my power to convince the boys that they have built-in, God-given, life-long best friends ready made in one another. In the end the experiment may not work of course: ultimately the choice will be up to them. But it won't be from lack of effort on my part. And I know most fathers wouldn't be keying in on that as a huge priority, so it's not obvious that other people will understand what I'm after: the beauty of lifelong best friends who are also brothers. But wouldn't it have been great if the policymakers in church leadership thought this central relationship, with all its long term potential for good—spiritual and temporal—was worth fostering? Wouldn't it have been great if they had even been willing to stop and consider it *at all*, consider respecting the wishes of a father for his own children?

Alas, but no. We still operate the Church by a system of top-down regulations and control, afraid—or unqualified—to enter into the messy and mysterious world of relationally-driven choices.

The generation has changed, but it would seem that little else has.

Yes, friends, the struggle is real.

THIS COULD CHANGE EVERYTHING

And although I'm in no position to offer a definitive answer to how to overcome this struggle, I think we've now come to the one thing that I wish the entire Church in America could hear. Hear, and take to heart. The one thing that I wish would become a basic principle of Christian thought, deliberately taught to the next generation of would-be ministers in every college, graduate school, and seminary across the country, across all denominational lines. The one thing that, if fully embraced, could lead to a seismic shift in both our philosophy and our practical approach to spiritual life, spiritual health, and genuine discipleship.

Deep breath.

Are you ready? Here it is:

Despite what we've mostly been led to believe, the most important spiritual influence in any individual's life (that is within the
realm of *man* to influence) is not great preaching, wonderful event
programming, intellectually sound Christian education, organized
religious activity, or even moderately successful small group ministry.
In other words, it's not to be found in ninety-eight percent of what
we as the modern church pour our efforts into.

No. *The most important spiritual influence in any individual's life
is their closest friends, their most intimate relationships.*

The clearest indicator of long term spiritual health is not how
great the teaching pastor is at the church you attend on Sunday
mornings. Oh, we've tried to convince ourselves that such was the
case. But we've been deeply mistaken—or willfully ignorant, in an
attempt to keep the 'professional ministry' at the center of the
Christian life. But no, the clearest indicator of long term spiritual
health—life-long spiritual health, really—in any individual's life is
*who it is that they spend their time with when they're free to spend time
with the people they love and cherish the most.*

That's it.

Look, I know we can have a really hard time with that. We tend to
think important things need to be overcomplicated things. But
sometimes the simple answer is the correct answer. Sometimes it is
right there, staring us in the face, even though we just refuse to see it
for the simple solution that it is.

Forget your educational theories, your pet programs, your favored
techniques. Sure, those things possess *some* power to effect *some*
change. But as a Church we've been huffing and puffing and striving
and laboring, pouring our time and resources into these plans and
schemes, thinking they offer the clearest pathway to seeing people in

our sphere of influence become 'fully devoted followers of Christ.' But every one of these pet programs and techniques has some pretty obvious limits, and if you've ever worked in full time ministry I don't think you need me to tell you that. They all flatter to deceive; they are perpetually disappointing in their effectiveness. In the end they never seem to be powerful enough: they rarely reach the escape velocity necessary to break out of the little 'religious' compartments in our life within which they were originally manufactured.

But the friend-to-friend influence factor *has no compartment*, because the really good friendships we are seeking operate at a level that is far above and beyond all compartments. They possess a power that transcends all barriers, extends beyond the boundaries of our mere 'church life'. Only the friend whom we have allowed beyond our defensive walls because he has proven himself faithful time and again—only such a one as he is granted unlimited power to impact our lives. As the proverbs point out, "Faithful are the wounds of a friend" (Proverbs 27:6). Indeed we *will* suffer his wounds—his intervention, his tough love—because it *is* love and we know it.

Iron sharpens iron.

When done right, it's that simple.

When done right.

Oh, we use that phrase about 'iron sharpening iron' a lot in the Church; I'm sure you've noticed. In all likelihood you're sick of hearing it by now. But most of that internal shrug of indifference you're feeling right now stems from the fact that the phrase is not just *over*used in the Church, but entirely *mis*used. Let me show you what I mean with a little mental exercise. Try to forget all the misused ways you've experienced the metaphor in the past just for a moment. Now close your eyes (no, really: give it a try) and allow your mind to create a mental image for what 'iron sharpening iron' would look like in a *literal* sense. What do you see?

I see two very strong objects—much tougher and unmoving than mere human flesh—being drawn across one another with such force that sparks of fire shoot in every direction. I see swords being sharpened against a whetting stone, sharpened to a razor's edge. I see the fires of the forge, the hammer and the anvil and the forming of something new that could have been created by no other means than heat and force and repetition.

Now, does any of that sound like the way things get done in *your* Church? Is that the kind of intensity that defines the men's ministries *you've* been a part of? Honestly, most of us, with our Lone Wolf attitudes and our independent spirits, wouldn't even put up with a group of once-a-week acquaintances that tried to live up to the true image of 'iron sharpening iron'. That sort of unyielding and abrasive treatment, when not among the friends whom we love and who love us in return, would mostly just feel...*harsh*. Which is why I suppose most church groups know better than to even attempt it.

And yet, the latent power is there. Iron does sharpen iron.

In the right context.

I began the chapter by telling you about 'the guys', my young friends who I've spent at least one evening with every week for most of the past three years. Well, just this week one of the guys, Daniel, a young but accomplished filmmaker, was talking about how much hypocrisy there is in the Church because the pressure to 'have it all together' keeps people from admitting any of their struggles or deeper questions about life. I couldn't stop myself from laughing. "Of course that's the way it is at church," I replied. "People hide behind an image, but not because it's some weakness unique to a religious setting. You haven't uncovered a hive of hypocrisy that throws doubt on the truth and goodness of Christianity, you're just witnessing basic human nature. People hide and pretend at church *because a gathering of people you barely know never was the right context for getting real*. Not until 'The Church' means the four of us sitting around this kitchen table just being ourselves will I expect 'The

Church' to be a place where people don't need to hide or pretend.""

Nothing else shapes the convictions and actions of a man to a greater degree than the company of men he has chosen as his own, that he has chosen to walk through life with. As Lewis yet again clarifies for us, it is the praise of these chosen few that we strive for, their censure that we dread above all else. Herein, amongst these dear brothers, resides almost all hope of personal transformation or genuine revolution.

> Alone among unsympathetic companions, I hold certain views and standards timidly, half ashamed to avow them and half doubtful if they can after all be right. Put me back among my Friends and in half an hour - in ten minutes - these same views and standards become once more indisputable. The opinions of this little circle, while I am in it, out-weighs that of a thousand outsiders: as Friendship strengthens, it will do this even when my Friends are far away. For we all wish to be judged by our peers, by the men "after our own heart." Only they really know our mind and only they judge it by the standards we fully acknowledge. Theirs is the praise we really covet and the blame we really dread. The little pockets of early Christians survived because they cared exclusively for the love of "the brethren" and stopped their ears to the opinion of the Pagan society all round them.
>
> (C.S. Lewis, *The Four Loves*)

Theirs is the praise we really covet and the blame we really dread.' This is the power that exists within an intimate fellowship of friends, be they a circle of two, three, or a dozen. This is the power that exists when a man believes that he is truly free, truly among his peers—and not simply interacting within an imbalanced relationship, playing the role of someone else's 'ministry', 'project' or 'friend not freely chosen'.

And this is the power that almost all the Church's formal attempts at 'community' actually hinder, because we are hardly ever left to ourselves, hardly ever left free among our peers. The organized Church's love for hierarchy and its mistaken belief that the Church is divided between highly educated professional experts and 'the congregation' are much to blame for this poverty of peers. We dare not be left alone: how could we hope to ever 'get it right' without professional guidance? We are the spiritual 'amateurs'; our little Fellowship is not officially acknowledged—it has not been endorsed by the People in The Know.

Friends, this attitude has nothing to do with spiritual maturity. Of course there is a place for mentoring, for discipleship, for the young believer to sit at the feet of the Wise. But that isn't all that's happening here. What's happening is that we are worshipping expertise: 'position', 'power' and 'professionalism', in a situation where we ought to primarily be concerned about the depth of someone's relationship with Jesus. The seasoned pastor of twenty-five years faithful service and many advanced degrees may be no more intimate with Jesus than the unknown 'common' man he passes in the church lobby with barely a nod of acknowledgment. Believe me, this idea that the 'professional' exists on some higher plane than the rest of us permeates the entire modern church, doing far more damage than we realize. Only when 'the expert sharing his knowledge' ministry paradigm is replaced by 'the-pilgrim-travelling-in-fellowship-with-other-pilgrims' paradigm will there be hope for any lasting change.

And let me dare to add this: only when our Christian leaders, church pastors and Religious Powers that Be admit that there is something stronger, deeper, and more powerful than all their best-laid plans and programs—only then can we expect to see Friendship return to its high and holy place in God's Kingdom here on earth. When the sacrament of friendship is once again preached from the pulpit, when we admit that The Fellowship must become greater, and our programs must become less—only then will we stop asking whether the church (little 'c') is relevant to the current era, and remember that the Christian, the 'little Christ' going about his normal life in the company of two or three like-minded brothers, never has, or ever could, lose his relevance.

> Men are mirrors, or "carriers" of Christ to other men. That is why the Church, the whole body of Christians showing Him to one another, is so important. You might say that when two Christians are following Christ together there is not twice as much Christianity as when they are apart, but sixteen times as much.
>
> (C.S. Lewis, *Mere Christianity*)

Can I say it again?

The most powerful spiritual influence in any individual's life is their closest friends, their most intimate relationships.

THE COST WE CANNOT AFFORD TO PAY

And the implications of this truth for most of us are, to be frank, simply frightening. Think with me for a minute. Consider what this means in a culture that now breeds the Friendless Adult Male by the millions. If a man's greatest resource for spiritual health and wholeness comes through the time he spends with his most intimate fellowship of friends, and most men alive today don't *have* an intimate fellowship of friends—well, you can see where this is going, can't you? We have effectively allowed ourselves to be cut off from our greatest resource, right here, in our most desperate hour.

Can I just ask: who is there in your life that would jump down a dragon's throat for you? That would hunt you to the gates of Hell to save you from yourself if need required? That considers your physical and spiritual health and happiness as an indivisible ingredient of his own health and happiness?

No one? Maybe your parents? Ideally that would have been the case, but I don't think I need to point out that it didn't work out that way for all of us. And are they even around anymore—as part of your daily life, anyway? It's great to have someone who thinks of you with love, maybe even says a prayer for you each morning. But at this point they're a thousand miles away and you see them twice a year if you're lucky: what of your *daily* need?

Okay then, maybe it's your spouse who knows your daily life inside and out? Growing up, during our most formative years, the culture certainly did its best to convince us that one day marriage was going to meet our deepest needs to be fully known, fully understood, fully loved. So...how has *that* been working out for you in your own life? I know the national divorce rate—even within the body of Christ—is still heartbreakingly high. What of the other half of all marriages, the ones that stay together? Would it be fair to assume that not every couple that chooses to remain married is in fact experiencing the deep relational intimacy and soul-satisfying interconnectedness we were created for? Think about the marriages *you* know. Would you say that even *half* of them have lived up to those lofty expectations? And yet, weren't we all led to believe that letting go of all our friends was the right and necessary 'adult' thing to do in order to gain this prize of great worth that would replace them all?

Friends, it's not my intention to downplay the importance of marriage, or family. Our parents and our spouses *absolutely* were intended to be permanent, glorious channels through which a large portion of our soul's relational needs were to be met. But it is rarely the case that they in fact *do* live up to their original design. And yet we still continue to bank all our hopes on them for the intimate, satisfying companionship through life's many adventures that our heart dreams of, even to some extent demands. For whatever reason, we refuse to admit that these channels have fallen short, and we remain blind to the suggestion that a great deal of our heart's needs were always intended to be met through a third stream other than just family and marriage—specifically, through Friendship.

As a result we enter into the harrowing trials of adult life having left one of our greatest resources for strength, courage, and happiness behind in the days of our youth. Is it any wonder that the inner journey towards wholeness of soul and holiness of spirit feels like an uphill slog that never quite goes the way we had imagined it would go back in the May-time of our youth when hearts were high and "we sang of revolution"?

> There's a grief that can't be spoken
> There's a pain goes on and on
> Empty chairs at empty tables
> Now my friends are dead and gone
>
> Here they talked of revolution,
> Here it was they lit the flame,
> Here they sang about tomorrow
> And tomorrow never came.
>
> Phantom faces at the window
> Phantom shadows on the floor
> Empty chairs at empty tables,
> Where my friends will meet no more.
>
> Les Miserables, "*Empty Chairs at Empty Tables*"

The chairs at our table are empty too—not because our friends have given their lives to some great cause and are now "dead and gone". The chairs where we once talked of spiritual dreams that bordered on a kind of holy revolution—and might well be talking of such revolution once again even now—are empty simply because *our friends* are gone. Not as in 'departed from this life'. Just departed from *our* life. Oh, they're still out there, somewhere, chasing the American dream, living the culturally acceptable role of the Lone Wolf. Probably even putting a good face on things, making it look like it's working for them. Based on their Facebook profile, you'd have to say they are apparently happier and more successful than you've ever felt in your whole dysfunctional life.

But trust me, friends: it's all an elaborate lie meant to fool the world of men, because *as* men in this society we've been trained from the earliest age to "never let them see you sweat". *Make it if you can, but by all means, fake it if you can't.* That's just the next step in this dizzying dance of mistaken masculinity. To some degree or another we have all given in to this madness, this pretentious game of putting bold faces on aching hearts for fear that otherwise we can never take our place at the council fires of the 'real men' in whose number we so long to be counted among.

I have warned that there are some frightening implications to the double-edged truths that our greatest spiritual resource is to be found in our intimate friendships, and that contrarily, for the most part we have in fact grown up and left those same friendships behind us. But I can speak of more than just mere implications, mere theoretical concerns. I am also able to speak from deep personal experience, deep personal failure, and ultimately deeply painful loss. I can do all that because, sad to say, I can tell you the stories of no less than *four* once deeply devoted followers of Christ that I have at one time or another counted among my closest and dearest friends, who have walked away from their faith in the years after our individual journeys brought, not our friendship, but our *active* fellowship to an end.

Now, I'm not suggesting that these dear friend's heartbreaking choices were all my fault. I wouldn't dare imply that I possess some sort of sovereignty over the fates of men. I'm not even suggesting that my qualities as a friend are that much different than what any other person would have to offer had they been in my place. I certainly don't claim to have some powerful aura of holiness that guarantees these dear old friends would still be walking with Jesus if I had remained in intimate fellowship with them. But, then again: we *did* fail to hold true to one another through thick and thin, as great friends ought. I *wasn't* there for them when they needed some wise counsel from someone they knew and trusted. So ultimately, how will I ever know how much things might have been different?

WE ARE WEAKER ALONE

It all makes a sort of wicked sense really, when we look at things from Satan's perspective. Remember, our Enemy has been around a very, very long time. Long enough to make a comprehensive and diabolically thorough study of God's beloved children. What makes them tick. What hits them where it hurts. What brings them to their knees. Satan may be powerless to lay siege to God's throne (he tried that once, and was thrown down in defeat and shame, see Revelations), but he knows that he can deal a blow to God's heart by destroying His children whom He loves so dearly. And he's got at least one overarching strategy in his arsenal for dealing with us that can be summed up in the simplest of terms: Divide and Conquer. And boy, has that tactic never been easier for him to pull off than it is in today's society. Hell rejoices every time one of God's children swears allegiance to the vow of the Lone Wolf. And we—we have no idea what ground we are giving to the Destroyer when we make this feeble attempt to protect ourselves through the pursuit of independence and autonomy. Legend has it that once upon a time the famed Spartan warriors of ancient Greece went into battle believing in the necessity of *interdependence*: believing that despite all their individual training and prowess, ultimately they were "only as strong as the man on their right". Today, even though we possess a fraction of the strength, discipline, and prowess of these great warriors, we somehow have convinced ourselves that *we* require no one in our own bid to successfully conquer our world. Honestly, when you look at what we've accomplished with our Lone Wolf mentality and what the Spartans accomplished with their spirit of interdependence... well, it's a little embarrassing, to tell the truth.

There's a scene in the fifth Harry Potter film, *The Order of the Phoenix*, that says it perfectly. Now, it doesn't always get portrayed in the movie adaptations (thankfully), but the way J.K.Rowling wrote Harry's character, he's actually extremely emotionally immature, prone to think the worst of everyone, and constantly interpreting situations through a lens of defensiveness and suspicion. Much of his response—especially to those who care most about him—comes across as downright peevish. It's really a wonder that in spite of the way Harry treats his friends, the moviemakers were able to turn the whole franchise into something that actually glorifies and exalts friendship, something that could be considered worth watching for that reason alone. But in this particular scene from the fifth film, we see a bit of the true Harry coming through. In textbook teenage style, he's decided that he's all alone in his struggles—that nobody understands either him or his actions. He's allowed his immature emotions to alienate himself from his dearest friends. He's embracing once again the deeply entrenched belief he's made continuous agreement with (remember he had to live 10 years of his life with relatives who utterly reviled everything about him), the belief that it's always going to be "Harry against the world". Then along comes his oddest, quirkiest friend Luna Lovegood. Quite unexpectedly she offers him some rare (for her) intelligible and insightful advice:

> Luna: That's what I'd do, if I were You-Know-Who.
>
> Harry: What?
>
> Luna: Separate you from your friends. Make you feel alone.
>
> You're less dangerous alone.

Yes. We are all less dangerous when we are alone. Voldemort knew that about Harry; your Enemy knows that about you. But will our stubborn worship of independence allow us to even see the truth of it in time to shore up our weak defenses before it's too late?

THE DEVIL'S PLAYGROUND

Of course I may be wrong, but I can't help believing things would have been different for my friends who lost their way in recent years had I been there. Had we respected the lifelong nature of relationships. Had we maintained the sacred responsibility to "be devoted to one another in brotherly love" (Romans 12:10). I've talked with a few of them since their loss of faith, and it was pretty clear to me that the doubts, disappointments, and struggles with conflicting worldviews that stole over them like slowly gathering storm clouds through the erosion of years upon years of personal crisis—that all of it could have been dispelled through some very simple, wise and faithful counsel from a dear and trusted friend. I can tell you that I'd been around, they sure wouldn't have fallen away from walking with Jesus without an all-out fight for their hearts.

Now, I'm sure every one of these old friends would deny that my friendship in those crisis years would have made any difference. I'm sure they think that what they believe now about the universe is the more 'intellectually honest' approach to understanding Reality. But friends, if there's one thing I know, it's that isolation is the Devil's Playground. And I know for certain that what some of these old friends had enthroned as an 'irrefutable' arguments against the Christian faith are not irrefutable at all. Those arguments would have been blasted away like a strand of straw in a Kansas cyclone long before they ever could have sunk down their vile roots, if we had still been in that old place where deep, serious, honest conversation together was a common weekly—if not daily—occurrence.

Nothing clears the air and washes away the clouds of confusion and cynicism that so easily gather in later years than a refreshingly sane talk with an old friend who has 'known us of old'. Nothing ties us to our younger selves more powerfully than a continued friendship with the people who shared those early adventures with us, who remember us from the days when "hope was high, and life worth living." We are far more likely to make rationalizations about our own abandoned ideals than we are to forget the hopes and dreams of those we have known and loved when they were at their strongest and best.

Now, those friends that lost their way: I'm not suggesting that their struggles were groundless. They all had life hit some pretty rough patches, faced some truly bitter disappointments. Mostly they were surrounded by a lot of the wrong kind of people espousing the wrong worldviews. And, yes, it is a dark and dangerous world. I get that. In many of our lives the gravitational pull towards discouragement and doubt can be so strong, and the wild and wonderful hopes of the Christian faith can appear so comparatively indefensible in this mad, mad world. An eventual loss of faith can seem almost inevitable. I totally get it. My life has not been free of such dark nights of the soul. I too, at some points have skirted that precipice, walked that harrowing mountain ledge between loss of faith and stubborn commitment to the Christian explanation of universal existence. And yet, somehow, by the grace of God, here I stand.

THE MAN ON MY RIGHT

Yes, by grace alone my own story didn't end in heartbreak and disillusionment like some of the dear friends that I've known. And I'm confident that I know one of the main reasons why my story has been different than theirs. I can tell you it wasn't primarily because of Christian books, Christian preaching, or even the Bible itself—

although they all were there to play their part when the time came. It certainly wasn't a church small group. (Honestly, the desire to attend organized church events is one of the very first things to 'go' when your struggling, isn't it? Despite what was intended by those who developed the program, the church-based small group can really come to *represent* everything that you are struggling with, rather than offer a pathway through it.)

No, the thing that held me to the sane course in a world gone mad—the specific medium God used to hold me to the sane course —was my steady, daily intimate relationship with my oldest and dearest friend, who never doubted, never wavered in his faith in God, or in his faith in me. David knew who I was at my best, who I wanted to be, and like a true friend he wasn't about to let me settle for something less—even when I was tempted to do so myself. Through many years, through rough patches too numerous to count, my wildest flights of existential angst had always been quickly brought to ground over a simple game of pool, a good workout, a pizza, a late night session of video game snowboarding, or an afternoon fly fishing on the South Platte River. Depending on the particular personal demon I was battling at the time, I might have said something like, "I know God loves everyone, I just don't think that includes me." Then David would just give me that look (a mixture of bemusement, disbelief, and impatience—like you see in the face of a weary parent forced to remind a small child of some rule they certainly had no excuse to have forgotten), and then he would reply with something refreshingly sane while nonchalantly sinking the eight ball in the corner pocket yet again. Something like, "Do you hear yourself right now? How can God love 'everyone', but not you—as by definition you would necessarily be included in 'everyone'?"

He may not have always been able to convince me instantaneously, but sooner or later his words—within the context of our years of friendship—always had the same effect; and that effect, in a word, was *grounding*. I'd like to think that at some points along the way I've been able to play that same role in his life as well. I hope that I have. I've seen him at his best, and I can vouch for the truth that it is far easier to let oneself slip away from where one needs to be than it is to watch your best friend do so. Chesterton may have been correct to say we are no closer to knowing ourselves than a distant star, but there is a friend that knows us "closer than a brother."

Now I can't claim to know what strength and encouragement, if any, our friendship has been able to offer to David over the years. What I do know is what he has been for me. In a constantly changing world where nothing remains the same for long, simply by being who he had always been, David often (at just the right times in fact) served as a stalwart reminder to me of the person that *I* had been, and honestly, really wanted to remain. I could say the same thing about David as C.S. Lewis had once written about one of his earliest Oxford friends, A.C. Harwood: "He was my one Horatio in a world of Hamlets."

To borrow from Robert Frost's enduring mental image: "Two roads diverged in a yellow wood, and I, I took the one less travelled by (the road of Friendship), and that has made all the difference."

> Alone among unsympathetic companions, I hold certain views and standards timidly, half ashamed to avow them and half doubtful if they can after all be right. Put me back among my Friends and in half an hour - in ten minutes - these same views and standards become once more indisputable...Theirs is the praise we really covet and the blame we really dread.

Can I just say it one more time?

The most important spiritual influence in any individual's life is their closest friends, their most intimate relationships.

Denied such intimate friends, a great portion of our soul must remain forever unknown. Apart from them we live far more alone than God ever intended, untethered from the dreams of our past, unsupported in the storms of our present, disconnected from our greatest spiritual resource and one of life's greatest joys.

BEFORE ANYTHING ELSE

We set out at the beginning of this chapter to answer the question, "Can the 'Real Deal'—deeply meaningful relationships—be expected to grow and thrive within even the best organized attempts at 'manufacturing' relationships?" To some extent, the answer is probably too complex to fit into any neat categories of 'yes' or 'no'. We've seen many of the challenges, but if the answer was emphatically 'no', then how is it that we can justify continuing our own ministry?

But I think there *is* a more conclusive answer. And that answer is that we've been asking the wrong question. Because the fact is we never should have been looking to 'organized religious programming' to bring us the Real Deal in the first place. No, this always *was* the proper province of the individual; this always *was* something we were meant to handle for ourselves. Here more than anywhere we must remember that, strictly speaking, you and I *are* the Church. Where two or more of us have gathered with Jesus presiding over our shared life together—there we have *become* the Church. Perhaps even we have become the Church at its very best, its intended form, its most glorious manifestation.

> ....whatever else you do, you must have a small fellowship to walk with you and fight with you and bandage your wounds...This is essential. This is what the Scriptures urge us to do. First. Foremost. Not as an addition to Sunday. Before anything else.
>
> (John Eldredge, *Waking the Dead*)

No programmatic attempts to provide us with a company of noble-hearted peers, brothers, and allies with whom to travel life's road is ever going to do a better job at meeting that need than we can do for ourselves. Than we *must* do for ourselves. Do for ourselves by the grace of God, of course: by the grace of the God who knows that we need it, who created us to desire it, and who—dare we believe it?—has made provision for us to have it.

> But, for a Christian, there are, strictly speaking, no chances. A secret Master of Ceremonies has been at work. Christ, who said to the disciples, "Ye have not chosen me, but I have chosen you," can truly say to every group of Christian friends "You have not chosen one another but I have chosen you for one another." At this feast it is He who has spread the board and it is He who has chosen the guests. It is He, we may dare to hope, who sometimes does, and always should, preside.
>
> (C.S. Lewis, *The Four Loves*)

TEN

DOWN THE
DRAGON'S THROAT

God is calling together little communities of the heart, to fight for one another and for the hearts of those who have not yet been set free. That camaraderie, that intimacy, that incredible impact by a few stouthearted souls - that is available. It is the Christian life as Jesus gave it to us. It is completely normal.

(John Eldredge, *Waking the Dead*)

Without more words, the two boys, still holding each other's hands, knelt together by the roadside. And they vowed to be true to each other so long as life should last; to share together whatever fortune might betide, whether it should be good or ill; to meet all dangers together, and to undertake all great enterprises in company; to rejoice together in success, and grieve together when sorrow should come; to devote their lives to the succor of the helpless and to the defence of the right; and, if need be, to die for each other.

(James Baldwin, *The Story of Roland*)

Looking back, I'd say we've been on quite a journey together through these pages. A meandering one at times to be sure, but hopefully each turn, each lazy bend in the river has carried us that much closer to our destination, that much further towards the waiting arms of the welcoming sea. If nothing else, I pray that your appreciation of, and desire for, deep, life-long friendships has increased exponentially as a result of the journey we've taken together through these pages. I doubt there is a better comparison, you know, than the enjoyment of an enduring friendship and, as C. S. Lewis put it, "the offer of a holiday at the sea." I think he would have fully agreed that a refusal to take this proffered path to joy was truly equivalent to an "ignorant child who wants to go on making mud pies in the slums because he has no idea what is meant by the offer of a holiday at the sea." (Lewis, *The Weight of Glory*)

Now as we come to the latter chapters of the journey, I suppose this is where you might expect me to offer some really 'helpful' and 'practical' tips and tools—maybe even an infallible step-by-step guide—for finding a fellowship of soulmates and bringing you a lifetime full of intimate, satisfying friendships.

Unfortunately I'm not a big fan of 'infallible' formulas—or formulas of any kind really. Consequently I don't spend much time trying to visualize life in formulaic terms, nor am I remotely qualified to offer them to my readers, who are no doubt far more familiar with their uses than I am. The very word 'formula' puts one in mind of scientific things, and I'll freely confess that I have neither the aptitude or even too much interest in the sciences. God bless those who do fill their mental space with such considerations: I'm sure we need them on our team. It's just not a position on the field I'm interested in playing. Now, I'm not apologizing for my unscientific mindset: I have been quite deliberate in focusing what little attention span I have at this age on experiencing things rather than on dissecting them. For example, I don't care nearly so much about people's theories of who *actually* wrote Shakespeare's plays: I just want the pleasure of reading them. And while there may in fact be a 'science' to building good friendships, treating the process with a scientific mindset is almost guaranteed to lead one down the wrong road. Philia, like all the loves, is a matter for the heart far more than it is a matter for the head.

You will have to forgive me, then, that this last portion of the book does not read like a 'how-to' manual for developing intimate friendships. For those that like such things, that manual is probably worth more attention than merely a few passing chapters at the end of this book. I'd say it's worth a book of its own; for the moment I leave the writing of such a book in someone else's much more well-suited hands than mine.

But I do want to leave you with something tangible, some attitude or approach or reorientation that will aid you in working towards the death of the Lone Wolf in your own life, and, hopefully, the resurrection and return of true friendship into your daily world. I pray that these somewhat random and by no means exhaustive musings will be more than enough to set you off down the correct path. Whether you choose to continue that journey we have been on—and what new and greater insights you may discover along the way—will of course be up to you.

THE DREAMS THAT WE DREAM

I confess that I remember very little of the thousands of sermons and messages I've heard preached in my lifetime. Now I don't know if that's a fairly common experience you can relate to or if I have incredibly poor recall for someone of otherwise normal intelligence. Considering that David has always claimed that I possess a superhuman knack for remembering every detail of some trip or event from the chronicles of our teenage adventures, I doubt that my powers of recall are really what's at issue. But for whatever reason, most of the messages I've heard through the years didn't offer the kind of catchy, lifelong 'handle' necessary for me to permanently hang on to them. I suppose knowing just how easily the world's great sermons are forgotten by the average man-in-the-pew has been one of the key reasons I've never wanted to be a head pastor. And why I've always thought it strange that as a church culture we hire our head pastors mostly for their speaking ability, and not for a great many other more important Christ-like qualities. But that's probably a discussion for another time.

Now, of the handful of messages that I do still remember, the oldest hails all the way back to my tenth grade church summer camp experience. The words that I have not forgotten from that week's opening talk were these: *"Life does not consist of the dreams you dream, but the choices you make."* I suppose they stuck with me to some degree because, honestly, I didn't like them very much. You see, if there's one thing I've always known about myself, it's that I'm a dreamer. I love to dream. And I love big dreams: the bigger the better. Doesn't matter if we're talking about mine or someone else's. In fact I enjoy few things more than encouraging other people's dreams—most especially because we live in a world of cynics, cranks and pessimists (of course they call themselves 'realists'), and it can be so hard to find anyone willing to give you something other than cautious, 'responsibly realistic' advice. Which is why if I could be compared to any character in the Bible, I'd be strongly tempted to choose Barnabas. Who wouldn't want to have the sort of reputation that led everyone to call him 'Son of Encouragement'?

Now at the same time, I do understand where that summer camp speaker was coming from all those years ago. Dreamers are often accused of coming with a factory installed fatal flaw: that they can be absolutely rubbish at follow-through. They have glorious visions, but lack something essential, something required for 'getting it done.' Or so the accusation goes. They can have the devil of a time getting the bright universe inside their head to come out and connect with the material universe around them. They may dream big, but they all too often end up living small.

I get all that. But as one of their number, I feel the need to defend the fact that it's not the fault of the dreaming that so many dreamers fail to convert their dreams into reality. The simple fact is that it is incredibly hard to turn *anything* new, fantastic, or unexpected into a reality. Ever. *For anyone.* So the problem isn't really that some people dream such bold dreams and then don't have what it takes to bring them about. The real problem is just the opposite. The real problem is that so few people dare to dream at all. And without having faced head-on the challenges of bringing one of their own dreams to life, they fail to see the inherent difficulties in doing so.

Now, whatever my defense of the matter, over the years I've rolled that old message around in my head like a pebble I can't quite shake out of my shoe, and I've discovered that there's a very opposite truth to my summer camp speaker's intended message, one that I think is equally important to consider. And that truth is this: life very much *does* consist of the dreams we dream, because it is our dreams that inform our choices. Do you get that? Our best choices—our most deliberate, intentional choices—are mostly made in the pursuit of some specific goals that we have set for ourselves. But how is it that we come up with these goals? Isn't it obvious that to a great extent, we come up with our goals in response to our dreams?

The boy who dreams of being a business tycoon one day is the boy who starts his own lawn mowing business at age twelve; who hires his little brother and his friend down the street in order to expand his growing empire; who keeps his books religiously and saves his hard earned dollars assiduously. But the boy who dreams of a professional sports career may not do any of those things: he will be too busy spending every free moment on the court or on the field, perfecting his game. Clearly the choices each of these boys make are merely an extension of the dreams that drive them.

Now, I take the time to mention all this because for me it holds the central answer to the question, *"How do we go from where we are—living in relative relational poverty compared to almost every culture and every era that has gone before us—to a place where we can personally experience deep, satisfying, lifelong friendships?"* And my answer is this: the first step towards experiencing great friendships is simply to set our hearts on finding them.

The first step towards experiencing great friendships is to set our hearts on finding them.

We must seek passage out of the relational desert we were born and raised in and somehow retrain ourselves to dream new dreams— dream them, and then allow our most significant choices to lead us in the direction of those bright dreams. We must raise Friendship back to the place of honor it once held for our ancestors, which requires that we become captivated by its beauty and goodness once again, as they had been. We intentionally romance our own hearts and fill our own minds with the old stories that dare teach us to dream once again of the great joy found in traveling through life with soulmates, kindred spirits, epic Fellowships. We go there by believing that the journey is worth taking, no matter the cost. Because sometimes life really *does* consist of the dreams that we dream.

THE SUMMER OF '89

When you grow up in the Midwest, far from either coast and thus far from the glamour of the entertainment industry, it's only natural that certain places you've never visited but have seen depicted count-less times in film and television become infused with a romantic aura hardly befitting their extremely mundane reality.

Such a place for me in the summer of '89 was the Los Angeles

International Airport. The first glimpse with my own eyes of the iconic space-age restaurant standing imposingly at the center of the hub of terminals felt like I had wandered onto the set of my favorite childhood show, *Remington Steele*. I half expected to see Steele and his beautiful and intelligent associate Laura Holt leap out of a long black Lincoln Continental limousine and pelt across six lanes of dangerously unconcerned airport traffic in pursuit of some white collar criminal desperately trying to flee the country with a suitcase full of purloined jewels, pilfered *objets d'art*, plates for counterfeiting money, or a million dollars in fraudulent insurance payouts. (The crimes and the criminals who committed them came and went, but—in the most comforting way imaginable—the story arc never significantly varied. It was truly the golden age of 80's romantic crime shows at their delightfully predictable best.)

Although my first visit to one of the most recognizable of t.v. landmarks didn't include the sighting of any famous personages, it hardly fell short of all my romantic feelings of awe and excitement. After all, I was still an eager youth of nineteen, and setting out to embark on the adventure of a lifetime. David had just made the five hour flight from Detroit, and was waiting for me inside the terminal, luggage in tow, lamenting the exorbitant cost of a glass of airport orange juice. Impatiently we waited together for the boarding call that would invite us to climb aboard the massive Boeing 747 that was to carry us to Hong Kong in search of romance and adventure.

You can imagine that four weeks on the far side of the world at such a raw, youthful age was more than adventure enough. But what took the whole trip to an emotional intensity unparalleled in all my life's adventures since was the fact that we were to be spending those four weeks in the home of the girl we had both been in love with for most of our teenage years. Yes, *both* of us. Madly in love with the *same* girl. Nor was it a passing craze: I had been hopelessly in love with her since the first moment I had met her six years prior. David had grown to love her more slowly, but no less ardently than I as the years had passed. So there we were, two best friends, both in agreement that they had found the woman of their dreams. Unfortunately, it was the same woman. Quite a pickle indeed. It all makes for a great, sad story really—if, like me, you happen to be a hopeless romantic who enjoys great, sad stories.

Mostly that's a tale for another time. What matters here is the depth of my friendship with David, the strength of our commitment to one another, and our sincere vows to never let 'the girl' come between us. Truth be told, I was already ninety-eight percent sure that she wasn't interested in me romantically. She might have viewed me as one of her best friends in the whole world, but something essential lacking in the area of physical attraction kept our love story a very one-sided affair. At the same time, I knew for absolute *fact* that she had liked David from the very beginning. In short, I knew my suit was hopeless. I knew that the great love of my life would not choose me, that the greatest love story of my life—up to that point—would most certainly end in the bitter pain of unrequited love. And even when during the long transpacific flight over, we toasted one another's fortunes in love and agreed 'may the best man win'—even then, I knew the words were nothing but 'good form', for the results had never been in doubt: this love triangle never had been a two horse race.

And yet..and yet, even in the knowledge of all the heartache that lay in store for me, my one hope—my ardent prayer—was that if she had to love another, that other might be my best friend. It just *had* to be David, and not some other random guy whose victory could not be vicariously enjoyed. I was one-hundred percent in David's corner. In fact I was resolved to aid them in coming together in whatever functions a best friend and intimate confidante was expected to perform in such situations, even if it meant disregarding the most powerful emotions I had ever experienced.

And you know what? Crazy as it sounds, I knew it was going to be okay. *I* was going to be okay, because although I was sure to lose 'the girl', I wasn't about to lose my best friend in the process. I know that may sound like a consolation prize to most modern readers, born and bred as we all are into a culture that worships romantic love while barely acknowledging friendship. But I was different. I *wanted* to be different. I wanted to live my life according to the Old Ways; I wanted to be a 'romantic' about more things than just romantic love. Of course my romantic worldview included the incomparable wonders and delights of falling in love; but it was not so impoverished that it held this one thing in view and nothing more: it also included a great many other wondrous things besides. Unbreakable oaths of friendship, for instance. Heroic sacrifices for the happiness of others. Jesus of Nazareth had been recorded as saying that greater love had no man than the one who laid down his life for his friends, and I, for one, was willing to believe that He knew something about great love that the modern world did not. Chivalry in victory, nobility in defeat, the courage to aim high, to dream impossible dreams: all these mattered to me as well.

EROS VS. PHILIA

As a matter of personal fact, it had always seemed strange to me that of all the great things our ancestors thought worth living for, that *Eros*—romantic love—alone had survived as the final remaining relic from the wreck and ruin of their once proud civilization. As moderns we can readily accept that Romeo Montague might reasonably choose to die for the loss of his fair Juliet. Why could we not also see that Damon was equally reasonable in offering to die for the saving of his dear friend Pythias? Again, though we certainly don't condone it, we may have some sympathy for the kind of romantic desire that caused King David to gamble his whole kingdom for the love of the beautiful but forbidden Bathsheeba. Why could we not have equal sympathy for King Saul's son Jonathan, who was willing to relinquish his prior right to that same kingdom for the sake of his friendship with that very same David? If a common ingredient of the human experience was a willingness (though of course not always the opportunity or the necessity) to forsake all to win or gain the love of the Golden Haired Beauty, why could we not see that it was of similar pathos and grandeur (though not a similar experience) to forsake all for the love of a noble-hearted and dear Brother?

I realize we've all been pretty much born and bred into a world that venerates and idolizes romantic love as life's greatest experience. We've been weaned from our earliest childhood on an endless stream of stories telling us to prepare, look out for, and seek with all our will for the day that the siren call of inexorable Eros resounds in our own hearts. Nor was I any different. Siren call indeed! At age six I fell in love for the first time—not with a person exactly—but with the mere *suggestion* of a person, a suggestion that appeared in the shape of a song. In the shape of the voice of an angel. It was music appreciation class at Randolph Elementary School, and we were watching a filmstrip of the Broadway musical *Annie*. (Yes, a filmstrip, if you even know what that is. Prehistoric times were those.) By the time the cassette recorder had finished playing the now-famous song *"Tomorrow"*, I was in love with whatever angelic being was behind that voice. A couple of years later Olivia Newton John sang *"Hopelessly Devoted to You"* in the now classic movie-musical *Grease*, and I was head-over-heels in love again. Seriously. By that time I figured I was worldly enough to understand all about love. After all, I had grown up since Annie: I had reached the wise and venerable age of eight!

So, yeah. I get it. If anyone was ever a child of a culture that enthroned Eros (romantic love) as a god to be worshipped with unquestioning obedience, that child was me.

In an age of Reason that has forsaken its belief in both the Fairy Tale and most of the wild and wonderful magic that goes into making the sort of world where Fairy Tales are viable explanations of Truth, it is odd that somehow this Fairy Tale of the 'golden-haired beauty' who promises everlasting happiness yet survives. And survives in the face of the mass of actual human testimony, mind you. Statistics certainly can't affirm this wild assertion straight out of fairyland that finding, falling in love with, and marrying the man or woman of your dreams has any more direct influence on one's ultimate happiness than the tossing of a coin: both actions appear to offer no better than a fifty-fifty chance of a positive outcome.

Now, I don't mention this to suggest that there needs to be an either/or battle between the two ideals of romantic love and highly prized, lifelong, deep male (or female) friendships. The two need not—must not—continue to be viewed as if they are mutually exclusive lifestyle choices. My temptation to place the two in juxtaposition at all is driven by the fact that we happen to live in a society that treats the one like it's the Holy Grail of all earthly happiness, and the other like it's merely the province of immature college frat boys. Clearly there's some glaring inconsistencies with this grossly unfavorable comparison. There's way more that's going on in this popular perception than just an honest rendering of the actual human experiences we have personally known or seen played out before us in the lives of others. And yet, somehow, this worship of romantic fulfillment coupled with a comparative denigration of platonic friendship has become the dominant narrative of our Age, one we have swallowed hook, line, and sinker. As we all know by heart at this point, the popularized fable of our day follows along these lines: Boy meets 'The Gang'. Then Boy meets Girl. Naturally Boy falls in love with Girl. Then Boy forsakes everything (including 'The Gang') to be with Girl. Finally Boy and Girl live happily ever after, fully experiencing all of life's wonders and delights by staring exclusively into one another's eyes for all of eternity.

And of course, in the end, by enthroning Eros we have ruined not only the hope of Philia (brotherly love), but also Eros itself. By demanding that it satisfies every last one of our wildly various relational needs, we have created an environment where it is destined to fail, destined to disappoint.

Despite the actual facts however, we all have been raised as children of our modern society and steeped in its prevailing relational myth. How can we ever hope to balance the scales until our hearts and imaginations are being fed on the epic beauty of Philia with the same consistent intentionality that our culture uses to train us up into the prevailing obsession of our Time?

We *need* to balance the scales. We need to re-imagine what relational happiness could look like, and from what quarters it is to be found—what the province of Eros, and what of Philia.

We need to dream the right dreams.

And then we need to feed those dreams.

How do we feed them?

One epic story at a time.

AN UNBEARABLE LOSS

When the final installment of *The Lord of the Rings* film trilogy hit the theaters I happened to be visiting family in California for the Christmas holidays. A group of extended family members went to see the movie together—I don't really remember exactly who all was there that day. What I do remember is that when the movie ended, the entire theatre had emptied before I had even stirred from my seat. I was just sitting there, glassy eyed, watching the credits roll to the last note of the closing song. I was absolutely wrecked. Gutted. No movie has ever left me feeling that emotional drained, and yet in some way still so full of emotion at the same time. Not *Braveheart*.

Not *Schindler's List*. Not *Gladiator*. Not even *The Mission*. (I name the top four contenders that might have dared come close in my memory. But not close enough for a fair comparison.) And yes, some of that emotion was surely because after three consecutive years of releases, there would be no more installments to look forward to. And some of it was no doubt because of what an epic adventure it was—the perfect mythical telling of all I believe to be true about the real universe which we inhabit. A small Fellowship of the faithful, fighting against all odds to overcome a terrible Evil that threatened to engulf the world and enslave every living thing to its dark purpose. And then, the great 'eucatastrophe' as Tolkien himself named it: an unexpected turn of events that brings light and joy and ushers in a Kingdom of delight and goodness almost too good to be true.

But if this were all I was experiencing, why the blankness? Why the feeling of being totally gutted?

No, the thing that left me slumped in my theatre chair, fighting back sobs from some deep place in my chest was the parting of the friends at the end of the story. "Well, here at last dear friends, on the shores of the Sea comes the end of our Fellowship in Middle-Earth. Go in peace! I will not say: do not weep; for not all tears are an evil." (Tolkien, *The Return of the King*)

Their dear friend, counselor, chief motivator and guide was leaving forever, crossing over the sundering Sea on the last tall ship to depart from the Grey Havens. There would be no more adventures together. Ever. The finality of this parting between the four hobbits and their beloved Gandalf was sorrow enough to cast a bittersweet light over the story's ending.

But there is more heartache to come. We watch as it begins to dawn on Merry, Pippin, and Samwise—even as it begins to dawn on us in the theatre—that Frodo also intends to depart into the Undying Lands as well.

And that's when I lost it.

You see, for me the entire epic story—despite being such a complete, mythic tale full of so many essential themes—had really been ultimately about one thing above all others. It had been about *Friendship*. Never-say-die, come-what-may, follow-you-to-the-gates-of-Mordor type Friendship. And of all the many such friendships thus woven throughout the tale—Merry and Pippin, Legolas and Gimli, Gandalf and Aragorn—even that central theme had narrowed down to one particular point of ultimate emphasis: the friendship between Frodo and Sam. At the very heart of Tolkien's magnificent fantasy world, resplendent though it was with great warriors, powerful wizards, massive forces of both good and evil arrayed for battle in numbers beyond reckoning, we find exalted above them all the power inherent in the love between two friends—the smallest and most unassuming in fact, of all the peoples that have gone to war for the fate of Middle Earth. More than anything else it is here, in the relentless loyalty and stubbornly determined love of the little gardener from the Shire, Samwise Gamgee, that we discover the power strong enough to bring down Sauron's kingdom of darkness and save all the free people of Middle Earth. I don't think I've ever seen portrayed a more powerful depiction of epic friendship than this one between the two simple hobbits, Frodo and Sam.

Which I hope goes to explain what I was feeling when Sam suddenly realizes that Frodo is leaving—that after all their shared journeys he's now going where Sam cannot follow, going to a place where there is no hope of return, no possibility of ever seeing him again through all the long ages of the world to come. And as I sat there long after the final scene had faded, alone in the theatre, my heart rebelled with rising anger against the way the movie had ended. *No, you can't do that. You can't pretend that this is a happy story when Sam has to lose Frodo, when he has to live the rest of his life without his best friend. If that's how it ends, what was the point of it all?*

Now, I know. There *was* a point to it all. The story had been about saving the entire world from destruction. And that had been accomplished. So my own feelings betrayed a definite bias on my part, a projection onto Frodo and Sam's story something of my own approach to the world, an approach that perfectly echoed Lewis' words yet again: "Life, natural life, has no greater gift to give."

Music, art, poetry, literature, nature, beauty in all its forms: fantastic, extravagant and undeserved gifts, all of them. God surely had not been frugal in scattering His good gifts, but had done so with a hearty will, with a lavish abandon none could have predicted, no mind could have conceived. To live at all was to embark on a grand romp through fields strewn with delights scattered abroad by a liberal hand, like partaking of a never ending Easter egg hunt. And yet, there in the midst of all these pleasures I had discovered, for my money crowning them all, the gift of True Friendship.

I think that when Sam lost Frodo, I felt the sting of the loss so sharply because I too had been blessed with a Frodo. And to have a Frodo was to understand what it would be like to lose a Frodo. And losing my Frodo was not a loss that I thought I could bear.

BROTHER TO BROTHER

Sometimes, when you do turn to the great, old tales for inspiration, you will notice a curious oddity, a relic of other times completely ignored in the mainstream of our culture today: the oath of friendship, the vows of brotherhood. Now, I know if I were to suggest that our world is the poorer for the loss of these, the knee-jerk Christian reaction would be to disagree—to point out that Jesus told us making oaths was a bad thing. "Do not swear an oath at all, either by heaven, for it is God's throne, or by the earth." (Matt. 5:34).

And yet, right there in the heart of one of our most cherished sacraments—a very present reminder of the beauty and significance of such ancient things—we continue to highly revere the most famous of all oaths: the wedding vows, made between millions of brides and grooms each and every year. And yes, I realize those vows are perpetually being broken. And I'm sure a great many are spoken out of good form, with no real intention to be bound by them if the winds of romance begin to blow from another point on the compass in the years ahead. But for all that, there are also countless families that have remained intact because of those vows, because of a noble commitment to stand by them no matter what, because some cour- ageous men and certain good-hearted women still want their word and their oath to mean something, still want their 'yay' to be 'yay' and their 'nay' to be 'nay'.

In our society today judges also still take oaths. People holding certain public offices take oaths. Witnesses in court take oaths. Military personnel, I believe, are still proud to be bound by oaths of honor and duty. Many doctors still swear to, and attempt to adhere to, the ancient oath of Hippocrates. Monks and nuns, though much marginalized in today's world, still exist, and still are bound by oaths of poverty, chastity, and obedience—oaths that have changed very little in a thousand years and more.

Most of those examples are of oaths to duty and to society as a whole. But there have also always been very personal, very relational oaths—more akin to the marriage vows—oaths made to friendship, to the Fellowship. The fabled cry of the Musketeer I have mentioned so often already is in itself more of an oath than a mere sentiment, a public pronouncement of a private agreement: that no matter how one of their company might feel in the moment, their actions will be ruled by their unwavering commitment to give their last breath to always protect the King and, more to our point, swiftly come to the defense of their brother musketeers at need.

My favorite oaths of Fellowship though are those that were a part of the chivalric traditions of the knighthood—both fictional and historical. The film *First Knight* portrayed this aspect of the famed

Arthurian Legend so powerfully that it remains to this day a central image for me of everything that epic Friendship can be, when at its very best. In the film Richard Gere plays a free-spirited 'lone wolf' version of the well-known hero Lancelot (very much a change from his traditional role in all the oldest legends) who comes to Camelot because he has inadvertently fallen in love with the King's bride-to-be, Lady Guinevere. He comes to the King's court for Guinevere: but he stays because he falls in love with something even harder to resist than her beauty. He stays because he falls in love with Arthur's great dream, his vision for a better world: at the center of which is a band of mighty warriors that have been offered a glorious cause worth living for and a fellowship of noble hearts worth dying for. After having cared for nothing or no one but himself most of his life, Lancelot is deeply moved—beyond even his romantic desires for the Queen—at the invitation to join such an epic gathering as that of Arthur's Round Table. His desire is granted, and in an unforgettable scene (for anyone who dreams of such things), each of Arthur's knights welcomes the new addition to their fellowship, *Sir* Lancelot, by placing their hand on his shoulder and repeating the vow, "Brother to brother, yours in life and death."

In one swift moment we see Lancelot, the consummate lifelong Lone Wolf, reintegrated into not just *a* pack, but into perhaps the most epic, heroic, devoted 'packs' ever to grace the pages of human history or legend. Whether you are thirteen, thirty-seven, or fifty-five, you cannot watch that scene without a longing awakening inside to have some similar adventure fall to your lot. Oh, how the heart inside of us all longs to be noticed by some Great King: chosen, called forth, invited to join his heroic mission and take our irreplaceable and much needed role standing alongside his band of equally heroic and devoted warriors, our true brothers.

And you know what?

That's *exactly* the story that God is telling.

And it's the message that our own ministry exists to share with all the lost and wandering—but brave—hearts dying to hear that this is really what Christianity means.

What Christianity is.

What Christianity offers.

> God is calling together little communities of the heart, to fight for one another and for the hearts of those who have not yet been set free. That camaraderie, that intimacy, that incredible impact by a few stouthearted souls—that is available. It is the Christian life as Jesus gave it to us. It is completely normal.
>
> (John Eldredge, *Waking the Dead*)

Completely normal? Intimate friendship that is also missional, purposeful, significant to the very core? How the world will be shaken when such a lifestyle becomes 'normal' for us!

FAITHFUL TO THE END

One Christmas a dozen years back or so I took a shot at writing a sort of oath of my own as a gift for David. Although I've always considered myself a pretty good writer, I've never dared to claim any ability at poetry, so it was a bit of a stretch for me. This was during a time of explosive spiritual growth that David and I were journeying through daily together—despite living nearly fifteen-hundred miles apart. The oath sums up both the depth of our friendship during that period, as well as the epic vision of that friendship that we were deliberately nurturing as we labored to come out of the 'fog of the familiar' and learn to see the world from a more glorious, significant, and ultimately truer perspective. It perhaps even predates the first crude visions of our ministry, The Warrior's Path, that was yet to grow out of our own experience with Epic Christianity.

Through darkest night and deepest woe
Though demons howl in pits below
And twists of fortune sad to know
Call to account the debt I owe

Yet debt and oath and bonds shall hold
Me to your side when night grows cold
For Friendship old makes hearts grow bold
And proves the warriors worth in gold

Hope shall fail, the way more bleak
Ere we shall find the Path we seek
But blackest night and evils grim
Will bind us closer, we and Him
To death's dark door you can depend
I will stand faithful to the End.

And further still, if we shall roam
Beyond the walls of earthly dome
To meet on shores beside the foam
Our bond reborn in celestial home.

So raise the helm and set the lance
Wipe the tears, strike up the dance
Square the shoulders, firm the stance
No strength, no virtue left to chance.

Side by side and back to back
We'll weather every foul attack
And break the spells of darkest Hell
With songs of joy like ringing bells
When laughter falls in cataracts.

When you think about the beauty of oaths of allegiance and the impact they can have in our lives, you must remember that for most of us, our commitment to the life of a Lone Wolf always had something to do with protecting ourselves from loss. At the heart of it you can almost always find a broken relationship—whether that experience of loss came through abandonment, betrayal, or even death. It was this above all else—the sense that no one could be trusted to stick around—that drove us to determine to need no one, to make life work on our own. You can understand, then, how the healing of that old wound begins to happen in that moment when you realize *here* is someone who would dare to bind themselves to you in vows of undying friendship, *here* is someone you can depend on through thick and thin. Much like the marriage vows, such promises between friends can be the firm foundation upon which trust and intimacy can build.

Somewhere around the same time that I wrote that poem, David related to me a vision of his that I found to be even more moving than what I had myself deliberately put into words. The vision itself referenced the opening scene from the Daniel Day Lewis film version of *The Last of the Mohicans*, a scene that we both knew well and felt deeply drawn to as an ideal display of masculine friendship in action. The opening sequence depicts the three heroes Hawkeye, Chingachgook and his son Uncas (for whom the story is titled) racing together through the woods, dodging, cutting, leaping, rifles in hand, chasing after their prey in silent unison—an image of determined purpose in the context of relational dependence and perfect understanding of one another. "As I was pondering all this this morning," David wrote, "I had a vision of you and I and Jesus running in unison through a beautiful wood—one in fellowship, motive, plan, goal. I don't know where we were going, but it was important, and it felt incredible. It was epic. And it is coming. Your brother for eternity, David."

Wow. Can you imagine? Having something like that to look forward to one day in the restored Kingdom of God? It's exciting, and hopeful beyond description—I know it would radically transform my attitude towards daily life if I were able to keep a future like that always fresh in my heart and vividly real before my mind's eye. And to be honest, I have to point out that it's also *radically* different from what most organized religion is offering up in today's world.

I don't want to beat a dead horse, and we've already said plenty about the kinds of groups the church mostly has on offer in the last chapters. But I think the deprivation we tend to experience in those settings is once again deeply tied to the weak and insipid nature of our dreams of *what those little fellowships could be*. Inspire the dream, and you change the reality. That is to say, inspire the dream and you raise the expectations; raise the expectations and soon people are demanding that the experience comes nearer to those expectations. At least somewhere in the same ballpark. They become, as we ourselves have become, *spoiled for the ordinary*. (Which, by the way is a *good* thing.) Simply paint an alluring picture of the Real Deal, and I think you will find that wild horses would not keep men (and women) from chasing hard after that vision.

OUR TRUE HEART'S DESIRE

You've got to understand that men don't want to be told that their highest glory and purpose in life is merely to 'be good', 'stay in line', go to church and get 'plugged in' to some organized church activity, as if they are some sort of toaster oven or kitchen appliance. No, a man wants to be, needs to be, handpicked. Chosen. The invitation into the Fellowship needs to be personal, it needs to be tailor-made to the man himself and to his irreplaceable place in God's battle plans to redeem the world from darkness. It needs to demand the very best of him—all his passion, all his strength, all his resources.

In his now classic fairy tale *Phantastes*, George Macdonald painted what has been for me the most complete and enduring picture of
the kind of epic, intimate, purposeful Friendship that I believe I was
made for—that I believe *you* were made for. Macdonald's main
character, Anodos, has awoken one morning in his ancestral High-
land home to find a river running through his bedroom. Following
its course, he stumbles across the border of our world and into the
wild and unpredictable land of Fairie, where an unimaginable series
of adventures befall him. Somewhere near the end of his fantastic
sojourn, after he has undergone many trials and learned many lessons,
he comes across a lonely tower occupied by two brothers. They are,
in fact, princes of the realm: the only sons of a beloved, aging king.
The brothers welcome him into their fellowship with unexpected
warmth and eagerness, and a surprised but flattered Anodos soon
discovers that this is because he has been *expected*. Unbeknownst to
Anodos, a great Providence has sent him to the brothers so that he
might aid them in the heroic task they have pledged themselves to
accomplish—or die trying. It turns out that the brothers' kingdom is
enslaved by three terrible giants whom no one has been able to
defeat—though many have tried and died in the attempt. The two
noble brothers have sworn to dedicate their life to defeating the
giants and freeing their father's lands from their tyranny, but being
only two knights against three giants, they have been waiting for a
'brother' worthy to share with them in the perilous adventure. And
although the fight is nothing to him personally—although he could
easily have packed up and moved on—Anodos happily agrees to join
them. Without hesitation he agrees to risk his life by accepting the
role of the missing third hero.

Considering the risk, for goodness sake *why*? If there was ever a
time to invoke the old advice to 'pick one's battles', to remind the
others that this simply 'wasn't *his* fight', wouldn't this have been the
time?

Some of his response, I suppose, was simply his allegiance to the vows of all knights errant (though he, like you and I, had only read of them): which, in part, was the vow to always take the adventure that befalls you without hesitation. But I also think he was motivated by something more—if I can judge by the feelings that arose in me when I read the story for the first time. I think that perhaps the offered invitation, for all its danger, was the sort of thing he had been waiting for his entire life: "Now if you will join us, we will soon teach you to make your armour, and we will fight together, and work together, and love each other as three never loved before." (George Macdonald, *Phantastes*)

That, my friends, in so concise a form you could almost consider it poetry, is everything I have meant to say in this chapter, everything I hoped to communicate. Macdonald's hero, young Anodos, would happily sell everything—even his own life—for the rare chance he has been offered to live in such heroic fellowship among such noble hearted brothers. He understood that, journey far and wide though he might, no better possible life was to be found. He could echo Cicero, that most famous of Roman statesmen, who said in his classic treatise *De Amicitia*, "All I can do is urge you to regard friendship as the greatest thing in the world; for there is nothing which so fits in with our nature, or is so exactly what we want in prosperity or adversity."

And my question to you is this: if the same invitation offered to Anodos was given to you, how would you respond? Has the dream of epic friendship been fostered and nurtured deeply enough in your soul that you would recognize the voice of one of your true heart's desire when it called? Would you have the courage, the hopefulness, the willingness to let go of the Lone Wolf persona you hide behind, to answer the call?

I pray that you would.

The world is waiting; the heavens are watching. Will you find your true-hearted brothers in time to defeat the darkness and free those many in need of rescue? Will you see, before it's too late, that "the powerful play goes on, and you may contribute a verse?"

I pray that you will.

ELEVEN

THE RETURN OF
THE PACK

And so at length Eomer and Aragorn met in the midst of the battle, and
they leaned on their swords and looked on one another and were glad.
"Thus we meet again, though all the hosts of Mordor lay between us,:
said Aragorn. "Did I not say so at the Hornburg?" "So you spoke," said
Eomer, "and never was a meeting of friends more joyful...you come none
too soon, my friend. Much loss and sorrow has befallen us." "Then let us
avenge it, ere we speak of it!" said Aragorn. And they rode back to the
battle together.   (J.R.R. Tolkien, *The Return of the King*)

There are a great many more things that could be said, that *need*
to be said—if we are to begin to open our hearts to the possibility of experiencing more of God's love and goodness through the
sacrament of satisfying, lifelong friendships. There is so much to be
said, for the simple reason that we are going to find that the path
forward is anything but clearly marked. The relational terrain ahead
is covered with generations of overgrowth. We are going to have to
become lone trailblazers in our own corners of the world, our own
little spheres of influence. Perhaps at first deeply misunderstood

trailblazers. Returning Friendship to the place of significance it was meant to hold will be an adventure of the heart we must dare attempt in a world that is hostile to the very nature of our task—a world that can offer us almost no frame of reference for how we are to proceed.

With that in mind, I want to offer a few more things to be aware of that may help pave a path forward into experiencing so much more of this gift from God than we have thus far known.

YOU'LL HAVE TO FIGHT FOR IT

Now, I'm under no illusion that my experience with friendship is very common in today's hyper-paced world. In case you've forgotten, this is Lone Wolf country, remember? Most people don't enjoy lifelong, intimate, central-to-their-life's-journey type friendships. Did I say *most* people? I don't think I know *anyone* that has the kind of relationship that David and I enjoy. If it was a more common experience, I certainly wouldn't have felt the need to write this book. No, being blessed with a lifelong best friend is certainly not something I have ever taken for granted—and less so with each passing year. And although mostly I view that friendship *as* a blessing from God—an undeserved, unmerited gift—it is also in many ways a living work of art: one that I have had a key role in bringing to life. I don't say that to boast. Again, mostly I see it as a sheer undeserved Gift. I am honored by the friendship of one of the healthiest, happiest, most enjoyable human beings on the planet. And I am often amazed that of all the other more fascinating, entertaining, lovable people in the world to choose from—all the people whose personalities bubble with charm, wit, intelligence, culture—I have somehow been blessed to get to play the partnering role of 'Butch Cassidy' to his 'Sundance Kid'. It is certainly for no excellencies of my own—of that I am sure.

But at the same time, what you need to hear in your own pursuit of epic friendship is this: you just don't maintain a vibrant, intimate, vitally central-to-your-life friendship for thirty-five years *by accident*, by letting things simply 'play themselves out'. There are too many impediments, too many interruptions, too many twists and turns in life's path for that to just somehow 'work'. I've no doubt, looking back on the story of your life, you can attest to the truth of it. It's undeniable: the modern world is simply not set up to be conducive to great friendships.

It wasn't a no-brainer that David and I would survive being in love with the same girl in our teen years, you know. That type of situation has spelled the end of many, many friendships. Leaving home to attend different colleges was another natural breaking moment. New adventures, new horizons, new and very dear friends. But we fought on, strove to maintain the old life while incorporating the new one. We survived those first few years by resorting to handwritten correspondence! (Yes, those were the days before the invention of the cell phone.) Then my parents moved the family home to Southern California, at which point we no longer even had school holidays to look forward to. After grad school our paths both returned to Michigan for the better part of seven years, but then it was his family's turn to move away to the foothills of the Rocky Mountains, leaving me behind. Just too many challenges to overcome? Certainly would have been, if the dream of 'Butch and Sundance'—the dream we talked about in the last chapter—hadn't been so deeply written on our hearts.

Indeed, like any specially great relationship, *you've got to be intentional* if you are going to make a great, lasting friendship. And that intentionality will be tested at every turn in this world of ours—this world that doesn't hold the same values, doesn't understand what motivates you to make the choices that you do. And because there is so little sympathy, you won't be able to go to the modern world

looking to get your motivation rejuvenated, either. You'll be completely on your own. (How often will you even find that the other
person in the relationship is of no help to your pursuit?) Which is
precisely why you will need deeply implanted in your imagination a
robust, epic and captivating vision of the glorious thing you are
pursuing, and an unswerving commitment to keeping at it when all
feels set against you. Because, in today's world...it pretty much is.

I CHOOSE YOU

Speaking of the world being set against you, another thing we'll
have to come to terms with is that true Friendship, by a sort of sad
necessity, is always going to require and include a certain amount of
'exclusivity'. Now, I know: the present cultural mood is *always*
against exclusivity in any form. The mere word itself is usually met
with suspicion, if not violence and hatred. And yet, I repeat: all the
really good friendships are built upon it. Is it any wonder then that
in this cultural climate real, deep friendships are on the decline? All
the talk these days is heavily biased towards the very opposite—
towards inclusiveness. It's sort of the watchword of this generation.
Again, that's not something I need to point out to you—I'll bet
you've run up against some campaign for inclusiveness in one of its
several manifestations this very week.

And that's fine, as far as it goes.

As far as it *ought* to go.

But it has obvious limits (well, they should be obvious to anyone
who can think for themselves). Do we really want, for example,
inclusiveness *in our marriages*? (All playful joking aside, I hope the
answer to that one is pretty obvious to you.) When we choose a
woman to marry, by necessity we are excluding all other women from
holding the title of 'wife' in our family. All choices, for that matter,
by nature have an element of exclusivity about them. It is inherent in

the very idea of 'making a choice'. When we turn left, we exclude from our present situation whatever adventures might have been waiting for us if we had in fact chosen to turn right. When you come to a fork in the road, you cannot take both the left fork and the right fork at the same time. It is permissible that you fall in love with two women, but according to New Testament morality and the laws of our nation, you are constrained in your choice to marry but one of them.

Now, relationships are in one sense inherently exclusive for the very simple reason that they are not judgements of worth, but *descriptions of how two people stand in relation to one another*. Thus the word 'relationship'. When I state, for instance, that a particular woman is *not* my wife or the mother of my children, I am not implying anything about her *objective* beauty, goodness, or importance to the world. I am merely stating that I did not marry her, that she did not bear our children. Search though you might, you will not find her name on their birth certificates. And when I meet such a woman, as my appreciation for her good qualities grows, I don't show that appreciation by calling her 'wife'. No matter what Christ-centered relationship we may develop, she is forever excluded from standing in this one particular *relation* to my universe that has already been filled—quite exclusively—by someone else.

So, too with Friendship. Because it is a choice between an endless number of available options, it is inherently exclusive and extremely limited. Not intentionally. Not maliciously. But there's simply no avoiding it. Because the very heartbeat of any deep and lasting friendship is summed up in this one simple-to-remember phrase: *I choose you*. Again, and again, day after day, I choose you. Surrounded by an endless sea of humanity, with new relationships constantly waiting to be formed, I still come back to you. I choose you to sit with in a cafeteria filled with other people, all of whom are equally as special as you in the eyes of God—perhaps even better suited as a choice for lifelong friendship. But I choose you nevertheless, and I stand by my choice, because that's what it means to be friends. I choose you when I've got a free afternoon on my hands. Or even when I'm so busy that something else will have to go undone: I still choose you anyway. I choose you when I reach for my phone, to connect with the outside world via text—even though I have two hundred other contacts readily at my fingertips. I make that same choice again and again—a dozen times a day.

Now, that is not to say that friendship speaks with the promise, "I choose *only* you." Where walking through life with one soulmate is a fantastic prize beyond our normal expectations, walking in the same intimacy with a fellowship of three or four like-hearted allies is yet better still by far.

> In each of my friends there is something that only some other friend can fully bring out. By myself I am not large enough to call the whole man into activity; I want other lights than my own to show all his facets...Two friends delight to be joined by a third, and three by a fourth, if only the newcomer is qualified to become a real friend.
>
> (Lewis, *The Four Loves*)

And yet there *is* a limit to how far the fellowship can grow and still remain personal, intimate, and bound by mutual affection. The exclusivity, at some level, must remain. But then, if we've bought into the cultural narrative that opposes all exclusive behavior, we won't have the courage to make the kinds of decisions necessary to build a robust and meaningful friendship. We must understand that here, in this particular pursuit, is neither the time or place to be worrying about pleasing 'the crowd'. If we insist that, in order to be 'fair', we will only go as deep with the one or two individuals that we most prefer to spend time with as we are able to also go with all of our acquaintances, we are not improving anyone's situation by being thus 'inclusive' in our behavior. Doing so won't give anything to the masses besides 'fair and equal treatment'. But we will have deprived a chosen few—and ourselves—of one of life's greatest treasures. "People who bore one another should meet seldom;" wrote C. S. Lewis, "people who interest one another, often." (The Four Loves)

It is curious to note that even in Lewis' life you will occasionally read a report from someone who knew him personally down through the years that dares to argue Lewis didn't know how to do 'good' friendship! Of course such reports came from people on the outer fringe, the ones that a lack of time or space or mutual interest kept just beyond the warmest glow of Jack's inner circle. (All who knew him at a personal level called him 'Jack'.) The accusation can hardly be taken at face value: not of the man whose friends meant so very much to him, whose literary fellowship with J.R.R. Tolkien and the other 'Inklings' will probably live in popular legend for many ages to come. It can hardly be believed of the man who kept up a correspondence consisting of over three hundred letters spanning nearly a fifty year period of his life with his teenage best friend from his childhood home in Northern Ireland, Arthur Greeves. How moving it was for me to read through their correspondence from childhood beginnings to the very end, and then, coming to the last letter very near Lewis' own death, read what were to be his final words to his oldest friend: *The only real snag is that it looks as if you and I shall never meet again in this life. This often saddens me very much...Tho' I am by no means unhappy I can't help feeling it was rather a pity I did revive in July...But oh Arthur, never to see you again!..."* (*They Stand Together*, Walter Hooper, Editor)

TRAVELING AT THE SPEED OF FRIENDSHIP

Another thing we have to take seriously in our pursuit of deep friendship and brotherhood is the fact that it is not only the culture that is set against us, but also the pace at which we are choosing to live our lives. I know: it is so easy to take the only world we have known as being the normal human experience down through the ages of history. But in this we have never been more mistaken. It may be the only way we know how to live, but the times we have been born into are anything but normal. Thousands of years of human history lived at 'impulse speed', (to use a term any trekkies will understand) and in comparison we of the current era are now racing through the days of our lives at 'warp factor seven'.

Sure, we're getting a lot of stuff done. (Even though you've probably discovered that the quicker you get stuff done, the longer the list of things you still need to do seems to become. There must be a name for this, something akin to 'Murphy's Law' that reads, *"The distance to the end of the to-do list remains equal regardless how fast you work, regardless of the number of items you cross off the list."*) And once again, I too understand a lot of this drive to run at top speed, blasting through the to-do list like a buzz-saw that's been souped up by Tim 'The Toolman' Taylor and then rewired to run on Red Bull Energy drinks. For one thing, it just feels good to be 'doing stuff', getting things accomplished. We live in a task-oriented society, remember? That doesn't just mean we are mostly bad at relationships, 'task-oriented' merely being the alternative option you find at the far end of the chart from 'people-oriented'. It also means we do in fact derive a sense of fulfillment from getting stuff done. It's what we've rewired our minds to think about. Constantly.

For that matter, we need to be honest about our other motive: isn't being constantly busy the best way to not have to face the deeper questions of our existence, the unmet longings of our hearts? I know the inner voice's whisper as well as you do: *Keep busy, don't stop to think about anything beyond the to-do list, because ignorance really does offer up it's own temporary form of bliss.* The key word, of course, being *temporary*. No amount of busyness will ever move us one step closer to answering our deepest questions or filling the aching void within.

Now, one of the many, many problems with this hyper-paced lifestyle we've adopted is that great friendships—or any other great relationships really—are fundamentally and unequivocally time-intensive. No time? No life-giving intimacy.

It's simple math really.

Although most of us find it hard enough to learn. We want so badly to live in a world where the basic laws of subtraction don't apply, where we can envision a pie chart where the sum of the parts equals one-hundred and fifty percent of the whole rather than merely one hundred percent. *Our ancestors often had deep friendships and mean-ingful family relationships,* we think to ourselves. *Why can't we have them too? Well, no, we don't want to give up anything else that is burning up our daylight right now. We've got to stay ahead, pursue excellence, keep up with the neighbors. Can't we just squeeze some great relationships in there somewhere? Why can't we have it all?*

Well, if those words don't put you in mind of a song by the rock legends Queen, I don't know what would:

I want it all,
I want it all,
I want it all,
And I want it now.

Now, I know what you will say, but the claim that one can replace 'quantity' of time with 'quality' of time is a claim I suspect was never made before the modern era, before overly-busy people began to search for some way to justify the way they were deprioritizing their most important relationships in the mad rush to squeeze more 'stuff' into their calendar. The quality vs. quantity discussion is mostly a construct of this age we live in: put it out of your mind entirely. There is nothing to it being a valid approach to building and maintaining deep relationships. Of course the quality of the time we spend with people is important. But juxtaposing quality and quantity always was a category mistake. *Of course* quality. Interacting together through conversation or shared activity is always going to do more for the relationship than sitting in a movie theater together, staring silently at the action on the screen in front of us. And equally so, *of course* quantity. Because the thing that is required to build a great friendship is both: *a quantity of quality time.*

Make no mistakes, friends: *Time* is the commodity here. And it is always going to be in short supply. But you and I both know that we've got a priority list of things we want to accomplish with our time, and even though we never get to all the things we'd like to, we work pretty hard at finding time for the things we think matter the most. And in a world that praises accomplishments and undervalues relationships, you must know that you'll be running upstream against the culture if you start giving the necessary time to building great relationships, because that means you'll be giving less time to 'accomplishing stuff'. To some extent, the trade-off is inevitable. You can't really hack the system on this one, so don't even try. You simply have to accept it as a basic fact: people with great relationships have less time than other people for 'getting stuff done.' Just take your best friend to work with you for a day, and then tell me if I'm wrong.

There was a moment in my own life that will stay in my memory forever—a moment when I saw with rare clarity what this battle for our most precious commodity would boil down to in the years ahead. It was early in my freshman year at college, and I was passing through the first floor lobby on my way to my room on the fifth floor to do some much needed studying. Wilkie, who was not yet my roommate, but spent more time on the couch in our dorm room than he did in his own room, was hanging out in the lobby, chatting it up with people as he was prone to do. He latched on to me as I passed by, asked if I wanted to get a pizza, maybe make an evening of it—just hanging around in the lobby together, spending time with whoever might happen to be free. The problem was that *I* wasn't free: I had a mountain of studying to do, and I knew it. Getting straight A's in high school had been a breeze, but a month into my first semester and I could already tell that hitting those same heights in college was going to take considerable time and effort. Standing there in the dorm lobby that afternoon, I was internally aware that I had reached a crossroads of decision: I could place the accomplishments of better grades as my first priority, or I could place spending time with people as my first priority. (This wasn't about being a good student, mind you: there's a world of difference between wanting to receive an education, and needing to jump through all the hoops required to get the highest G.P.A. possible.) I couldn't just float from one decision to the next: I felt like there needed to be a hierarchy of priorities, a deliberate and purposeful guide to all the choices that would lay ahead of me over the next four years. I was aware that all of my upbringing was telling me I needed to chase the accomplishments. But I knew the kind of person I wanted to be, and I knew that people were truly the most important priority of all.

Needless to say, I chose pizza with Wilkie that fall evening of my freshman year, and I really haven't looked back since. And you know what? I've never met anyone who cared that I got a few B's on my college transcript.

WE MUST BE INTENTIONAL

I think we can all admit that we live in a modern world that is accomplishment-driven, goal-driven, success-driven: a world where friendship is looked at as a mere happy accident of circumstance. And of course, circumstances change; and when they do, so does the immediate circle of people we cross paths with on a daily basis. Now, having grown up in such a culture, in such a world, one of the hardest things to adjust in our thinking is to come to realize that *deep and lasting Friendship requires intentional effort.* Especially when the priorities we've been living from up until now mean that we probably no longer live anywhere near many of our favorite people. C.S. Lewis once advised that university students seeking their path in the world after graduation should consider making their 'fellowship' their top priority, rather than their careers. *Get a flat somewhere together,* he suggested, *and then seek your career options from within the absolute non-negotiable of keeping your fellowship together.* But that is rare advice indeed in today's world. No one was there to make such a beautiful suggestion when my college fellowship parted ways. Or yours, I imagine. Instead we allowed our individualism to sweep us far away from each other, down vastly divergent streams. And at this point in most of our lives years and years of water has flowed under that particular bridge. I'm afraid it's simply not enough to wait for fate or chance or a career move to throw us back into one another's path. It's not enough to wait another five years for your next college reunion. On the contrary, we are going to have to go out of our way to fight for our friendships. We are going to have to be intentional.

The message of Intentionality by the way—the need to do the hard work to stay close to our dearest soulmates—is one of the truths that stands very near the center of what our ministry, The Warrior's Path, exists to communicate to the Church—and to the world. As men, we may have been told (or it may still be news to us) that we desperately need to walk through life in a Company of Men. But the missing piece of that message which we are endeavoring to bring is this: *it's not just any* Men that will do. They need to be *our* Men: the ones we have come to love and cherish, the ones that have been tried and tested time and again and shown us their qualities at every turn. The ones whose praise we covet and whose censure we dread. Who know our hearts and love us, even in the midst of our brokenness: yet, who somehow, inexplicably seem to be just as honored in our company as we feel in theirs. Who see the same things, share the same bright visions usually shrouded in darkness to most of the people we meet. Who bring out the very best in ourselves, and motivate us to find something within that is even better than our best.

Lewis, once again, spoke well of exactly such a Company:

> Every step of the common journey tests his metal...hence, as he rings true time after time, our reliance, our respect, and our admiration blossom into an Appreciative love of a singularly robust and well-informed kind...In a perfect Friendship this Appreciative love is, I think, often so great and so firmly based that each member of the circle feels, in his secret heart, humbled before all the rest. Sometimes he wonders what he is doing there among his betters. He is lucky beyond desert to be in such company. Especially when the whole group is together, each bringing out all that is best, wisest, or funniest in all the others.
>
> (C.S. Lewis, *The Four Loves*)

Rare indeed it is to find such a Company—rarer still to find them all living within an hour radius of your current address. (Even if they do live near, you know how hard it still is to get the whole 'gang' together in the course of your normal schedule. For as often as you actually end up seeing them, they might as well be living on the other side of the country.) Near or far, without an aggressive and un-yielding intentionality we simply are not going to end up spending nearly enough time with 'our' Men.

So we *do* need to be aggressively and unyieldingly intentional. And this need is the driving force behind one of the unique dreams we have at the Warrior's Path: the dream to see the base assumptions of our Christian culture reoriented so radically that it becomes *taken for granted* that a man needs to get together with his closest friends, his deepest spiritual resource, *a minimum* of twice a year. *A minimum* of every six months. So much the better if that includes not only getting together, but also getting away, out of 'the matrix', out of the familiar, the hum-drum, the soul-starving Shallows of modern life as we know it. (And yes, the same goes for the women in our lives as well. On the average they may understand this need a bit more than we do, but it's still not to the point of being a universally understood spiritual and relational imperative even among most women. Certainly not among many of the women that I know.)

Did you catch that? Don't let your eyes skim over it and just quickly move on to the next paragraph. We are talking about re-orienting our lives around an *intentional rhythm* of consistently returning to the Company of Men (or Women) that mean the most to your heart. This is *central*, it is life-changing, and yet it has been marginalized in both the culture and in the modern church to the point of near extinction. I don't know about you, but I have *never* heard a sermon on the essential necessity of getting away from your busy life at least every six months to not only refresh the intimacy of your relationship with God, but also to drink deeply from the un-tapped reservoirs of joy and refreshing He intended us to experience through the gift of our dearest friendships.

Yes, here and there you will find a church or ministry that offers the occasional retreat, mission trip, or adventure for the men (or women) they are trying to reach. But how often do you hear them being promoted *as if they are essential*? As if the church culture as a whole has finally admitted that the pace of modern life is insanely out-of-balance, and you're going to get totally fried at the soul level if you don't make these 'escapes' a huge priority? And, even if this was the attitude that the church leaders were adopting and successfully projecting regarding these events, if the atmosphere at those events they are offering is such that 'putting a good face' on your life seems like a far more appropriate option than getting painfully genuine and transparent, then it's not going to accomplish the sort of soul healing that most of us are in such desperate need of. Or if the offered event is a curriculum driven one—little more than a series of Sunday morning sermons that have been relocated to the woods or the mountains to shake things up a bit—then your heart's journey is not going to be the central theme of the weekend, and that's not what we're talking about either. And if you attend these events as a virtual stranger or casual acquaintance, instead of experiencing the time away in the company of some of your most cherished companions—well, that certainly isn't anywhere *near* what we are talking about. And since that pretty much sums up the nature of almost all the 'get away' events the local church currently offers...well, you can see what a radical shift in Christian culture it is going to take to fulfill the relationally-driven vision that is at the heart of what we do.

GETTING AWAY, GETTING TOGETHER

Now I know that your schedule doesn't exactly allow for two escapes a year above and beyond your family vacations (which *are* part of our culturally accepted assumptions as to what our life rhythms should include, but can turn out to hardly be genuinely refreshing in any significant ways, as we talked about earlier). So what exactly are we suggesting? *Two weekends every year spent...how? Running off to the mountains with the 'old gang' in search of something as hard to quantify as the refreshing of the fried places in our soul? Really? As busy as we are? As thin as we've stretched our resources? As much in our sphere of influence that depends on our presence simply to hold things together and avoid utter collapse?*

I know: to our current way of thinking it sounds like an extremely expensive and disruptive self-indulgence, doesn't it? You can see why making this a standard necessity for living a healthy Christian life will require a radical shift in Christian culture as a whole.

But you can absolutely trust me on this: once you start living like that you will feel that *even six months* is far too long between such times of refreshing. A soul can take a lot of damage in the course of six months, you know. A vibrant relationship with God can stutter, stall, grow stale in far less time than that. Our faith, our virtue, our courage, our determination to live and love from out of the good heart Jesus has now given us—all of it can all take more hits through the course of half-a-year of our overly frenetic lifestyle than we have the capacity to shake off. With no one beside us to stoke the flames in our soul, we lose our intensity and passion for the Kingdom. Without ample iron with which to sharpen our edge, we lose our momentum. With no strong warriors on our left and on our right, we lose our heart for entering into battle, allowing ourselves to drift with wherever the tide around us happens to be flowing. Finally, alone and adrift in the middle of a life we can't quite make sense of, wave after wave of disappointment and confusion descend upon us until we are too dazed and confused to remember who we are, or what significance we once thought our life was supposed to have.

Can anyone tell me why it takes us three years—or five, or even ten—of this sort of aimless wandering before we think, *Man, I need to get off this merry-go-round, if only for a weekend. I need to get away with God, let Him heal this mess that's been gathering in my fried soul. And I need to get with the guys, finally let someone know about the private war I've been losing. Maybe even—heaven forbid—admit that I'm not the island I appear, and ask for a little help?*

Friends, there are simply moments in life (many of them, if I am any judge of it) where the change, the much-needed breaking of the unhealthy cycle you are stuck in, demands that two things must happen. The first is that you must get off the merry-go-round. Leave the environment. Slow down. Breathe. Back far enough away from the day-to-day that you now consider 'your life' to gain some rare perspective. I know it sounds impossible: too good to be true, and impossible at the same time. But it *has* to happen. The lie that we've bought into is that none of it *can* be stopped—that the current is too swift and the shore too distant to even dream of escape. And the sense of hopelessness *that* lie ushers in is a very big part of our problem, because now we are living in a form of bondage, bondage of our own making, bondage that exists only in our own imaginations. Trust me: I'm not remotely suggesting that it's *easy* to break away from all that holds you down to your own personal daily grind. Quite the opposite actually. I'm just suggesting that these little 'escapes' that our lives demand for clarity's sake *are* available if you just have the courage to go after them. Sadly, as you know, most people never do.

The second thing that must happen is this: you must receive input from outside your own 'stuck', cyclical patterns of thinking. As Einstein said, "We cannot solve our problems with the same thinking we used when we created them." Your brain may be like an organic supercomputer, but if it keeps endlessly crunching the same data using the same program, the results are going to stay the same. A new piece of data needs to be entered into the system, or some new software uploaded. A new voice, a new perspective, needs to speak into the problem. In short, we need some wise counsel from someone who knows us well, who understands our situation. Who understands the complexities of our unique personality that got us into that situation in the first place. Who knows us well enough to understand why we are 'stuck' and what it will take to break the cycle we have fallen into. When that happens, it can almost be embarrassing how simple the solution to your problem always was—only you couldn't see the forest for the trees.

Now, does getting those two things feel impossible right now? A modicum of respite from 'life', and the wise input of ones you love and trust? As badly as you know you need them, have you given up on ever being able to call a brief halt to the madness that is 'your life'? Have you told yourself that no help can be expected to come from that quarter? That you'll just have to figure all this out on your own, right here in the midst of the storm—the storm that has you so disoriented you're not sure where you're headed or who you even are anymore? Is this what you're telling yourself, even though you and I both know that 'figuring it out alone in the midst of the storm' never has worked for us in the past?

I think we've all been there. We've all felt this, that life is 'too much' and we are 'not enough' to handle it; that we are far too alone to realistically expect much help. So where exactly are we as a Christian community on all this, knowing it as deeply and personally as we do? Well, to put it bluntly, *we've gone missing*. In fact we've gone into hiding. Hiding behind an individualism that has invaded every aspect of our Christian beliefs. *I have my battles, you have yours. Your battles are your responsibility. Your journey is between you and God. I'll help, if you ever get desperate enough to ask. But really I hope you never do, because I've already got more trouble of my own than I can handle.*

WHY WON'T WE ENGAGE?

And as I write this I am feeling a very unpleasant emotion rising up inside of me:

Utter disgust.

With myself.

Because I see so much of myself in that description. I don't think I ever knew how deeply affected my attitude was by this individualistic approach to life. Even with the people I'm the closest to, the people for whom I long for all the joy, wholeness and holiness that can be found in this world: how often do I actually *engage*, dive in, intentionally go 'there', and how often do I instead shrug and say, *"It's all between them and God. They've got to find their own way. My own journey is trouble enough"?* How many times have I excused myself from any responsibility by calling it 'minding my own business'? An inherent leaning towards the comfort of passivity, and the permission offered by an individualistic worldview to live from out of that passivity make for a pathetic end product, let me tell you. I can see that now. And I know that something fundamental about the way I go about my relationships needs to change.

Allow me to pause here. I'm aware that I've really stumbled across a pretty crucial self-revelation here, and I can't simply sweep it under the rug and just move on. I've got to take a long, hard look in the mirror and ask myself: *Am I deeply committed to being engaged in anyone's heart's journey to the degree I wish someone would be engaged in mine?* Knowing how badly I long for that sort of engagement myself, how can I possibly justify not offering it to others?

Of course, this is hardly just a private issue for me alone. The Church as a whole is to some great degree in need of the same kind of change that my own life requires. If I've subconsciously accepted the 'every man for himself' approach to life—in spite of my hatred for it, and my hunger for something better—you can imagine how deep this must run in every aspect of our society, including the Church. I mean, we all know people in our personal sphere of influence that are probably stuck in some pretty awful places, (we know because of how often we've found ourselves stuck in those places ourselves) but what are we offering to do about it? Hope they find a good pastoral counselor somewhere along the way and leave it at that?

Understand, I've got nothing against counseling. I think when done by a Spirit-led, wise and caring professional it can be powerful, even life-changing. But how much of what we think demands professional help is really just the sort of stuff that we could be working through on a regular basis if we were intentionally engaged in deep relationships with people personally invested in our journey? With people who know us intimately and love us deeply? With our true Friends? Because, the real question that we must have an answer to—if we hope to have any shot at living the abundant life Jesus offers—is the question John Eldredge posed in his book *Waking the Dead*: "Who will fight for your heart?"

Who will fight for your heart?

For far too many of us, the answer, sadly, is *no one*. That's why there is still so much work left to do: so many allies to be sought for and found, so many epic friendships yet to be born. There are many, many more souls out there waiting to be noticed, to be known, to be called forth and invited into deep fellowship—one little band of 'merry men' at a time. It is for the hope of these things that I have written this book, and why at The Warrior's Path we continue to do what we do, and pray for this new dawn that we earnestly seek to break upon the church at last.

> Honestly, though he is a very brave and true hobbit, Frodo hasn't a chance without Sam, Merry, Pippin, Gandalf, Aragorn, Legolas, and Gimli...He will need his friends. And you will need yours. You must cling to those you have; you must search far and wide for those you do not yet have. You must not go alone.
>
> (John Eldredge, *Waking the Dead*)

You must not go alone.

SO VERY FAR TO GO

Oh, how I wish I could say that this message was taking stronger root in the Christian culture through our efforts, and through the efforts of those small pockets of good-hearted allies who have also seen the destructive force that living in a friendless adult world has had on so many souls. I wish I could say that the alarm had been raised sufficiently, the warning 'beacons' lit, calling the Church to war against the isolation and loneliness that is resulting from our impoverished view of True Friendship.

I wish I could say that.

But I can't.

Personally I have yet to see much of the shift that I long to see—a vibrant and joyous celebration within the Church of that glorious Stream of grace called Friendship that God intended to use to bless our lives for now and for eternity. Yes, for eternity. For though we have been taught to look forward to 'treasures' that await us in God's Kingdom one day, we have mostly pictured them as the sorts of 'treasures' we are in the habit of storing up for ourselves here in this life. In doing so we have missed the clue that the great Apostle Paul left us as to what those riches truly look like:

> "For what is our hope, our joy, or the crown in which we will glory in the presence of our Lord Jesus when he comes? Is it not you?"
>
> (I Thess. 2:19)

For Paul, it was those dear friends he had made along the way of his many missionary journeys, those for whom he "longed for with the affection of Christ Jesus" (Philippians 1:8), that were to be the crowning joy awaiting him in the Life that was yet to come. Lewis, we've noted many times, called Friendship "the crown of life". Through the words of Paul, God informs us that Friendship—and all our deepest earthly relationships—are also one of the crowns of *eternal* life. And that is both beautiful, and disturbing, when you consider how differently we value our own relationships in comparison. Honestly most of us don't even have a *category* for making sense of the apostle's deep, passionate affection for—not just 'the mission'—but the people that 'the mission' has brought into his life.

In a couple of days David and I are headed up into the mountains again for one of our retreats—a time of healing, conversation, laughter, tears, renewed intimacy with dear brothers and, most of all, with God. Another year has passed, and Fall has come once again. I can't wait to get away from the soul-numbing busyness and go to see the mountains while the aspens are in their golden glory: can't wait to take a three day blast from a fire hose of God's breathtaking beauty, let it have the healing influence that the dry, parched places in my soul so desperately need.

But as much as I am looking forward to it, I find myself thinking about all the dear friends we invited whose life simply would not release them from it's vice-like hold—even when they knew what a time of restoration and joy they would surely be missing. I am saddened knowing what they will miss—for what *I* will miss by not getting to share the experience in the company of their wise, spiritually gifted, encouraging presence. Our long term goal of changing the culture seems as far away as it ever has.

THE NOW AND THE NOT YET

And here, I think at last, we must come to an end.

And yet there is still so, so much more to be said. Some encouragements, some key concepts, even some necessary cautions. Not every Lone Wolf you meet, for instance, is even *capable* of changing his lifestyle simply because he has seen that there is another way to live. For some deeply wounded people it may take a significant amount of soul healing before they can even begin to open themselves up to intimate friendship. And those of us that *can* open ourselves up to it—just be forewarned that there is heartache and disappointment ahead. The intimacy we seek will be thwarted at every turn. There will never be enough time; our *ability* to 'unveil'

will never be as developed as our desire to do so; our level of commitment to pursuing that intimacy won't match up to what the other
people in our relationships are either willing—or perhaps able—to
offer in return. And even the very best of friendships will hit rough
patches. Because they are relationships between two imperfect individuals, even the best of friends may go missing at just the moment
when we need them the most. They will disappoint us; we, in turn,
will disappoint them. When we are at our very best we will grow in
our desire to seem them achieve their perfection—to see them become the person God created them to be, to see their glory fully
restored and shining for all to see—and they in turn will desire our
True Self to shine forth as well. In these moments we may experience
a new and unbearable heartache as we stand by and watch our friend
choose to live beneath that glory, as we are all so very prone to do so
very much of the time. Heaven be praised that we have grown up
into the type of creature that is finally capable of seeing the glory
hidden in another soul, capable of aching with a vicarious and self-
forgetful longing to see it blossom into its fullest expression. It is a
sign that we are beginning to see the value of another person other
than ourselves as God, in His omnipotence, sees each and every soul
that has ever sprung from His own heart, sees each dear one that
Jesus bled and died to save and restore unto Himself. As Lewis
reminds us again, "Friendship...is the instrument by which God
reveals to each the beauties of all the others. They are no greater than
the beauties of a thousand other men; by Friendship God opens our
eyes to them."

    We *do* see the beauties, the latent image-bearing glory, of our
dearest friends, and we *do* desire for their sake to see their glory
increase, *and for our sake*, that we might be blessed to walk through
these Shadowlands in happy Fellowship with such radiant sons of
God. And it really would be unfair of me to pretend that both these
desires wont be challenged, assaulted—yes, even thwarted—at every

turn. And yet, none of these waiting heartaches and disappointments is cause to hesitate, to turn back and renew our vows to the
life of the Lone Wolf. Neither marriage nor the relationship between
parents and children are any less fraught with danger and
disappointment, and yet that does not stop us from believing that
they are worth the effort, worth the risk. Relationships are always
risks, and the life of the Lone Wolf is essentially the life of a coward.

And so we do not lose heart, we do not turn aside. Whatever
dangers may lurk along the path of giving ourselves to intimate
relationships, the dangers of living without them are always greater.
"It is better to have loved and lost than to never have loved at all"
wrote the poet Alfred Lord Tennyson, and though very few who
have not read *In Memorium* know the story behind those famous
words, Tennyson penned those words not in memory of a lost
romance, but in memory of a lost friend.

In these words of the poet, in fact, I think we have an approach to
relationships that is the antithesis to the vow of the Lone Wolf.
Though we may lose, we must not miss out on the love. That love is
the rescue of our hearts, and sometimes, it may even be the rescue of
the world. Frodo lost his trust in Samwise (in the film version) on
the very steps of Cirith Ungol, just when he needed him most. All of
Middle Earth might have paid an eternal price for that misunderstanding. But Samwise returned, restored Frodo's faith, saved the day
and...well, everything that could be saved. Peter disowns Jesus three
times only hours before the crucifixion. But on his return, Jesus goes
out of his way to restore the love that binds them—and once again,
through the work that lies ahead for Peter, a world is in some degree
saved because of Jesus' refusal to leave the relationship in tatters.

And so we must press on, in spite of the heartaches and the disappointments. And we accept that no relationship is going to be
perfect. Despite personally having been blessed with the kind of
relationships that most people could only dream of, my heart knows

that the relationships in my life still have a very long way to go. We have yet only reached the foothills of a far greater country still, where we will at last be as fully known, as fully understood, as fully loved by each and every one of those who matter to us most as we are now, in these Shadowlands, by God and God alone. It is a country that one day we fully intend to reach; and is, we can be assured, no country for Lone Wolves. *That* broken, guarded, diminished version of humanity will finally and everlastingly be swallowed up by something so much better we can only now begin to grasp a portion of it in the vaguest outline, as "through a glass darkly".

This, my friends, is a destiny worth striving towards. Worth dreaming about. Worth living for.

It *will* be incredible.

It *will* be epic.

And best of all, as David once said, *it is coming*.

AFTERWORD

There can be no friendship when there is no freedom. Friendship loves the free air, and will not be fenced up in straight and narrow enclosures.

- William Penn

Today we are faced with the preeminent fact that if civilization is to survive, we must cultivate the science of human relationships.

- Franklin D. Roosevelt

There is still so much more to say, so much deeper that I wish we could go. No one will argue, I suspect, with my self-assessment that this book has been far from comprehensive: fragments—musings really—nothing more. Regardless of it's original internal failings however, I am aware of one thing: I set out to write this book more than four years ago, and I finish it in what may prove to be a vastly different world than the one in which it began. Never has a message calling us back to the simple human pleasure found in deep friendships been more timely, more vital, more central to human health. Never has such a basic God-given privilege—one responsible for more than half of all the happiness in the world—

been more scandalously pushed to the margins of life. At the time of this writing we have, as a global community, just passed through an unprecedented period of isolation. We have passed through something the world perhaps has never known before: a government mandated limitation on human interaction brought about in response to the COVID-19 virus. Right or wrong, the impact of these lockdowns and quarantines is something that will surely threaten to define an entire generation's approach to human interaction. If the Enemy of Mankind ever hoped to perfect his plan to divide and conquer—to get people at their weakest point of isolation and then pick them off one-by-one—we have just handed him the perfect opportunity on a silver platter. Adolescent counselors and crisis workers can attest to how much damage that isolation has already done—the increase in teen suicide alone was an undeniable statistical fact of the lockdown period.

But what of the long term effects on the rest of us? For one defining year we were bombarded with an endless stream of propaganda claiming to define for us which activities were and were not 'essential' to human life. And one message came across crystal clear: spending time physically in the society of other people was *not* essential. Whatever faint homage the modern world has pretended to pay to the essential significance of relationships to our overall health and well-being...well, the curtain has been pulled back and all that lip service is now well over.

Biological existence—the only type of existence that a Materialistic worldview can scientifically prove—is all that matters in such a world as this. Is it any wonder that a society which questions the very existence of the human soul would in time lose its high valuation for the moment when two kindred souls meet? The reality of having a 'soul' has become a mere metaphor; the metaphor is near to becoming a fable. As William Shakespeare so aptly put it to Phillip Henslowe in the film *Shakespeare in Love*, "Henslowe, you have no soul. How can you understand the longing that desires a soulmate?"

Such talk of soulmates and kindred spirits may be fine figures of speech during peacetime, but what about now, when we have gone to war against a disease, and been warned that every other human we meet is a potential carrier—is in effect, to be treated like the enemy?

I don't pretend to know what the future holds for our society, and perhaps time will tell that my fears are unfounded. But I think we have all seen the way people have taken to the ease and comfort of doing so much from the safety of home, and there is much to suggest that things will not easily return to the way they were before. For many the technology they were forced to embrace has now become their norm—work remotely, study online, have every meeting via Zoom, even 'do church' from our own sofa in the comfort of our bathrobe and slippers.

Friends, I don't think we can underestimate the inroads made against what remaining relational values our society had left that all this fear-inspired use of long-distance technology is having. Sure, Zoom may be functional. And it can be used for relational purposes. Sometimes. But only a fool would suggest that it is any sort of an improvement to our innate hunger and search for human connection. For deeply moving, deeply satisfying personal relationships. For the knowing of one another's stories, the intertwined sharing of one another's journeys. For the great joy of truly 'doing life together'.

Now, I'm not saying that before the events of the past year and a half we could have been satisfied with the way things were going in our world, relationally speaking. The position that relationships held in most of our lives needed rehabilitation long before current events ran their course. But now we stand on the cusp of a 'brave new world' that glorifies anything but bravery, and offers to our hearts far less that is truly good than the old world did. If we thought some of these highly touted 'technological advances' were going to advance human civilization, it is a gross understatement to say we may have been mistaken. Our isolation and experience of feeling utterly alone are increasing exponentially. Depression and hopelessness are at an all time high. Where will it all end?

My friends, the only hope for the aching abyss of the human heart has always been found in relationships. One heart meeting—and experiencing true, lasting connection—with another heart. Being completely known. Being completely loved: uniquely adored, passionately desired, intentionally pursued.

Because, when all is said and done, it was this for which we were created.

For Relationship.

For Love.

That's it. That's the whole deal in a nutshell.

In half a century of sampling just about every version of Christianity known to the current era, I have finally come to see that most of it is huffing and puffing over the peripheral, the forms, the ideas, the outer trappings of religion. The real truth of it (we use the words, but again, mostly as a pleasant sounding metaphor) is all about the relationship. Fall daily in love over again with your Abba Father, with His Son Jesus, and you will be amazed at how all the rest of what we call 'religion' will sort itself out. Or vanish from your mind completely. It really is that simple. And freeing. And beautiful. And you know what? A relationally oriented person in a relationally oriented society would have figured that out a *whole* lot sooner than most of us—if we ever even *do* figure it out. Which is why learning to view the world relationally can change everything.

Can I help you move one inch closer to finding this to be the rock-bottom reality of human existence? I pray that I can; I pray that I have. Here I have dedicated an entire book to the great significance and deep beauty of human friendship, and I stand by every word of it. Your life will be forever impoverished until you raise Friendship back onto the pedestal carved for it by our ancient ancestors during the simpler, more relationally aware ages of the past. That is a fact. But in the end I cannot fail to make clear that all that I have said about Friendship is only a foretaste, a shadow of the ultimate significance and far greater beauty to be found in experiencing the One Friendship that was meant to be the ground and root of our lives: friendship with our Maker, our Creator, our Sustainer, our God and our True Father. Find this, and you find the greatest treasure in the Universe. Miss this, and you miss the central purpose of your existence—the central purpose and the deepest pleasure, the very best thing that has ever been or ever could be in this or any world that could be imagined.

Of course it will be argued that 'friendship' paints only one picture of what it means to find this intimacy, this proper relation to our Maker, and perhaps not the fullest, most life-like portrait at that. Nevertheless it is a true likeness as far as it goes, and one we are encouraged to make full use of, for it is Jesus Himself who invites us into such a bold intimacy. "I no longer call you servants...I have called you friends..."(John 15:15).

So may all of our lives be marked by a clear, observable pursuit of an ever-deepening intimacy with both God and Men. And may it be said of us, to borrow from Charles Dickens memorable ending to *A Christmas Carol*, that we became "*as good a friend* (italics mine), as good a master, and as good a man, as the good old city knew, or any other good old city, town, or borough, in the good old world..."

ACKNOWLEDGEMENTS

My undying gratefulness to my wife Robyn, and to my children Tristan, Nathaniel, Cody, and Gwendolyn. Every moment spent working on this project was a moment that stole my undivided attention away from you, and I thank all of you for being patient with me and allowing me to pursue this lifelong dream. Dream though it is, what I write will never be as important to me as the time that I get to spend with you each and every day. Thank you Jesus, for giving me back this long-surrendered hope: the unexpected freedom and the chance to do what I've always wanted to do.

ABOUT THE AUTHOR

DERRICK STEELE is the co-founder of The Warriors Path, Ltd., a ministry devoted to helping people discover the epic and wonder-filled nature of the story that God is telling and the role that He has given each of us to play—if only we dare to seek it—in the unfolding drama of the redemption of the human race. Derrick is a young adult pastor, an accomplished film writer, a youth soccer coach, an avid gardener and unabashed Anglophile—but above all else he is a proud father to his four children: Tristan, Nathaniel, Cody, and Gwendolyn. Derrick and his wife Robyn Love, together with their four children, live in Farmington, Michigan.

To learn more about Derrick, David, and The Warriors Path, visit their website:

www.thewarriorspath.org